Revising State Theory

Essays in Politics and Postindustrialism

Fred Block

Revising
State Theory

Essays in Politics and Postindustrialism

TEMPLE UNIVERSITY PRESS
Philadelphia

TEMPLE UNIVERSITY PRESS, Philadelphia 19122
Copyright © 1987 by Temple University. All rights reserved
Published 1987
Printed in the United States of America

The paper used in this publication meets the minimum
requirements of American National Standard for Information
Sciences—Permanence of Paper for Printed Library Materials,
ANSI Z39.48-1984

Library of Congress Cataloging-in-Publication Data
Block, Fred L.
  Revising state theory.
  Bibliography: p.
  Includes index.
  1. State, The. 2. Capitalism. 3. Business and
politics. 4. Industry and state. 5. Economic
history—1971–   . I. Title.
JC325.B574   1988   306'.2   87-9983
ISBN 0-87722-465-X (alk. paper)

Contents

vi   Contents

Preface

The chapters of this book are essays that were written at different times over the period from 1976 to 1986. The essays are organized around two central themes. The first is the relationship between the state and society and the determination of state policy. The second is an analysis of current economic and political problems as aspects of a transition from industrial to postindustrial society. While most of the essays in Part I take up the first theme and most of the essays in Part II take up the second theme, the issues become intertwined in the introductory chapter and in several of the chapters in Part II.

I have chosen not to revise the individual essays—other than correcting errors—since I do not want to disguise the evolution of my position over time. Instead, I have written an introductory chapter that addresses the development of my views of the state and political economy in relation to specific historical developments and the work of other scholars. State theory, as is true of most intellectual work, emerges in response to very concrete circumstances, and I have tried to illuminate the development of my own work by exploring some of those circumstances.

In writing the essays that I have collected here, I have been sustained and supported by many colleagues; some of the particular debts are acknowledged in the individual chapters, but there are some debts that are more general. Larry Hirschhorn is the coauthor of Chapter 6; he has been my friend and sometime collaborator since 1970. Larry was an advocate of the postindustrial perspective when I first met him, and after several years of argument, he persuaded me that the reality of postindustrial transition requires a reconsideration of many of the basic assumptions of the social sciences. It is difficult to exaggerate the extent of my intellectual debt to him. Theda Skocpol bears a particular responsibility for this volume; it was she who gave me the idea to collect my essays in a single volume. Moreover, her support for my work in state theory has been extremely important to me. Michael Ames provided strong encouragement and sound advice in his role as friend and editor. I have also had the benefit of other close friends on whom I have been able to rely for intellectual feedback in the period in which these essays were written. These include Karl Klare, Magali Sarfatti Larson, David Plotke, Margaret Somers, Ann Swidler, and Bob Wood. In the last few years, Jerry Jacobs has been a valued colleague and critic of my drafts. Finally, I have relied on Carole Joffe, wife and colleague, for her infinite stores of intellectual good sense and emotional support.

I am also grateful to the German Marshall Fund of the United States for financial support during the time that I prepared this manuscript for publication.

Introduction

1

State Theory in Context

This introduction is intended to provide an overview of the issues discussed in the subsequent chapters of the book. The argument is organized in two parts. In the first part, I situate my own work in state theory in relation to other lines of analysis. This gives me the opportunity to explain the genesis of my own contributions to state theory (the essays of Part I) and to discuss some of the limitations of this work. In the second part, I have sought to place the recent debate about state theory in a broader historical context. I am interested in reevaluating this work, in particular, in relationship to the rightward shift of American politics in the eighties. This requires discussing the implications of the theory of postindustrial transition (elaborated in the essays of Part II) for understanding the role of the state in advanced capitalist societies.

Part I: The Development of the Argument

My interest in questions of the state and its relationship to capitalism developed within the student movement of the sixties. As an undergraduate at Columbia College from 1964 to 1968 and as a graduate student in sociology at U.C. Berkeley from 1968 to 1974, I was immersed in debates about the inadequacy of liberalism and the need to construct an alternative radical social theory. While much has been said about the anti-intellectualism of the student movement of the sixties, the circles that I traveled in were militantly intellectual. Although we sometimes felt guilty about not being full-time organizers and activists, we were extraordinarily serious about the project of radical social theory. As early as the late sixties, we defended the importance of left intellectual work by relying on Gramsci's arguments about the centrality to revolutionary politics of mounting challenges to bourgeois ideological hegemony and of elaborating an oppositional intellectual position that could become hegemonic.

Within the student movement, discussions of the state were dominated by the theory of corporate liberalism. As I argue in Chapter 2, the theory of corporate liberalism was one of the American New Left's major intellectual innovations. The core of the theory was that much of the history of American liberalism in the twentieth century could be understood as a facade covering the self-interest of corporate capitalists. Domestically, liberalism meant limited reforms that farsighted capitalists acquiesced in to maintain social order but that were shaped to assure continuing corporate dominance of the society. Internationally, liberalism meant an American foreign policy that opposed any social movements that could interfere with the maximal freedom for American corporations to trade and invest as they pleased. This "liberal" foreign policy, it was argued, led directly to support for repressive right-wing dictatorships and to bloody military interventions. By bringing the foreign and domestic components together under one rubric, the theory of corporate liberalism made it possible for the New Left to form its identity in radical opposition to the Democratic Party liberalism out of which many of its activists had emerged.

While the theory of corporate liberalism was new, it built on a long tradition in American society of populist distrust of the domination of politics by business elites. Such distrust was a central theme of nineteenth-century populism, and it continued into the twentieth century in both popular and academic forms.[1] For example, the progressive historiography of Charles Beard and his followers stressed the domination over American politics of business elites. In fact, these ideas are so deeply rooted in American society that at the same time that the New Left was creating the theory of corporate liberalism, right-wing conspiracy theorists were pointing to the malevolent impact on U.S. foreign policy of such business-dominated groups as the Council on Foreign Relations.[2] And in the seventies, writers on both the left and the right denounced the Trilateral Commission as the latest ploy by narrow elites to dominate American society.

Drawing on this tradition required that theorists of corporate liberalism directly attack the pluralist analysis of American politics that had become the conventional academic wisdom in the fifties. Pluralists argued that power in American society was broadly diffused among a variety of different interest groups, no one of which held a position of dominance.[3] Actual governmental policy outcomes reflected the multi-sided conflicts among these divergent groups. New Leftists, building on the arguments of C. Wright Mills in *The Power Elite*, bitterly attacked the pluralist argument, insisting on the existence of dominant elites that shaped both political agendas and political outcomes.[4] The membership of these dominant elites was disproportionately drawn from the business community, but even those from other kinds of backgrounds shared the world view of the businesspeople due to common social background or school experiences. Within the student movement these arguments developed very concretely through research showing that university boards of trustees were dominated by powerful businesspeople.

Tying the critique of pluralism to the theory of corporate liberalism simply involved showing the disproportionate influence of "corporate liberals" within the most important elite circles. During the sixties, at the level of national politics, and particularly foreign policy, this was a relatively easy exercise to carry out because of the continuing dominance over major policy positions by members of the "Establishment"—scions of established WASP families, trained at elite prep schools and the Ivy League, and occupationally rooted in finance, law, or a handful of major foundations. This group that included Dean Acheson, the Dulleses, the Bundys, Dean Rusk, and many others of "the best and the brightest" personally embodied "corporate liberalism."[5]

The theory of corporate liberalism began to lose its luster in the early seventies at the same time that the New Left fell apart as a political movement. Part of the reason was the coming to power of the Nixon administration, which abandoned much of the domestic liberalism of the Kennedy–Johnson years[6] and began to displace *some of* the "best and the brightest" from governmental positions. In fact, the old Establishment group became bitterly divided over the Vietnam War and ceased to loom as large as it had before. But at the same time, New Left intellectuals had their own reasons to rethink their positions. In an effort to regroup in the face of the collapse of the student movement, New Left intellectuals turned toward European Marxism for theoretical guidance. But there were obvious problems in assimilating theories of corporate liberalism and elite dominance into a sophisticated Marxist framework.

This effort at assimilation would appear to be relatively simple. What had previously been defined as a corporate liberal elite could be redefined as the vanguard of the American capitalist class based in the most powerful internationally oriented firms. Yet this synthesis was empirically and theoretically problematic. At the empirical level, it could not make sense of many of the central issues of American politics of the time. First, there were the intense divisions within the Democratic Party between more hawkish and more dovish factions that dominated both the 1968 and the 1972 Presidential campaigns. It was unclear whether both factions were dominated by corporate liberals or whether one faction represented something else entirely; either way, it was clear that something more than a synthesis of corporate liberal theory and class analysis was needed to explain these conflicts. Second, there was the unfolding of the Watergate crisis with the growing divide between the Nixon administration and the press, Congress, and significant parts of the federal bureaucracy. Again, it was unclear how the parties in this conflict related or failed to relate to corporate liberalism.[7]

At the theoretical level, the turn of New Left intellectuals toward European Marxism was a search for a more sophisticated way of looking at the world, one that went beyond the superficial level of appearances to find the underlying realities of social life. This project was exemplified by Marx's aphorism that if appearance and reality were the same thing, there would be no need for science. The problem was that no matter how one phrased it, the familiar idea that American politics was dominated by a small group of people based in the largest corporations seemed to be an observation at the level of appearances. The synthesis of corporate liberal theory and traditional class analysis was simply not theoretically sophisticated enough; it seemed pedestrian and unmistakably American.

It was in this context that Poulantzas' work came as a revelation. For the American audience, the most widely read work was his critical review of Miliband that was published in *New Left Review* in 1969.[8] In that essay, Poulantzas argued that Miliband's efforts to show the dominant position of capitalists in staffing the state apparatus and in influencing political outcomes was misguided. He argued that in accepting the importance of individual agency, Miliband had moved on to the "epistemological terrain" of his opponents. The alternative, he argued, was to understand that the relationship between the state and capitalism was a structural one.

Poulantzas argues that the relation between the bourgeois class and the State is an *objective relation*. "This means that if the function of the State in a determinant social formation and the *interests* of the dominant class in this formation *coincide*, it is by reason of the system itself: the direct participation of members of the ruling class in the State apparatus is not the *cause* but the *effect* and moreover a chance and contingent one of this objective coincidence."[9]

For Poulantzas, the essence of this objective relationship was that the state served as the point of cohesion of a class-divided social order—organizing the capitalists and disorganizing the working class.

Poulantzas' contribution succeeded in shifting the discussion to the more sophisticated level that American New Left intellectuals were looking for. While there were serious problems in Poulantzas' formulations, his intervention did two things. First, it posed the question particularly sharply of why the state in capitalist society functions as it does. Second, it allowed for a shift in focus toward the state itself. When analysis was centered on business domination of the state, the things that the state actually did received only secondary attention. But by placing the state at the center of analysis, Poulantzas made it possible to focus attention on what the state actually does.

As Domhoff has noted,[10] the shift in the American discussion that followed Poulantzas led to a period of neglect of the empirical analysis of business dominance of the state.[11] This was hardly surprising—if focusing on the role of capitalists in staffing the government and influencing politicians put one on the epistemological terrain of pluralists, who would want to do it?

Sorting Out the Issues
Thus far, I have emphasized the role of intellectual fashion in influencing the debate, but there are real substantive issues in the evaluation of Poulantzas' position and those of the business dominance theorists. Poulantzas made an important contribution in shifting the debate, but I will argue that his arguments at the time were basically misguided. There were good reasons for moving away from an exclusive focus on business dominance, but they were quite different from those that Poulantzas cited.

The first problem with Poulantzas' 1969 position was his acceptance of the Althusserian idea that individuals were mere bearers of structures, and that the structures acted. It was this position that underlay his contempt for Miliband's focus on the actions of individuals. But from the vantage point of current social science, it seems clear that structures act only through individuals and that the willingness of individuals to reproduce a particular structure requires explanation. Adam Przeworski and others have persuasively argued for the indispensability of the stance of "methodological individualism," which traces all action to individuals and sees all arguments in which structures act as exercises in reification.[12] From this standpoint, Poulantzas' attack makes little sense.

Poulantzas' second central claim about the state's objective function amounted to a form of "hyper-functionalism," as Miliband argued in reply.[13] The state was, by definition, reduced to fulfilling a functional need of the capitalist order. The formulation left no room for the state to be more or less successful in serving the needs of capitalism. In fact, Carnoy argues that Poulantzas quickly left this formulation behind as he developed a perspective that placed much more emphasis on class struggles within the state apparatus.[14] The latter perspective then made it possible to understand variations in state actions.

In short, Poulantzas' arguments against the empirical research of business dominance theorists were mistaken. In the rush to embrace Poulantzas' more sophisticated formulations, a valuable research tradition was neglected. This was unfortunate because it is valuable to know more about the specifics of the ways in which business power influences policy outcomes.

Nevertheless, the impulse of Poulantzas and those who were influenced by him to go beyond the business dominance tradition were fundamentally sound even though Poulantzas' early formulations were mistaken. As I see it, there are three reasons for going beyond the business dominance tradition in analyzing state policies. All these arguments are consistent with the basic empirical finding of the business dominance theorists—that businesspeople in the United States exercise disproportionate influence over state policies through staffing of key government positions, through lobbying and campaign contributions, and through direct personal contact with policymakers in private clubs and policymaking organizations.[15] But when taken together, these arguments suggest the limitations of a business dominance perspective.

Structural Sources of Business Power

Beyond the shores of the United States, it is not uncommon in parliamentary democracies for parties of the left to dominate the legislative and executive branches of government for longer or shorter periods. Many of these left parties are relatively closed to direct business influence. When they are in power, there is little staffing of government offices by capitalists, business campaign contributions are limited, and the effectiveness of business lobbying is diminished. Yet we also know that with relatively few exceptions, such governments have avoided taking strong anticapitalist actions. Not only that, they have tended to be preoccupied with pursuing policies that will maintain economic stability, and this usually means making significant concessions to the business community.

These experiences suggest that there is something important going on in addition to the processes that business dominance theorists emphasize. It appears that even when the business community is not able to influence the state in the traditional ways, policy outcomes tend to be favorable to business concerns. This suggests that there are "structural" factors that operate at a different level from the exercise of personal influence. These "structural" factors are still the consequence of behavior of real human beings, but it is not necessarily the kind of purposive, instrumental action that business dominance theorists emphasize.

In the United States, it is still difficult to imagine the election of a national administration that would not be directly subject to business influence, but the hypothetical possibility has important political implications. As we have noted, the business dominance perspective builds on a long American tradition of populist distrust of business interests. Within that tradition, the proposed cure is "to throw the bums out"—to retire from public office all those who represent or have been subservient to business interests. With a purified government in power, it is then imagined that policies far more favorable to the "little people" would be pursued. However, European experiences with Socialist and Social Democratic governments suggest the limitations of this scenario. Important reforms might occur at the margins, but even with a change in governmental personnel, the power of business would continue to have a large influence over governmental policies. In short, there is more to business dominance than is captured in the usual studies of recruitment of state officials and personal forms of influence.

The Limited Rationality of Capitalists

The business dominance approach tends to understate the shortsightedness and irrationality of the business community. This problem is most obvious in the tradition of corporate liberalism, but it runs through almost all versions of business dominance theory. The problem derives from the joining of two commonsense observations. First, the United States through most of the twentieth century has been unusually successful in pursuing state policies that maintain social order and that contribute to economic growth. Second, as business dominance theorists argue, the business community has had inordinate influence over the shaping of state policy. It follows from these two premises that the business community, in general, has pushed the state to carry out policies that have been good for economic growth and good for maintaining social order. The consequence is an image of businesspeople, or of key groups within business, as being rational and sensible in their pursuit of self-interest.

One problem with this image is that it neglects the intense divisions within the business community that impede the process of developing common interests and common programs. Within a particular industry, there will be significant conflicts of interest between small firms and large firms, and there will often be intense rivalries among the large firms. There are also conflicts between industries that have conflicting interests on fundamental questions such as the different perspectives on gasoline costs between the automobile industry and the petroleum industry. Such conflicts can also occur over fundamental areas of state policy such as the tension between firms oriented toward international trade and firms oriented exclusively to the domestic market; such firms are likely to lobby for very different foreign trade policies.

Some business dominance theorists are well aware of these internal divisions, and they have sought to locate mechanisms that allow the business community to formulate policies in its collective interests. Domhoff has stressed the role of social clubs and policymaking organizations; Mintz and Schwartz have emphasized the special role of large banks and insurance companies whose members sit on many major corporate boards; and Useem has stressed the role of an "inner circle" of corporate managers who sit on multiple corporate boards and play an active role in major business lobbying groups.[16] While these analyses are important for understanding the way that the business community is structured, they tend to exaggerate the ease with which the business community is able to locate its collective interests.

Part of the problem is that the process of attempting to formulate a coherent business position on a particular issue is itself a highly political process. Decisions have to be made about whose interests will be taken into account and whose will be neglected. Moreover, considerations of what is politically possible become extremely important in this process of aggregation. For example, in a business policy forum attempting to develop a unified proposal on tax reform or foreign trade policies, it will be necessary for Company X or Industry Y to make some concessions; they will have to accept some losses from the new proposal in order to secure other gains. However, the willingness to make these concessions depends on an assessment of what legislation is likely to pass. If Company X or Industry Y is afraid that the provisions legislating losses will be enacted, while the gain provisions will be tabled, they are likely to take quite different positions within the policy forum.

This concern with what kind of measures the state will actually enact means that attempts to form common business positions are shaped by the immediate political climate. If, for example, popular pressures for a particular reform measure seem overwhelmingly strong, business interests who actually oppose any version of the reform might throw their weight behind one version that seems least threatening to their interests. At another time, when popular sentiment is more positively disposed toward business, the consensus business position might push strongly for a reversal of earlier reform measures. The business community makes strenuous efforts to influence public opinion in particular directions, but the success of these efforts varies enormously. The result is that business opinion will appear more or less liberal or more or less conservative depending on the general political climate and what appears to be politically possible.

Processes of interest aggregation, in short, do not produce *the* business position, but *a* business position that is the result of political debate and strategic calculations. Many times, different business policy groupings have come up with quite different positions on a particular issue. But even when there is one position that appears to draw the support of the most important parts of the business community, that position could well have been different with a different political climate or a different process for aggregating interests. Consensus business proposals that emerge from such groups might diverge significantly from what the average businessperson favored before the political process began. These political processes mean that the reality of business dominance is quite different from a simple imposition of previously existing business views on the state.

How different can be seen from looking at the dominant political views within the business community. Most American businesspeople in the twentieth century have subscribed to a free market ideology that is basically hostile to governmental interference with business decision-making.[17] The basic outlines of this ideology are all too familiar since it is the same ideology that the Reagan presidency has espoused. At its core is the idea that the market, by itself, will produce rational outcomes, and that government regulations and provisions for social welfare tend to interfere with market rationality.

Businesspeople's support for this ideology does not prevent them from seeking help from the government for their own profit-making activities in the form of trade protection, subsidies, tax benefits, punitive treatment of strikers, government contracts, and so on. But despite this hypocrisy, the ideology of free markets allows them to reject the idea of any *quid pro quo* for the government support they receive. It would be logical for state managers to assume that in exchange for favorable treatment on issue 1, a firm or an industry would agree to help achieve state objectives on issue 2. But the free market ideology makes it possible for those firms to resist any linkage between the issues. Managers insist that their favorable treatment on issue 1 was necessary for sound business reasons, but that government interference on issue 2 would interfere with market rationality.[18]

But the critical point about the quintessentially capitalist ideology of the free market is its utter inadequacy as a basis for organizing a society. (See Chapter 9.) Karl Polanyi described the idea of a society organized around a self-regulating market as utopian because of its impossibility.[19] He argued that if markets were left to regulate themselves, society would quickly be destroyed. In the absence of any effort to regulate the conditions of labor, there would be a progressive lengthening of the working day and reduction of wage levels until the working population was unable to reproduce itself. Any capitalist who attempted to resist this intensified exploitation of the labor force would be unable to survive the competition. Also, in the absence of environmental regulation, there would be a complete degradation of the environment since firms would have every incentive to lower costs by increasing pollution and by reducing product quality, often in dangerous ways. As long as one assumes a competitive market of many firms, it is unlikely that an ethical firm would survive long enough to establish a reputation for more reliable products. Polanyi's point was that capitalism survived because the movement toward market freedom was combined at the outset with what he calls "the protective counter-movement"—the effort to protect society from the market in the form of government regulation and trade unionism. For example, the limits on the length of the working day that Parliament imposed in the Factory Acts served to protect the working class and, as Marx showed, created powerful incentives for technological innovation in capitalist production.[20] While it is unlikely that supporters of the free market will acknowledge that the Factory Acts played this critical role in capitalist development, the reality is that at every stage of development, the vitality of capitalism has depended on these types of governmental interference in the market.

Why do businesspeople continue to adhere to an ideology that does not provide a sound basis for organizing the society? Part of the answer is that by the very fact of governmental forms of regulation, they are insulated from living with the consequences of their ideology. Without having to suffer the reality of a self-regulating market society, they are left free to blame government intervention for all the defects of the capitalist economy. But the deeper reason is that the ideology of the free market is an extraordinarily powerful framework for defending their own freedom of action. In a society that professes democratic principles, it is not at all obvious why decisions to close a particular factory or to develop or not develop a new medication should be the exclusive prerogative of corporate managers. But free market ideology provides a powerful justification for that prerogative, and it is a justification that is bolstered by the "science" of economics that has shown that such decisions are likely to serve the general welfare when they are made by corporate managers responding to the market.

But this view of business ideology requires some modification of the business dominance thesis. It leads directly to the hypothesis that in those historical periods in which the hegemony of the business community is most absolute, when it is required to make fewest compromises in imposing its free market ideas on the state, the choice of policies will be most irrational. This would seem an apt description of the twenties, when business reigned supreme and created the conditions for the stock market crash and the Great Depression. If the Reagan administration had been more successful in its efforts to dismantle the welfare state, the long-term consequences of business hegemony in the eighties might have been as disastrous as in the twenties. As it is, the partial victories of the Reaganites—in weakening the regulatory apparatus, in undermining trade union strength, and in cutting spending for social welfare and social infrastructure—have done considerable damage to the vitality of American capitalism.[21]

In short, the capacity of the U.S. state to pursue policies to strengthen a capitalist social order cannot be attributed to business dominance alone. When the business community is able to impose its free market views, the consequences are far from rational because of the utopian idea of the self-regulating market and the irrationalities of the short-term pursuit of profit. On the contrary, the condition for effective state policy-making is that business dominance be constrained by other social groups and the state itself. Faced with these constraints, segments of the business community tend to push for policies that are more "realistic" in light of the existing balance of political forces. And under certain conditions, business loses almost all its influence over the policymaking process, opening the way for major reforms such as the Wagner Act, which granted collective bargaining rights to unions.[22]

Yet this approach points beyond the business dominance perspective because it stresses the importance of analyzing the processes within the state that mediate between business influence and policy outcomes. After all, state managers choose among business proposals: some business initiatives are implemented, others are rejected, and still others are modified. Often business dominance theorists are content to show the broad similarity between business proposals and policies that were implemented in a particular issue area.[23] Yet such an approach tends to ignore the political processes and calculations that were critical in the formulation of business positions, and it fails to examine the selection that state managers make among multiple proposals. It can also be that the broad similarity obscures some critical differences between business proposals and the policies that were actually implemented. Finally, such an approach is unlikely to examine the negative cases, important policy initiatives that began in the state in which business had little input or influence.[24]

All these considerations have been emphasized in the work of various state theorists who have pointed to such variables as popular mobilization, party politics, bureaucratic rivalries within the state, conflicts across different levels of government, and the existence or nonexistence of state capacities in order to explain policy outcomes.[25] It seems obvious that an adequate analysis must be attuned to the various forms of business influence and to the concrete ways in which popular mobilizations and public opinion intersect with those influences. Finally, attention must be paid to the ways in which the internal dynamics of the state filter and shape those varying influences.

Identifying Business Actors

Business dominance arguments often fail to make important distinctions between business and nonbusiness social actors. The basic reality of a business-dominated society is that many members of the middle classes—academics, lawyers, professional politicians, civil servants, employees of nonprofit agencies or foundations, and even reformers and union officials—will have some kind of personal links to the business community. They might come from business families, sit on boards of community or charitable organizations with businesspeople, or even be directly dependent on the largesse of philanthropists who made their money in business. But the existence of these kinds of personal connections do not—in themselves—prove anything. When people from upper-class families become committed radicals, it makes little sense to see that radicalism as an expression of their class interests. But when people from a similar background become committed to one or another type of reformist activity, it is all too common to treat that activity as a direct expression of their material position, as evidence of business commitment to reform.

The same problem presents itself in evaluating the role of academic experts. It is very likely that an individual who becomes a national advocate of a particular social reform will—as the reform approaches implementation—have a range of business connections such as foundation support for research and contact with businesspeople in a range of policy organizations. But what level of such contacts is sufficient to identify the academic as representing the interests of a particular sector of the business community? How do we know that the academic is not actually using businesspeople to advance his or her own agenda?

It is useful in such instances to recognize the distortions that can result from historical perspective. When we are talking about an upper-class reformer or an academic expert in the Progressive period, for example, it might seem quite plausible to imagine that the individual was representing the interests and concerns of the business community. But in thinking about contemporary politics, we can easily imagine comparable individuals—such as upper-class activists in the peace movement, academic experts on comparable worth, or consumer advocates—whom it would be implausible to label as representatives of business interests. There is, in brief, a danger of tautology in business dominance formulations. Since business activity is the key source of wealth in the society and many political actors can be linked to that wealth in one way or another, it is easy to show that virtually all political initiatives are business-dominated. But at this level of generality, the argument becomes meaningless because it is disconnected from any serious specification of what business interests are and how they are routinely advanced. Moreover, there is a failure to address the issue of whether a particular initiative that is being linked to one or another business interest has any kind of widespread business support.

Two steps are necessary to overcome this problem. First, it is important to specify more precisely the dividing line between business and nonbusiness actors, so that it is not true by definition that business dominates all of political life. Second, it is important to recognize that there is a long historical tradition of middle-class reformism that has a quite complex relationship to capitalism. At times, this middle-class reformism can have a significant anticapitalist edge; at other times, it can coincide with and reinforce the interests of particular segments of the business community; and sometimes, it lies between these two extremes or is a complex combination of both. But the failure to be able to distinguish between middle-class reformist impulses and business dominance results in an impoverished understanding of the complex politics of capitalist societies.

It follows from these three points that the debate between advocates of business dominance and their critics is one of the many disputes in the social sciences that cannot be resolved by simple appeals to the data. Each side is able to construct its own data that have been shaped by theoretical premises.[26] So each side might see the participation of a particular individual as support for its interpretation, since one side treats that individual as an independent academic expert and the other views him or her as a representative of a business-dominated policy group. Similarly, a particular business intervention might be seen by one side as reflecting fundamental business support for a policy initiative while the other side might see it as a form of damage control to change some features of an initiative that business sees as unstoppable. Most fundamentally, there is no way to measure what proportion of a particular piece of legislation can be explained by business dominance variables as opposed to state-centered or class struggle variables. Ironically, the closer the debate comes to actual empirical cases, the more sterile and less informative it becomes.

Situating the Work

My own contributions to state theory (especially Chapters 2, 3, and 5) were efforts to build on the first two of these critiques of business dominance formulations. I wanted to offer an alternative to the reductionism that characterizes much Marxist analysis, since it seemed that some writers in this tradition felt compelled to explain any particular state policy as reflecting the interests of one or another fraction of the capitalist class.

I began to develop this alternative when I was struggling to make sense of historical materials. My dissertation project (subsequently published as *The Origins of International Economic Disorder*) was an effort to understand United States international monetary policies in the three decades from World War II to 1971. This was a policy arena where divisions within the business community were often sharp and where different parts of the executive branch also had conflicting priorities. One of the most interesting aspects of the study was the discovery that the American policymakers who originally designed the International Monetary Fund did not share the vision of an open world economy that dominated the State Department and American foreign policy in the post–World War II period. In this and other cases, I could not satisfactorily explain historical developments within available Marxist formulations.

In the dissertation and the book, I was able to sidestep many of these theoretical issues by focusing on the policies themselves. But when I was done with the book, I felt a need to extract what I had learned about state theory from the historical materials. The results were a series of essays with two main emphases. The first was a greater acknowledgment of the autonomy of state actors in formulating and implementing policies than Marxists had generally acknowledged. The second was a sharp rejection of the idea that capitalists understand what is necessary to reproduce a capitalist social order. My argument instead was that the rationality of a capitalist order does not come from the understanding of capitalists, but that it is rather a consequence of the three-sided conflicts among capitalists, state managers, and the working class.

It can easily be argued that my approach was colored by the particular issue area that I had studied. United States international monetary policy is a particularly complex field that is distant from the immediate problems of running a business. Moreover, it is an issue area that intersects with the most important problems of statecraft—maintaining the nation's position within a capitalist world economy and a competitive state system. It seems logical that in this issue area, state managers would have a higher level of autonomy in formulating policies, and that most business interests would be either uncertain or confused about how to resolve the various tensions in international economic relations.[27]

While it is useful to recognize that the level of state autonomy varies by issue areas, I would still argue that the case of international monetary policy is by no means atypical. Once the focus is on national-level policies whether defense, foreign trade, energy, taxes, welfare, or labor, there is a comparable degree of complexity. In all cases, there are multiple business interests and it is not easy to see how they can be reconciled in a manner that will protect the nation's international position and maintain a reasonable degree of social peace. The result is that state managers have a good deal of freedom to maneuver in formulating policies, and businesspeople have a great deal of difficulty figuring out which policies would benefit them over the long term. In sum, while international monetary policy might represent an extreme case, it is one that effectively illuminates much of the terrain of national-level policy formation.[28]

New Developments

Since the articles of Part I were written, there have been two important developments in state theory that require some discussion. The first is the development of a body of literature that focuses on the irreducibility of politics and the second is the elaboration of state-centered theory, particularly in the work of Theda Skocpol.

The arguments about the irreducibility of politics have been elaborated most explicitly in the work of David Plotke, Ernesto Laclau, and Chantal Mouffe.[29] All these theorists have their roots in the Marxist tradition, but they are sharply critical of the Marxist tendency to understand politics simply as an expression of class forces. The critique begins with the idea that classes or any social groupings are themselves constituted through political processes; social groupings and social mobilization are not an automatic consequence of social structure.[30] Moreover political struggles have the potential to constantly reshape lines of political conflict or coalition; much political discourse can be understood as efforts to persuade people that their interests converge or diverge with those of certain others. It follows from this that it is misguided to see political outcomes as flowing in a determinate way from the mobilization of social interests. The political process itself shapes both perceptions of interest and the outcomes, and there is inevitably a high degree of indeterminacy to this dynamic.[31]

This line of argument pushes ideology toward the center of state theory, since political struggles are ultimately struggles over ideas. Contending groups attempt to generate support for their positions by drawing on one or another strand of ideology, and they challenge opposing groups by showing that their proposals are inconsistent with accepted ideological premises. This approach also leaves considerable room for the role of psychological factors, since the effectiveness or ineffectiveness of political leaders in these rhetorical struggles has much to do with personality and their capacity to respond to conscious or unconscious needs of various segments of the population.

This approach to politics indicates some of the limitations of my work. First, my articles tend to suggest that the only important actors—other than state managers—are class actors—either subordinate classes or the capitalist class. I would now revise that to include many other collective actors organized around race, gender, age, sexual orientation, religious orientation, or shared views about the environment or the arms race. In place of a narrow focus on "class struggles," the emphasis would be on a broad range of social struggles.

Second, the emphasis on the irreducibility of politics is a useful reminder that my articles simply lay out a model of some of the most important determinants of political outcomes within capitalist democracies. But this model will be of only limited use in making sense of any particular political outcome because it does not capture variations in political structures, political resources, and political ideas. Part of the problem springs from confusion over what a theory is actually supposed to do. American social science is torn between at least two competing conceptions of theory. In the first, the idea is to abstract from the specifics of different situations to generate a model that captures the most important dynamics. This is what economists do in building models, and they argue that if everything else is equal, the same results will hold across situations. In this tradition, the truth is in the model and not in the complexities of the particular situation because the model is supposed to capture the underlying laws that tend to be obscured by superficial variations. In the second tradition, a model is only a device to facilitate analysis of specific historical situations. Rather than beginning from scratch to make sense of the situation, the model provides a first approximation and then one looks at additional factors to provide a coherent explanation for the specific situation. In this second model, the truth is in the situation, but models are valuable to the extent that they provide initial illumination for a variety of situations.

Significantly, these different versions of theory cut across the division between mainstream and Marxist scholarship. While Marxists tend to be critical of the positivist bias of the first model of theory, it is also the case that much of the Marxist tradition rests on the idea that the analysis of the mode of production reveals the truth of a social order. Whereas I would now argue that the theory I was advancing was of the second type, the Marxist discourse of the pieces suggests that I was proposing a complete model. This confusion was costly because it made my work subject to a functionalist reading that I had not intended.

The argument I make in Chapter 3 can easily be interpreted to suggest that there is at work in capitalist democracies a selection mechanism that invariably chooses policy outcomes that are consistent with the long-term needs of the capitalist system. That reading is possible precisely because the article does not stress the openness of the model—the extent to which specific circumstances will shape policy outcomes. Above all, the model gives insufficient weight to the extremely unpredictable role of ideological struggles in shaping state actions. In this sense, the emphasis on indeterminacy by the theorists of the nonreducibility of politics is a valuable corrective.

On the other hand, there are also problems with the position of these theorists of the autonomy of the political realm. The first difficulty is most obvious in the work of Laclau and Mouffe, whose emphasis on indeterminacy is so strong that even theories of the second type are treated as potentially leading to reification—giving solidity to arrangements that are far more ephemeral. In their effort to avoid reification, Laclau and Mouffe appear to reduce all social structures to discourse. They appear to reject even a relatively open model of the political process that was designed to be only a first approximation of fairly typical political patterns.

Another problem is that Laclau and Mouffe never address the question of whether the level of indeterminacy is itself historically variable. Could it be that an analysis of social structural factors gives us less leverage for making sense of contemporary politics than a comparable analysis fifty or one hundred years ago? Such an argument seems plausible in that the greater material wealth of contemporary society both expands the range of choice for individuals and reduces the extent to which politics is a struggle over economic survival for the majority of people. The issue is whether these theorists are making a methodological correction of errors of past theories or simply building on the empirical observation that in our own historical period, it is the case that anything seems possible.

The systematization of a state-centered approach in the work of

Theda Skocpol has been the other important new development in state theory.[32] Skocpol has energetically argued that both the liberal and the Marxist traditions have been society-centered, explaining what goes on in the state as a function of what goes on in society. Her alternative is a state-centered approach that would provide a corrective to the standard view by stressing the diverse ways in which the state structures social life.

As with many intellectual positions, there is both a soft and a hard version of Skocpol's position. The soft version is quite close to the position I elaborate in Chapter 3; it stresses that states act in the context of social struggles between capitalists and subordinate groups. Hence, in her 1980 article, Skocpol explicitly builds on my model, but insists that to explain the actual policy outcomes in the New Deal, one has to place greater emphasis on state-level variables, such as the political capacities of state managers and struggles within and between the executive and legislative branches of government. This softer version of her arguments draws attention to variables that are insufficiently emphasized in my argument—the degree to which state action shapes and conditions social struggles. She is also able to incorporate many of the findings of business dominance theorists about specific means by which business influences the state, but she shows very effectively that those arguments are incomplete.

But there is also a harder version of Skocpol's argument in which she claims that state-centered variables are more important than society-centered variables in explaining particular historical outcomes. This version appears in a number of her case studies of particular policy outcomes, so there is ambiguity as to whether the superiority of state-centered variables is specific to these cases or is being invoked as a more general principle. But either way, she is in the position of arguing that for these cases, business dominance accounts are not just incomplete; they are simply wrong because they explain outcomes at the societal level that are more appropriately explained at the state level.

For example, in a recent essay, one key problem for Skocpol and her coauthor is to explain why Britain, unlike Sweden or the United States, failed to develop innovative Keynesian responses to the Great Depression.[33] The core of the explanation is that in Great Britain, new economic ideas were not able to develop a foothold for development within the state apparatus because they were "stifled from within the state by Treasury control and parried from without by the normal, self-enclosed functioning of British Government." This is in direct contrast to Sweden, where economists with innovative ideas were able to gain direct influence within the state apparatus. Yet no effort is made to link the Treasury's dominance over economic policy in Britain to the City of London's enormous influence over the British economy. Nor is there any serious acknowledgment that the Treasury, and in turn the City's, resistance to any economic innovation was linked to their defense of the pound's international economic role. But the reality was that the obstacles to economic innovation in Britain after the onset of the Great Depression were of a piece with the factors that precipitated the disastrous overvaluing of the pound in 1925—a story that had much to do with economic interests.

This harder version of Skocpol's line of argument is also vulnerable to critique because the sorting out between state-level and societal-level variables is ultimately arbitrary. The point is that state and society are interdependent and interpenetrate in a multitude of different ways. Even in the most extreme cases that we have of states that sought maximal control and domination of civil society—such as in Nazi Germany or in Stalinist Russia—we know that state initiatives were constantly either frustrated or reshaped by societal forces. The point, quite obviously, is that our analyses need to integrate societal-level and state-level factors and that arguments about which of these factors are more important tend to divert us from the more important issue of understanding the complex and changing interaction between state and society.[34]

Some of these difficulties in Skocpol's position can be traced to her emphasis on one dimension of the state-society relationship—the development of state bureaucracies with professional civil servants and considerable expertise. While there is no doubt about the importance of the development of public bureaucracies, an exclusive focus on this aspect can result in an inadequate understanding of the state–society relationship. It has to be emphasized that building a strong bureaucracy need not produce effective state action; the outcome depends on the particulars of the interaction between state bureaucracy and society. There are ample examples of highly professionalized bureaucracies that have interacted with society very ineffectively.[35] Moreover, there are also many instances of effective state actions that do not fit within the model of strengthening bureaucratic capacities.

The problem is that the idea of state-building that is often present in Skocpol's work is not the best metaphor for grasping the relationship between state and society. It is a metaphor drawn from construction that suggests that the more effectively the state is built, the more it will be able to shape and influence society. But if a well-built state is like a well-built house, it should keep out the social equivalents of rain and the wind—the influences from society. Yet the strong state is often quite open to societal influences like the development of new policy ideas. It seems more

accurate to use an organic metaphor in which the state–society relationship is controlled by a membrane that selectively permits some
influences, ideas, and resources to pass in one direction or the other.
Hence, when we seek to understand the capacities of a particular national
society, our attention is focused on the membrane, on the actual ways in
which state and society interact.

Part II: The Context of the Debate

One of the most striking aspects of recent work on state theory is that
ideas and arguments that developed initially on the leftward fringes of
American academic life are now part of mainstream discussions in political sociology and political science. In particular, the disproportionate
power of the business community is now widely acknowledged, so that
arguments about how that power is exercised are a critical part of mainstream discussions. It is tempting to explain this development as another
indication of a leftward shift in academic discourse that has resulted from
the incorporation of a generation of academics who were shaped by the
New Left. But this is too simple, especially because one can point to many
examples of leftist ideas that have far less resonance in the academic
community today than twenty years ago.

It seems more likely that the explanation has to do with a change in
the society that has led both leftists and mainstream academics to recon-
sider earlier positions, and that this reconsideration has brought them to
convergent positions. There is some anecdotal evidence for this. For
example, my essay that appears here in Chapter 3 was published at about
the same time that Charles Lindblom published his *Politics and Markets*,[36]
but the two works coming out of very different traditions emphasized the
structural power of the business community. Similarly, when Stephen
Krasner—a self-described conservative—published his book, *Defending
the National Interest* in 1978,[37] he had to acknowledge that it was difficult to
distinguish his position on the relation between business and the state
from that of structural Marxists.

But if there was such a change in society to which diverse theorists
responded in somewhat convergent ways, it does not follow that they
adequately grasped the nature of the change. On the contrary, it is
another case where the Owl of Minerva takes flight at dusk, where
theoretical understanding comes only at the very end of an historical
period. The irony, of course, is that the theoretical understanding illuminates the period that has passed but not the period in which we
actually live.

What is at work here is a relatively simple sociological dynamic—that institutionalized relations of power tend to become visible only when they weaken. When these institutionalized relations are most effective, they tend to be invisible, precisely because the justifying ideologies so dominate people's commonsense understandings.[38] The classic recent example is the existence of women's subordination. In the fifties, people would have responded to the claim that women were systematically discriminated against in American society with incredulity because they had so totally accepted an ideology that justified differential treatment of men and women as normal and natural. The full-blown analysis and critique of male domination emerges only in the seventies, when patriarchal arrangements are already weakening. And by the eighties, some feminists have come to recognize that analyses of capitalist patriarchy refer to arrangements that no longer exist.[39]

In state theory, the development is analogous. In the fifties, pluralist arguments dominate because the exercise of power has been rendered invisible. The relation between business and the state works so well that it leaves few traces. Moreover, there is little real debate about how the society should be structured, so the extent to which everyone's basic assumptions fit with the interests of corporate capitalism is not at all obvious. Since nobody was even asking the big questions of who should make investment decisions and how should income and wealth be distributed, it was not apparent that the narrow limits of debate fit exactly with the interests of business. Moreover, the pluralist model worked to make sense of the less weighty issues that formed the substance of actual political debates. To be sure, C. Wright Mills directly challenged this consensus with the publication of *The Power Elite*,[40] but the responses to him were as extreme as they would have been to a major intellectual figure advancing a radical feminist analysis in 1956.[41] Mills, in short, was perceived as outrageous because he questioned what were perceived as normal and natural features of the American social order. As mentioned earlier, the New Left took up Mills's critique of the pluralists in the mid-sixties, but pluralists continued to insist that business was simply another interest group. However, the cumulative impact of Vietnam and racial conflict in the late sixties, the drama of Watergate, and the growing economic difficulties of advanced capitalist societies in the early seventies served to make the exercise of power in American society widely visible. The previous functional relation between the state and business had been disrupted and the efforts by each side to advance its own interests became more apparent.

This is the context in which Marxists who were attempting to move beyond business dominance theories converge with mainstream analysts who were now willing to recognize the importance of the state and the disproportionate influence of the business community. Suddenly, this new convergent view appears as commonsensical as pluralist analysis did in the fifties. But what is interesting about the analyses at the point of convergence is that they have a bias toward functionalism; they are still seeking to explain the relative political stability of the period in which pluralist analyses were dominant. They fail to address the issue of why the exercise of power had again become transparent within American society. They do not tell us why the previously functional relation between state and business has been disrupted.

Dysfunctionality

The most visible factor in the breakdown of the relatively smooth relation between state and business were problems of macroeconomic management. In the fifties and sixties macroeconomic policies had succeeded in producing reasonable economic growth with relatively low levels of unemployment and inflation. But this changed in the seventies; macroeconomic policy in the United States took a number of different turns, but regardless of the policies pursued, growth appeared to slow, profits stagnated, and unemployment and inflation climbed. These policy failures produced increasingly intense conflicts over the nature of the state's role in managing the economy.

As I argue in Chapter 5, the business community's response to these developments was dominated by the fear of a further extension of the state's role in managing the economy. In the early seventies, an increased government role in national economic planning that included a relatively stable system of wage and price controls and some kind of measures for allocating capital among different purposes seemed a rather logical response to the nation's macroeconomic problems (see Chapter 2). Such fears were heightened when even the relatively conservative Nixon administration took the first step toward a more interventionist policy by imposing mandatory wage and price controls. But such a scenario of increased governmental intervention conflicted with the U.S. business community's particularly strong preoccupation with maintaining managerial freedom of action. The fear was that movement toward some version of national economic planning would fatally impair the freedom of firms to pursue profits as they wished.

The business community responded by mounting a campaign to shift the focus of blame for the macroeconomic problems from business to government. The basic premise of this campaign was that if it was government intervention that had produced the problems, then it would be illogical to opt for even more government intervention. This message was pounded home through paid advertisements, op-ed columns, and hundreds of studies produced by conservative think tanks funded by business. This campaign contributed to the 1980 defeat of Jimmy Carter by Ronald Reagan, who espoused free market economic arguments that had not been taken seriously since the early days of the Great Depression.

Before Reagan's triumph, the politics of the seventies were characterized by conflicts between business and the state. On the one hand, an assertive business community was advancing a general critique of government intervention in the economy and often found itself in conflict with the administration in power. On the other hand, the Nixon, Ford, and Carter administrations were hardly passive instruments of business purpose. While all three administrations—for quite different reasons— had severe problems of effectiveness, it was evident that they were struggling as best they could to develop policy responses to the macroeconomic problems. However, their responses were also obviously constrained by the considerable power of the business community. It was in this historical context that analyses that simultaneously emphasized the autonomy of state managers and the disproportionate influence of the business community made intuitive sense.

In sum, the problems of macroeconomic management of the seventies helped to generate a new consensual view about the relationship of business and the state. But the key question is why did these seemingly unsolvable macroeconomic problems develop in the seventies? What happened to throw the previous relationship between state and economy off the track? While there are a range of possible answers to this question, I will address two of the most widely held answers and then propose my own alternative explanation.

The answer advanced by the business community has been that the problem is rooted in an excess of government intervention in the economy—too much regulation, too much welfare spending, too high taxes. Ironically, the same argument has also been advanced by some left intellectuals who have argued that the reforms won by the working class have destabilized welfare capitalism.[42] There are many problems with this line of argument; its theoretical weaknesses are addressed in Chapter 9. But the empirical weaknesses are revealed by the failure of Reagan's free market economic policies to restore healthy economic growth in the United States. There was rapid growth in the Reagan recovery from 1982 to 1984, but this seemed to result more from the stimulus of accelerating military spending than the impact of "supply-side" tax cuts. Moreover, in 1985 and 1986, the economy was sluggish, unemployment remained at historically high levels, and the growing size of the foreign trade deficit was hardly an indication of dynamism. The fact that the results of Margaret Thatcher's somewhat different experiment with free market policies have been even worse suggests that "too much government" is not a persuasive explanation for the macroeconomic difficulties.[43]

Another possible answer is that the problem was precisely the failure to move toward national economic planning, toward a more interventionist economic policy in which the government would play a more active role in the allocation of capital. This has been the position of some of the American advocates of industrial policy who have argued that economic vitality can be restored by the government exercising more influence over investment. Since this path has not been taken, it is difficult to evaluate this line of argument. But the experiences of other countries leads to skepticism about the positive contributions that investment planning policies can make by themselves.

In recent years, there is a growing literature that points to the relative economic successes of some of the smaller countries of Western Europe—the Nordic countries, Austria, and Switzerland—some of which have extensive government involvement in the economy.[44] This literature is valuable as a further refutation of the claim that too much government is the problem, since some of these countries have performed better than the United States in controlling inflation and unemployment despite their higher rates of taxes and welfare spending. In Sweden and Norway, for example, mechanisms have been developed for controlling the growth of prices and wages that involve tripartite arrangements among government, business, and labor, but government planning of investment flows has not been central to their efforts and government tends to play a mediating role rather than a directive role. Moreover, it is easy to exaggerate the relative successes of these countries; they have done much better than anyone could have expected, but they hardly represent a new model of macroeconomic management.

Japan is, of course, the success story of government planning that is usually invoked by advocates of industrial policy. But the Japanese model of state planning is difficult to export to the very different institutional environment of Western societies.[45] Moreover, some of the Japanese industrial successes have as much to do with the internal organization of firms, such as the organization of the labor force and the systems of inventory and quality control, as with policies pursued at the national level.

The most glaring recent negative experience was that of France in the first years of the Mitterrand government. The government put in place a strategy to speed the modernization of the French economy through the nationalization of banking and key industries and direct stimulus to consumer demand. The idea was that the nationalizations would give the government more influence over investment flows and the spurs to consumption would make certain that both private and public firms would expand their capacities. But the plan had limited successes and no dent was made in the high rates of unemployment.[46] The French Socialists had to contend with unfavorable international economic conditions—other major nations were contracting their economies at the time—and with the hostility of the business community. Yet there seems little evidence that these interventionist policies would have succeeded had they been left in place for a longer period of time.

In sum, the two standard explanations for the macroeconomic problem are too little reliance on markets or too little reliance on government planning of investment, but neither of the implied solutions seems to represent an effective response to the problems. And this, in turn, has severely disrupted the state–business relationship because neither of the moves that have worked in the past shows much promise of success. On the one hand, a return to greater reliance on the market has not produced the desired results. On the other hand, greater government involvement in shaping capital flows—which seems to be the logical next step for those who have advocated the use of the state to rationalize the economy—does not represent a persuasive alternative.

Postindustrial Transition

My argument is that both the macroeconomic problems and the exhaustion of the traditional repertoires of policy responses can best be understood as products of a period of postindustrial transition. (For an early formulation of the idea of postindustrial transition, written in collaboration with Larry Hirschhorn, see Chapter 6). The idea of postindustrial transition is that a number of current trends—cultural, technological, and social—come into conflict with the patterns of social and economic organization that dominated in the period of industrialism. Among these trends are greater fluidity in the adult life course, the computerization of work, the accelerating shift from goods production to services, and the emergence of postbureaucratic forms of work organization.[47] This conflict between new trends and old patterns creates a period of social disruption in which institutions fail and people lack any clear sense of how social life can be reorganized. The very term *postindustrial* conveys the lack of any positive sense of new principles of social organization; it is simply that the society has moved beyond industrialism and there is a need to invent new patterns of social organization.[48]

Some of the ways in which postindustrial trends disrupt the economic concepts and the economic policies of industrial capitalism are addressed in Chapters 6, 7, and 8. I argue in Chapter 8 that even our accounting schemes for measuring economic growth are rooted in industrial assumptions, so they are inadequate for measuring new forms of economic growth based on services and computerization. The result is that there is an absence of an accurate picture of what is going on in the economy, much less satisfactory policy directions.

This is one of the key factors in undermining macroeconomic policies; the economy is qualitatively different from the one for which the dominant economic theories were devised. Hence, the policy prescriptions based on those theories tend to have indifferent or even contradictory results. For example, almost all currents of contemporary economics focus their concern on manufacturing as the key sector of the economy. But it turns out that in the United States, services constitute close to 60 percent of all consumer purchases, compared with 14 percent for durable manufactured goods.[49] This does not mean that policies should ignore manufacturing, but there is a need for a more accurate grasp of the structure of contemporary economies.

A closely related problem has to do with the shrinking of manufacturing employment, particularly production workers (see Chapter 7). This employment category was the central pivot of industrial society for more than a hundred years, but this traditional industrial working class is now contracting at a rapid pace as a result of new technological advances. This contraction makes it substantially harder—although not impossible—to achieve full employment. On the one hand, the sectors of employment where growth seems probable—public sector, trade, finance, and various services—are sensitive to specific institutional variables; there are wide variations among the developed capitalist countries in the relative growth of these sectors.[50] On the other hand, claims for jobs in these potentially expanding sectors are being advanced by women who were previously outside the labor force. The result is rising levels of labor force participation that makes full employment dependent on particularly vigorous growth in these highly variable tertiary sectors.

The problems of the labor market are one example of a general pattern; postindustrial developments place institutional problems at the center of the policy agenda. Traditional macroeconomic policies were purely quantitative—increase aggregate demand, slow the growth of the money supply, reduce taxes—but these measures fail to address the new problems. The new problems are institutional; how can firms be organized to make maximal productive use of human skills and technological advances; how can services like health care and education—which constitute a growing share of total consumption expenditures—be organized most effectively; how can we devise mechanisms for deciding about the allocation of capital to infrastructure development—transportation, energy, communications—in a situation where neither the market nor centralized planning has proven its effectiveness? In each of these cases, the problem calls for new institutional solutions rather than a simple extension of the state's power to regulate the economy.

In sum, I want to suggest that progress in addressing the macroeconomic problems created by postindustrial developments requires a fundamental change in the nature of the state–economy relationship. While a number of diverse ways of restructuring the state–economy relationship are imaginable, the path I see as preferable encompasses a number of initiatives that can be grouped under the heading of the debureaucratization of the state.

The debureaucratization of the state must not be confused with a libertarian or anarchist vision of a reversal of the state's central role in coordinating social life. On the contrary, a debureaucratized state could well be more influential and more indispensable than the bureaucratized state, but the ways in which the state exercises its power would change.[51]

Debureaucratizing the State
One of the main signposts of postindustrial change are the efforts by corporations to devise new forms of organization that diverge sharply from classical Weberian bureaucracies. It is now widely understood that classical bureaucracies with their elaborate hierarchies and precise specification of the responsibilities of each officeholder work best in situations in which the tasks to be carried out are stable over time. In situations where an organization faces a rapidly changing environment and must continually adapt its activities, the classical bureaucratic structure encounters numerous problems. Most important of these are slow responses to new situations, lack of adequate horizontal coordination among employees at the same level of the organization, and an inability to motivate lower-level employees to take initiatives.[52]

These problems have led to a variety of efforts to devise postbureaucratic organizational forms that are characterized by fewer levels of supervision, diminished deference to hierarchical authority, greater reliance on teamwork, and expanded decisionmaking responsibilities for lower-level employees. While these new organizational forms create new conflicts and new problems, these postbureaucratic organizations are more effective than traditional bureaucracies in situations where changing technologies and changing markets create high levels of uncertainty and unpredictability.

It seems only logical that similar organizational changes would be appropriate for government agencies that also face rapid changes in their environments. If one thinks, for example, of the normal procedures of government regulatory agencies such as the Environmental Protection Agency or the Food and Drug Administration, it seems obvious that even when the agencies are working to fulfill their legislated missions, they cannot possibly keep pace with the multiple hazards that they are supposed to protect against. Most importantly, they have very little organizational capacity to develop quick responses to new regulatory situations.

In fact, one of the reasons that the business attack on government regulation gains some resonance with the public is precisely that these agencies are often so rigid and bureaucratic in their responses. When lower-level employees must work with a fixed protocol, they cannot waive the completion of irrelevant forms nor can they respond to the uniqueness of the given situation. The whole structure of the organization leads to a much greater concern with following procedures than with assuring desirable outcomes.[53]

There are, of course, good historical reasons why state agencies have been confined by this kind of strict proceduralism. When agents of the state are free to respond to each situation according to their own subjective evaluation, those who are subject to regulation have little protection against arbitrary and capricious actions. In this respect, bureaucratic procedures were an advance over informal decisionmaking. But they are an advance that leads to paralysis when decisionmaking must continually confront an array of situations that do not fit precisely within the existing rules.

There is, however, an alternative to the arbitrary exercise of governmental power on the one hand and regulatory paralysis on the other. This is a shift from a procedural to a substantive concept of regulation that is implemented through links between state agents and organized groups in the society. There have been efforts in this direction in Scandinavia particularly in the area of occupational health and safety. The basic premise is that the goal of regulatory policy cannot be captured in formal goals such as reducing exposure to hazardous chemicals to a certain designated level. On the contrary, the goal is to create a progressively safer work environment, and it is understood that this is dependent upon creating different attitudes and behavior at the workplace. The key agents in the regulatory process become workplace health and safety committees that take on the formal role of monitoring management actions. These workplace committees work closely with government agents who are able to mobilize legal sanctions in cases where management refuses to cooperate to correct a dangerous situation. However, the use of legal coercion is a last resort; the basic idea is that government support empowers the health and safety committee to be able to negotiate effectively with management.[54]

A regulatory model that built on these experiences could be applied well beyond issues of workplace health and safety. It would place considerable responsibility in the hands of frontline government regulators who would work with workplace or citizens' committees. However, this model also provides protections for the regulated since legal sanctions can be used only when the government agents and the grassroots committee make an effective case before an independent tribunal. Yet the debate within this tribunal would not be narrowly procedural; it would revolve around what constitutes reasonable progress toward the regulatory goal.[55]

This model could be used to address fundamental issues of organizational efficiency. While there is considerable evidence that more democratic forms of work organization are more efficient under current conditions, many American managers are reluctant to abandon the familiar authoritarian forms of work organization. With appropriate changes in labor law, it would be possible for government agents to provide critical support for employees' efforts to force management to adopt more democratic and more productive ways of organizing the workplace. It could also be used for environmental regulation. One can imagine local environmental groups being provided with some of the technology and expertise necessary to monitor various environmental hazards so they could work with the support of government agents to negotiate steady improvements in environmental practices.

Similar kinds of reforms could be applied to social decisionmaking about basic infrastructural investment decisions like energy or transportation planning. In addition to the elite groups that have historically dominated such planning, the government would also fund the development of counterplans in which citizens groups, drawing on both public and expert inputs, would develop alternative plans for meeting the same objectives. Then the legislative decision would be a choice of one among several alternative plans, and if public support for one of the counterplans were sufficiently strong, there would be a chance of its implementation.

Another important area of debureaucratization are changes in welfare policies. The basic thrust of welfare policies throughout industrial capitalism has been compensatory, to provide income for marginalized groups—the old, the disabled, mothers and children—while minimizing the interference with market incentives. With compensatory welfare, the state is in the position of "regulating the poor."[56] The alternative model is of welfare as empowering—providing resources that people can use to upgrade their education and skills, to provide services to other family members such as children or aged parents, or to launch new business or nonprofit initiatives. In contrast to compensatory welfare, it is undesirable that empowering welfare policies be used to stigmatize and regulate recipients. On the contrary, the whole idea is to create an environment in which people will take initiatives. With rapid rates of job change and continuing marital instability, large parts of the population can and should take advantage of empowering welfare resources.

In recent years, many of the developed capitalist countries have made small steps in the direction of empowering welfare in response to rising unemployment levels. The Comprehensive Employment and Training Act in the United States and a comparable program in Canada made it possible for groups of people to receive grants to provide nonprofit services to a community. In a number of countries, provisions have been made to provide unemployment benefits in a lump sum, so an individual can start a small business, and there are a range of different efforts to provide resources to unemployed individuals for additional education or training.[57]

While these examples suggest that there are many dimensions to debureaucratization, there are three centrally important elements. First, there is a shift within the state apparatus from bureaucratic to postbureaucratic forms of organization, so that lower-level employees are able to respond flexibly to different situations. Second, there is a shift from procedural to substantive regulation; the goal becomes to solve a problem or to put in place mechanisms that can solve problems as they develop. Finally, there is a reliance on an increased level of activity and organization among nonstate actors. The state plays a critical role in facilitating the mobilization of these nonstate actors by providing resources, protection, and the exercise of its legal authority, but without this mobilization of nonstate actors, there is little likelihood that these new forms of state regulation will be effective.

This means that debureaucratization of the state depends on a renewal of political participation in which the citizenry plays a more active role in the regulation of social life. But this renewal need not take the form of nineteenth- and early twentieth-century mass politics; it does not have to mean huge street demonstrations and parties of radical opposition to the status quo. It could, instead, build on workplace organizations and on the rich tradition of civic and voluntary organizations that have always characterized American social life. But whatever form this revival were to take, it requires a reversal of the trends toward privatism and political apathy that draw individuals away from any sustained engagement with politics.

The argument, in sum, is that postindustrial developments create new problems of macroeconomic management that cannot be met effectively within the historic framework of state–society relations. A reshaping of this relationship—what I have called the debureaucratization of the state—represents a way to respond to the institutional problems of postindustrial development. While this debureaucratization of the state increases the state's capacity for effective action, it depends critically on a revival of political participation and involvement.

The debureaucratization of the state will be resisted by the business community. The same defense of management autonomy that has led managers to resist earlier forms of state regulation will lead them to resist these potentially more intrusive forms of regulation with even greater intensity. Moreover, any revival of popular political participation runs up against the growing dominance of American politics by big money media campaigns, in which business influence is magnified by the importance of campaign contributions. In the near term, there seems little likelihood of any alternative to the continuing stalemate between a powerful bureaucratic state and a powerful business community, neither of which has the policies or capacities to respond effectively to the problems of postindustrial transition.

In the longer term, however, the prospects are somewhat better. Albert Hirschman has persuasively argued that Western societies experience an alternation between periods in which private pursuits are dominant and periods of intense concern with the public interest.[38] His argument suggests that the current period of extreme privatism will not go on forever. Yet the critical issue is what will be the lasting political consequences of a new cycle of interest in public concerns. If extensive steps toward debureaucratizing the state are taken during that period, those changes can institutionalize a higher level of political involvement that could persist even into a new period of privatism. If, on the other hand, this new period of political engagement leads only to an increase in the power and responsibilities of a bureaucratic state, then the opportunity to break out of the stalemate will be lost.

Even if the debureaucratization of the state begins, there will still be intense conflicts of interest among various groups in the society. The fundamental issues of equality and social justice that the left has long struggled over will be undiminished in their urgency. The point is only to suggest possible political developments that would make it possible— once again—that those conflicts and struggles could produce results other than eternal stalemate.

A Final Note on Marxism

The intellectual evolution reflected in the essays and in this introduction raises the question of my current relation to Marxism. Since the essays that were written earlier use an explicitly Marxist discourse, while those that were written more recently do not, some explanation is in order. However, it is not a simple matter to clarify this issue.

As with other New Left intellectuals, my approach to Marxism, from the start, rejected the more positivist and reductionist strands of the tradition and favored the more critical and holistic currents.[59] Our collective project was to see if a coherent theoretical framework could be shaped out of the "unknown dimension"—the more or less underground tradition of critical Marxism.[60] But the task of producing coherence proved more intractable than we had expected. We found that many of the key concepts that promised to provide coherence to a Marxist analysis did so at the cost of an unjustifiable narrowing of the array of causal factors. The Marxist concept of class, for example, tends to exclude the possibility that nonclass social actors could play a significant role in determining historical outcomes. However, attempts to incorporate these nonclass actors into the theoretical framework result in reduced coherence and a position that is no longer recognizably Marxist. This problem is most apparent with Marxist economic concepts. As I argue in Chapter 9, Marxist analyses often rest on the idea of a logic of capitalist accumulation. This logic is used to explain why certain institutional arrangements have evolved in one way and not another or why certain policy choices were made. However, the concept of a logic of accumulation does not hold up under close scrutiny, since there are generally multiple strategies by which capitalists, both individually and collectively, might strive to attempt to secure profits at a particular point in time. The seemingly objective quality of these economic categories obscures the actual range of choices in a given historical situation. Even what capitalists perceive as an appropriate rate of profit is a variable that depends upon particular historical circumstances. In sum, it becomes apparent that Marxism's effort to explain phenomena in terms of underlying economic dynamics is incomplete; those economic dynamics are also socially and culturally constructed.

Those of us who have pursued this path from a search for coherence within the tradition of Critical Marxism to a more complex analysis face a serious dilemma in figuring out how to label ourselves. On the one hand, it seems like an act of arrogance to continue to claim the name Marxism for work that systematically criticizes many of the central concepts of the Marxist tradition. While there are aspects of the Marxist tradition that I can embrace unequivocally, it seems presumptuous to insist that those particular aspects are the "truth" of the Marxist tradition to which I remain committed.

On the other hand, the alternative of declaring that I am no longer a Marxist is also unappealing. For one thing, such a declaration could easily be misperceived as a statement that I have abandoned the political commitments that brought me to Marxism. Moreover, to claim that I am now outside the Marxist tradition would be untrue to the reality that in ways both conscious and unconscious, I continue to use the intellectual tools that I learned from that tradition. One of the major achievements of New Left intellectuals has been to persuade some of our mainstream colleagues that the Marxist tradition is an important part of the Western intellectual heritage. This act of persuasion has created a new intellectual climate in which it has been possible for diverse intellectuals to learn from Marx and Marxism. It would be inconsistent with this achievement to return once again to a situation where intellectuals routinely declared themselves to be on one side or the other of a divide between Marxists and non-Marxists.

In light of the defects of both of the obvious alternatives, my own choice is to opt for a new label that conveys some of the intellectual and political commitments of those of us who are seeking to build on, but also to go beyond, Marxism. The most appealing term for these purposes is *Post-Marxism*. The idea of Post-Marxism is that the questions that Marx posed remain central for understanding and transforming our social world. However, the answers that Marx offered no longer suffice, and just as Marx sought to transcend Hegel, so too, those who pursue the Post-Marxist project seek to transcend Marx.[61]

Part I

2

Beyond Corporate Liberalism

The theory of corporate liberalism emerged in the 1960s and continues to influence the thinking of many intellectuals critical of politics in American society. The core of the theory is a reinterpretation of the meaning of American liberalism. The traditional view was articulated most concisely by Arthur Schlesinger, Jr., when he argued that liberalism was the movement of other sectors of the population to restrict the power of big business.[1] In this view, the expansion of the role of the state during the twentieth century was a consequence of popular victories that succeeded in making capitalism a more benevolent system. The new theory reversed the old view arguing that liberalism was the movement of enlightened capitalists to save the corporate order. In this new view, the expansion of the role of the state was designed by corporate leaders and their allies to rationalize the economy and society. Rationalization encompasses all measures that stabilize economic and social conditions so that profits can be made on a predictable basis by the major corporations.

A great deal of work in the area of social policy analysis of the past five or ten years has been influenced by the theory of corporate liberalism.[2] Both radical and liberal scholars have recognized that there is often a close correspondence between the development of some social service institutions and social policies and the basic logic of accumulation in a capitalist economy. For example, relief policies are designed to create an adequate labor pool and the educational reforms of the progressive era

This essay is reprinted from *Social Problems* 24, no. 3 (Feb. 1977): 352–360. © 1977 by the Society for the Study of Social Problems.

were designed to meet the needs of firms for a more educated force. In accounting for this relation, there is a tendency to rely on the explanations of the agreement between capitalist firms and the state developed in the theory of corporate liberalism. Such arguments take the form that a particular institution or social policy fits the needs of the corporate system because of direct intervention by representatives of dominant corporate interests at a critical moment. This kind of argument serves as an easy substitute for an analysis of the more complicated causal processes involved. While such interventions do occur, no attempt has been made to specify under what conditions or whether they succeed or fail. The argument thus leads toward an inverted functionalism[3] where all social institutions fit the logic of capitalist accumulation because they have been so directed by representatives of an extremely powerful corporate class. Moreover, this type of argument leads to an exaggerated view of the corporate system's capacity to reform or rationalize itself. I will attempt to demonstrate this perspective by showing how the theory of corporate liberalism has itself led to incorrect expectations about the course of American politics.

The Evolution of the Theory

The foundation for the theory of corporate liberalism was a reinterpretation of the Progressive Period in American history. Gabriel Kolko's *Triumph of Conservatism*, first printed in 1963, argued that many of the reform measures of the Progressive Period that expanded the federal government's role in regulating business were designed by the dominant corporations themselves.[4] He rejected the earlier view that these reforms were the product of popular reform movements, and argued that they grew from efforts by the largest and most powerful corporations to protect themselves from the evils of unrestricted competition. In short, big business needed state regulation to stabilize the business environment because the persistence of small firms and high levels of competition endangered the newly formed corporate giants. The largest meat packers, for example, wanted federal inspection of meat because the adulteration of meat by smaller firms endangered United States access to foreign markets. Kolko's analysis was extended by James Weinstein[5] who argued that during the same period, some of the leading corporate figures favored federal welfare measures, such as workers' compensation, because they feared intense class conflict. The corporate leaders who met with conservative trade unionists in the National Civil Federation developed a vision of rationalized labor-management relations that would strengthen American capitalism.

These reinterpretations of the Progressive Era might have ended up as an obscure footnote, but for the fact that the theory became that of the emergent New Left of the 1960s. Its importance to the American New Left can be explained by two interrelated facts. The American student movement—in contrast to similar movements in Western Europe—lacked a living, Marxist intellectual tradition on which it could build. The only visible Marxism in the United States was the stale orthodoxy of the American Communist Party, and it was widely agreed in the early New Left that the Marxist tradition was largely inadequate to an understanding of the American situation.[6] But in the absence of a useful Marxism, the early New Left needed a theoretical justification for its break with traditional American liberalism, out of which it had developed.

The break with liberalism was necessary. The New Left quickly realized that the assumptions of New Deal liberalism interpreted by Democratic Party liberals of the 1960s were in conflict with the full-scale attack on racism and poverty that the New Left advocated. This point was symbolized for many by the role that Hubert Humphrey played at the Democratic Party convention in 1964 when he insisted that the Mississippi Freedom Democratic Party accept a compromise with the representatives of Southern racism. By 1965, the emergent New Left had realized that the liberal tradition was fully identified with the expansionist, interventionist foreign policy that produced the invasion of the Dominican Republic and the endless escalations in Vietnam. The theory of corporate liberalism made it possible for individuals in the New Left to understand that the liberal politicians, whom they might previously have admired, were not simply making mistakes but were consciously carrying out evil policies.[7]

The theory of corporate liberalism explains the lack of contradiction between liberalism and the pursuit of an expansionist foreign policy, culminating in Vietnam. In fact, the theory enabled a reinterpretation of the entire Cold War period, which remains one of the New Left's enduring contributions.[8] Furthermore, it provided the groundwork for a critique of Kennedy–Johnson policies on poverty and race that emphasized the essentially manipulative and cooptative intent behind those policies. In short, it justified the profound moral outrage of the American New Left because it suggested that conscious policies rather than an impersonal system were responsible for the defects of this society. In this sense, the theory played a transitional role for many. Their moral outrage facilitated radicalization, but once radicalized, it was possible for them to look more dispassionately at the evils of the society. Once this transition was made, many individuals recognized the analytic value of Marxism—a theory that took for granted the evils of a capitalist society.[9]

Paradigm Crisis

While the theory of corporate liberalism seemed tailor-made for an analysis of the Kennedy–Johnson years with the war against poverty, civil rights legislation, and Peace Corps, the applicability of the theory became problematic with the election of Richard Nixon. It is my argument that Nixon's illiberalism created a kind of paradigm crisis for the theory of corporate liberalism that has still not been resolved. The theory still explained U.S. foreign policy because of the basic continuity in goals from Johnson to Nixon, but problems emerged in domestic policy. The movement away from expanded social welfare programs for blacks and the poor, the effort to make the Supreme Court conservative, and Agnew's attacks on the liberal media were not readily explained by the old theory. If corporate liberalism's response to black rebellion, for example, had been the expansion of welfare and the development of cooptative social programs, then why was Nixon attempting to dismantle these programs and responding to black rebellion with intensified police repression? One response was the argument that political repression had always been used in tandem with cooptation,[10] but this did not explain why Nixon wanted to cut back the Great Society programs. Gradually, a new explanation emerged for Nixon's illiberalism that was completely consistent with the theory of corporate liberalism. This new explanation was the Yankee vs. Cowboy theory that was first developed by Carl Oglesby, a leader of SDS in its vital period, and popularized and elaborated by Kirkpatrick Sale.[11]

The basic premise of the revised theory was that corporate liberalism had a specific social base in the capitalist class—the old Eastern money, including Wall Street, and the established industrial firms. Yet during the post-World War II period, a new social grouping had emerged within the capitalist class with a different ideology—corporate conservatism. These corporate conservatives were based in the South, Southwest, and southern California and their economic base was defense industries, oil, and a number of other sources of new wealth. First Goldwater, and later Nixon, built a political base among these Southern Rim, corporate conservatives—the Cowboys—and it made sense that Nixon's policies should diverge from those of Yankee, corporate liberals.

While the Oglesby–Sale argument was a brilliant theoretical impro-visation, its empirical basis was shaky. Little was done to establish the nature of the policy conflicts between the two groups or the connection between policy conflicts and differing economic interests. Furthermore, the existence of a split in the capitalists class was not adequately proven. The weight of the evidence points to a high level of economic integration between "Cowboys" and "Yankees," and it appears that in both 1968 and 1972 Nixon received overwhelming support from capitalists in both groups or regional areas.[12] Finally, any attempt to account for Jerry Ford's conservatism by lumping him among the "Cowboys" stretches the limits of credibility.

Still another line of argument has emerged to explain Nixon's illib-eralism in a way consistent with the theory of corporate liberalism. This second line of argument focuses on the fiscal crisis of the state—the existence of a basic contradiction in contemporary United States capital-ism that takes the form of severe strains on governmental budgets at local, state, and federal levels.[13] The withdrawal of earlier concessions to the poor becomes intelligible in the context of a fiscal crisis that places limits on the state budget. Corporate liberal policies expanding the role of the state could no longer be afforded, necessitating illiberalism for the system.[14] While this argument does not explain all aspects of Nixonian illiberalism, it is more solidly grounded in empirical reality than the Yankee–Cowboy explanations.

The fiscal crisis argument leads to questionable predictions when it is placed in the framework of the theory of corporate liberalism. If the fiscal crisis is serious enough to cause illiberalism in domestic policy, then the theory would suggest that the more conscious capitalists would again favor an extension of state power to rationalize the economy and solve the crisis. The heart of the theory is the idea that enlightened capitalists recognize that crises of capitalism can be resolved through an extension of the state's role. Such a recognition would also accompany the unfold-ing of the fiscal crisis of the state. A number of radical commentators have accepted the logic of this position, and they have argued that we are on the eve of a new era of corporate-inspired rationalization of the economy through a further extension of the state's role in economic decision-making.[15] They are predicting that the major corporations and their allies will favor some form of national economic planning as a means to create an expanded flow of goods and services, resolving the fiscal crisis and making possible a renewed flowering of cooptative policies toward the poor and rebellious.

In the past year [1975], these predictions seem to have been verified. A prestigious group of academics, labor leaders, and business figures has emerged to advocate national economic planning. Senators Javits and Humphrey have introduced legislation in Congress to create a national planning agency. In short, for the first time since World War II, national economic planning has become an issue in American politics.[16] Despite these straws in the wind, I would argue that there is little evidence that the country will, in the next five or ten years, move toward national economic planning of a sort that represents a genuine effort at economic rationalization through the use of the state. I think a few pieces of evidence have been given an exaggerated importance because they fit with a prediction arising from the theory of corporate liberalism. When we free ourselves from that theory, it appears that there is more evidence of a serious long-term effort by the corporations to reduce the role of the state in the economy in the two areas most associated with liberal policies—the regulation of corporations and the provision of social welfare.

Evidence Against Corporate Liberal Rationalization

Since my argument conflicts with what is accepted wisdom in some circles, it seems worthwhile to examine the evidence for corporate opposition to any further extension of the government's role in the society. The Ford administration, since its inception, has had a strong bias toward free market policies, rather than expanded government regulation of the economy. William Simon, Alan Greenspan, and others in the administration have repeatedly argued that the solution to many of the economy's problems is trust in markets to restore equilibrium. As they see it, many of the current problems result from earlier efforts to regulate the market to achieve certain ends. Interference with the market impairs its workings while failing to achieve initial objectives. In a range of policy areas from energy, to international exchange rates, to the slowing of inflation, the Ford administration has opted for those policies most consistent with allowing markets to work with minimal interference. While the administration's capacity to pursue such policies is limited by political factors, the bias toward free market solutions is clear. Yet little corporate criticism of these policies has emerged. If there were a significant interest in corporate circles in rationalizing the economy through an expanded government role, then one would expect explicit critiques of the Ford administration's adherence to laissez-faire rhetoric and policies. To be sure, debate goes on in the business press about the merits of specific policy measures such as regulation of certain prices or the free floating of exchange rates. But there is no evidence of a fundamental critique of the free market by corporate leaders. It is always possible that such a critique is articulated only behind closed doors, but one would think, given the importance of the issue, that there would be evidence of debate.[17]

I emphasize that even the apparent motion in the direction of national economic planning falls far short of the advocacy of governmental rationalization of the economy. In fact, the major concern of the committee for national planning and the proposed national planning legislation is an improvement in the quality of the economic data collected by the government. The model of planning is one in which corporations make more information available to the government, so that it can provide the corporations with more accurate projections about developments in the economy. Corporations will then be able to plan more effectively.[18] Yet even this limited conception of planning has merited intense denunciation from key corporate figures. The president of General Motors argued in a recent speech that

Sooner or later, the Government plan, if it is going to serve any purpose at all, is going to mandate a different mix of goods and services than the free market would spontaneously provide. In other words, inevitably someone—maybe all of us—would lose some freedom. . . . Planned economies simply cannot provide the richness and diversity of new and better consumer goods and services that market-oriented economic systems are able to offer in such abundance.[19]

This suspicion that information gathering might lead to later efforts to direct the flow of investment explains the resistance of corporate leaders to the Federal Trade Commission's efforts to get profit information for various product lines. Since most large corporations produce a variety of goods, the federal government lacks information on the profitability of particular products. The Federal Trade Commission has attempted to gather such information, but it has encountered great opposition from the corporations.[20] Of 345 corporations surveyed for 1973 data, 117 have refused to turn over the information and are fighting in the courts to keep the FTC from demanding the information. The holdouts include such giants as DuPont, GE, GM, Union Carbide, and Philip Morris. If corporations resist efforts by the government to collect information, they will not support government efforts to coordinate the economy to shape the "mix of goods and services."

Another set of facts is perhaps even more significant—the actual response of the business community to the fiscal crisis of the state. This response has been an almost universalized support for cutbacks in government spending for social services and social welfare programs. *Business Week*, one of the more liberal business periodicals, has editorialized repeatedly for tax relief for the corporations, which would come at the expense of social spending, since opposition to higher personal taxes is strong. Bankers and corporate representatives played a critical role in forcing massive budget cutbacks on New York City, and the business press has praised efforts by such diverse politicians as President Ford, Governor Brown of California, and Governor Dukakis of Massachusetts to hold the line on social spending. The reasons for business response are simple—American corporations are experiencing a crisis of profitability.[21] The profit share of national income has been declining, and a reduction in the share of national income that goes to government might reverse the downward trend in profits. The corporations seem to favor a reduction in the role of the government, if only because they think it would be consistent with tax relief. The crescendo of rhetoric in American politics against big government fits closely with the perceived interests of the corporation.

Mistaken Assumptions

This evidence suggests that the theory of corporate liberalism exaggerates the capacity of corporate capitalism to rationalize itself through the use of the state. One would think that in an economy dominated by a few hundred major corporations, it would be relatively simple to develop a centralized planning mechanism adequate to overcoming a severe fiscal crisis. Its difficulty indicates that the corporate system is significantly less rational—even on its own terms—and well directed than many of us believe. This insight about economic planning has implications for other social institutions as well. If, in a certain period, the educational system or the health care system, seems to fit smoothly with the logic of the economic system, it might not be the result of conscious intent, but the consequence of larger structural factors or a temporary, almost accidental fit. In any case, serious strains could develop between the educational system, for example, and the economic system, and might prove difficult to alleviate. In short, strains and contradictions would tend to be endemic if the system's capacity to rationalize itself is as limited as we have suggested.

Because of some of the assumptions built into the theory it leads to an erroneous view of capitalism as a smoothly managed and organized system. One of the problematic assumptions has been noted elsewhere: the tendency to ignore how much reforms are forced on capitalism from below.[22] Kolko, in his *Triumph of Conservatism* is particularly vulnerable to this criticism because he fails to place actions by corporate representatives in the context of general pressures for reform. Corporate interventions are seen entirely as spontaneous efforts at rationalization rather than as efforts partially to channel reform in the least threatening directions. Specific reforms are a result of demands from below, combined with the efforts of the powerful to shape and control the process of change. This modification in the standard corporate liberal framework is useful in understanding such reforms as the extension of educational opportunities, which has often involved an intersection of working-class and corporate interests.

Another problematic assumption in corporate liberal theory is that the relationship between the state and the corporations is clear. Almost all examples of corporate liberal reform involve the extension of the powers of the state either in the form of regulation of business and the business environment or the provision of social services. Corporate liberalism as a business ideology is supposed to represent a dramatic break from traditional laissez-faire business views. While laissez-faire might continue as the ideology of small business and as part of Fourth of July rhetoric, the leaders of the dominant corporations are supposed to have discarded the distrust of governmental growth that is central to laissez-faire. But this argument obscures the continuing tensions between government and big business that serve to regenerate business distrust of government.

These tensions can be seen clearly in government regulation of business. Even though government regulatory agencies are notoriously likely to be captured by the interests they are supposed to regulate,[23] Corporations maintain a high level of vigilance to prevent the regulatory agencies from overstepping their bounds. From the corporate point of view, the danger is always present that an ambitious civil servant, a political appointee, or aggressive congressperson will attempt to expand a regulatory agency's jurisdiction past the limits acceptable to the corporation. Historically, there have been many examples of agencies that got out of control and had to be brought back into line by strong corporate actions.[24] The corporations depend on the regulatory agencies to stabilize the business environment, but dependence makes the corporations potentially vulnerable to undesired interference. The possibility of undesired interference is considerable, because the logic of government bureaucracies is to attempt to expand their own authority as a justification for larger budgets and more personnel.[25] Hence, the corporations must be prepared to prevent that logic from leading to increased bureaucratic interference.

This example can be generalized. Corporations often need governmental action to stabilize the business environment. However, an expanded governmental role always threatens diminution of the corporation's sphere of autonomy. Autonomy is one of the corporation's most precious resources; it is continually attempting to preserve its ability to make critical decisions, such as investment decisions, free of outside interference.[26] The corporation, therefore, has an ambivalent relation to governmental authority. It attempts to maximize what it can get from the government in the form of stabilization of the environment, subsidies, tax breaks, and contracts. But it also attempts to minimize governmental interference in its internal decisionmaking process. It should be clear that even corporations heavily dependent on government contracts still have a use for laissez-faire ideas when they are trying to avert intensification of governmental regulation of their internal affairs.

This corporate ambivalence toward government makes it imperative to understand what one means by national economic planning. For example, corporations that would benefit have no objection to plans such as the recent Rockefeller/Ford energy proposal, which would make billions of federal dollars available to firms in the energy industry. In fact, they would support such a plan even if it was called national economic planning. However, such a plan does not represent the rationalization of the economy necessary to overcome the fiscal crisis of the state. If the government doles out dollars to private industry in the form of incentives and contracts, it only makes the fiscal crisis worse. Rationalization requires that the government direct the flow of private investment funds to assure a rapid increase in the supply of needed goods and services. Only in this way can the total social product be expanded to reduce inflationary pressures and assure that future growth of governmental budgets can be financed from a continually expanding tax base. The problem is that the corporations resist this kind of investment planning vigorously, because it constitutes the most direct assault on their decisionmaking autonomy. In other words, the corporations are happy to loot the federal Treasury through subsidies, tax breaks, and research contracts, but they are loath to be told by the government where and how much to invest, unless, of course, the government bribes them into cooperation. Yet the essence of the fiscal crisis is that the government cannot afford to bribe corporations into making the necessary investments.

Ambivalence in corporate attitudes toward the state has existed for some time, but it has become acute in the age of the multinational corporation. Overwhelming evidence exists that the largest United States firms have become global in their operations, with a dramatic rise in the 1965–74 peiod in the percentage of their profits earned abroad.[27] These corporations exist by planning their investment on a global basis in order to maximize overall profits. Therefore these corporations would be strongly opposed to efforts to plan investment at the national level, because of the likelihood that such national plans would conflict with their own global planning process. These corporations attempt to gain the political support of their home government in relations with foreign states without constraints in their planning from the narrow interests of their home nations.[28]

This continuing, and perhaps intensifying, interest by large corporations in avoiding governmental intrusion in their decisionmaking processes makes it possible to understand the free market drift of the Ford administration as something other than anomaly or anachronism. The free market policies and rhetoric of the administration did correspond with the interests of the most powerful corporations. There are pressures within the society for the state to play a rationalizing role by extending its intervention in the economy. These pressures are likely to intensify as the seriousness of the economic crisis becomes more apparent, and have already influenced and limited the capacity of the administration to pursue its free market policies. But these pressures for an extension of the state's role do not originate in the dominant corporations. No matter how explicitly conservative the intent of those who advocate some form of economic rationalization today, their actions cannot be interpreted as a reflection of the conscious will of the dominant capitalists. Even those who would attempt to save capitalism by making it more "rational" must come into conflict with the present-day dominant corporations.

Conclusion

The capacity and willingess of corporate leaders to reform society has been exaggerated by the theory of corporate liberalism. The strongest corporations have an aversion to the interference in their internal affairs that an extension of government power would entail. While my argument has focused on the fiscal crisis and national economic planning, the argument has important implications for other areas of social policy. The system's inability to resolve the crisis through planning points to a long-term pattern of reduced government spending for social services and social welfare. But I would also suggest that the chances of thoroughgoing rationalization in the interests of the dominant corporations in other spheres is less likely than the theory of corporate liberalism has implied. For example, a corporate-inspired reorganization of the medical care system for overcoming the problem of skyrocketing costs does not appear likely, even though a multitude of efforts to patch up the medical care system can be anticipated.

I am not trying to argue, however, that conservative reform[29] is impossible. I am simply attempting to show that it is a mistake to assume that when conservative reform occurs it is a result of the conscious intent of corporate leaders. Past and present rationalizations of capitalist society are the product of a complex series of interactions among social classes and the state. The task is to develop a theory that makes sense of those complex interactions without reducing them to a single dimension. Marxist theory provides a starting point for the completion of this theoretical project. It was central to Marx's thought that social life in capitalism is a product of forces that occur behind the backs—without the conscious understanding of social actors, including those in the dominant social classes. The Rockefellers and their colleagues certainty benefit from capitalism as a social system, but they do not control it. While it is often comforting to believe the opposite, because it means that at least someone is in charge, the reality that capitalism is a system "out of control" is ultimately the strongest argument that can be made for its replacement by a different social order.

3

The Ruling Class Does Not Rule: Notes on the Marxist Theory of the State

The Marxist theory of the state remains a muddle despite the recent revival of interest in the subject.[1] Substantial progress has been made in formulating a critique of orthodox Marxist formulations that reduce the state to a mere reflection of economic interests. However, the outlines of an adequate alternative Marxist theory are not yet clear. This is most dramatically indicated by the continued popularity in Marxist circles of explanations of state policies or of conflicts within the state that are remarkably similar to orthodox formulations in their tendency to see the state as a reflection of the interests of certain groups in the capitalist class. Many Marxists, for example, were drawn to interpretations of Watergate that saw it as a conflict between two different wings of the capitalist class.[2] This gap between theory and the explanation of actual historical events demonstrates that the critique of orthodox Marxist formulations has not been carried far enough. These earlier formulations—even when they have been carefully criticized and dismissed—sneak back into many current analyses because they remain embedded in the basic concepts of Marxist analysis.

This essay proposes two elements of an alternative Marxist theory of the state. The first element is a different way of conceptualizing the ruling

This essay is reprinted from *Socialist Review* 33 (May–June, 1977): 6–27. Reprinted by permission of the *Socialist Review*.

class and its relationship to the state. This reconceptualization makes possible the second element—the elaboration of a structural framework that specifies the concrete mechanisms that make the state a capitalist state, whereas other structural theories have tended to analyze structures in an abstract and mystifying way.[3]

Although these two elements do not provide a complete Marxist theory of the state, they do provide a new way of thinking about the sources of rationality within capitalism. Contemporary Marxists have been forced to acknowledge that despite its fundamental irrationality, capitalism in the developed world has shown a remarkable capacity to rationalize itself in response to the twin dangers of economic crisis and radical working-class movements.[4] Since the present historical period again poses for the left the threat of successful capitalist rationalization, the understanding of the sources of capitalism's capacity for self-reform is of the utmost political importance. The traditional Marxist explanation of capitalist rationality is to root it in the consciousness of some sector of the ruling class. In this light, capitalist reform reflects the conscious will and understanding of some sector of the capitalist class that has grasped the magnitude of the problem and proposes a set of solutions. The alternative framework being proposed here suggests that the capacity of capitalism to rationalize itself is the outcome of a conflict among three sets of agents—the capitalist class, the managers of the state apparatus, and the working class.[5] Rationalization occurs "behind the backs" of each set of actors so that rationality cannot be seen as a function of the consciousness of one particular group.

This argument and its implications will be traced out through a number of steps. First, I intend to show that critiques of orthodox Marxist theory of the state are flawed by their acceptance of the idea of a class-conscious ruling class. Second, I argue that there is a basis in Marx's writing for rejecting the idea of a class-conscious ruling class. Third, I develop a structural argument that shows that even in the absence of ruling-class class consciousness, the state managers are strongly discouraged from pursuing anticapitalist policies. Fourth, I return to the issue of capitalist rationality and describe how it grows out of the structured relationship among capitalist, workers, and state managers. Finally, I briefly analyze the implications of this argument for capitalism's current difficulties in the United States.

The Critique of Instrumentalism

The major development in the Marxist theory of the state in recent years has been the formulation of a critique of instrumentalism. A number of writers have characterized the orthodox Marxist view of the state as instrumentalism because it views the state as a simple tool or instrument of ruling-class purposes. First, it neglects the ideological role of the state. The state plays a critical role in maintaining the legitimacy of the social order, and this requires that the state appear to be neutral in the class struggle. In short, even if the state is an instrument of ruling-class purpose, the fact that it must appear otherwise indicates the need for a more complex framework for analyzing state policies. Second, instrumentalism fails to recognize that to act in the general interest of capital, the state must be able to take actions against the particular interests of capitalists. Price controls or restrictions on the export of capital, for example, might be in the general interest of capital in a particular period, even if they temporarily reduced the profits of most capitalists. To carry through such policies, the state must have more autonomy from direct capitalist control than the instrumentalist view would allow.

The critics of instrumentalism propose the idea of the relative autonomy of the state as an alternative framework. In order to serve the general interests of capital, the state must have some autonomy from direct ruling-class control. Since the concept of the absolute autonomy of the state would be un-Marxist and false, the autonomy is clearly relative. However, the difficult is in specifying the nature, limits, and determinants of that relative autonomy. Some writers have attempted to argue that the degree of autonomy varies historically, and that "late capitalism" is characterized by the "autonomization of the state apparatus." But these arguments have an ad hoc quality, and they share an analytic problem derived from the phase "relative autonomy from ruling-class control."

The basic problem in formulations of "relative autonomy" is the conceptualization of the ruling class. Relative autonomy theories assume that the ruling class will respond effectively to the state's abuse of that autonomy. But for the ruling class to be capable of taking such corrective actions, it must have some degree of political cohesion, an understanding of its general interests, and a high degree of political sophistication. In sum, the theory requires that the ruling class, or a portion of it, be class-conscious, that is, aware of what is necessary to reproduce capitalist social relations in changing historical circumstances. Yet if the ruling class or a segment of it is class-conscious, then the degree of autonomy of the state is clearly quite limited. At this point the theory of relative autonomy collapses back into a slightly more sophisticated version of instrumentalism. State policies continue to be seen as the reflection of inputs by a class-conscious ruling class.

The way out of this theoretical bind, the way to formulate a critique of instrumentalism that does not collapse, is to reject the idea of a class-conscious ruling class. Instead of the relative autonomy framework the key idea becomes a division of labor between those who accumulate capital and those who manage the state apparatus. Those who accumulate capital are conscious of their interests as capitalists, but, in general, they are not conscious of what is necessary to reproduce the social order in changing circumstances. Those who manage the state apparatus, however, are forced to concern themselves to a greater degree with the reproduction of the social order because their continued power rests on the maintenance of political and economic order. In this framework, the central theoretical task is to explain how it is that despite this division of labor, the state tends to serve the interests of the capitalist class. It is to this task—the elaboration of a structural theory of the state—that I will turn after a brief discussion of the division of labor between capitalists and state managers.

Division of Labor

The idea of a division of labor between nonclass-conscious capitalist and those who manage the state apparatus can be found in Marx's writings.[6] Two factors, however, have obscured this aspect of Marx's thought. First, Marx did not spell out the nature of the structural framework in which that division of labor operated, although he hinted at the existence of such a framework. Second, Marx's discussion of these issues is clouded by his polemical intent to fix responsibility for all aspects of bourgeois society on the ruling class. Even when Marx recognizes that the ruling class lacks class consciousness, he still formulates his argument in such a way as to imply that the ruling class as a whole is in conscious control of the situation. Marx used the idea of a conscious, directive ruling class as a polemical shorthand for an elaboration of the structural mechanisms through which control over the means of production leads to control over other aspects of society.

The tension in Marx's formulations is clearest in *The Eighteenth Brumaire* when he is explaining why the bourgeoisie supported Louis Bonaparte's coup d'état against the bourgeoisie's own parliamentary representatives. He writes:

> The *extra-parliamentary* mass of the bourgeoisie, on the other hand, by its servility towards the President, by its vilification of parliament, by the brutal maltreatment of its own press, invited Bonaparte to suppress and annihilate its speaking and writing section, its politicians and its *literati*, its platform and its press, in order that it might then be able to pursue its private affairs with full

confidence in the protection of a strong and unrestricted government. It declared unequivocally that it longed to get rid of its own political rule in order to get rid of the troubles and dangers of ruling.[7]

The passage suggests a division of labor and a division of interest between the extra-parliamentary mass of the bourgeoisie, primarily interested in accumulating profits, and the parliamentary and literary representatives of that class, whose central concerns are different. Marx uses the notion of representation as a substitute for specifying the structural relationship that holds together the division of labor.

In an earlier passage, in a discussion of the petit-bourgeoisie, he states what is involved in the idea of representation:

Just as little must one imagine that the democratic representatives are all shopkeepers or enthusiastic champions of shopkeepers. According to their education and their individual position they may be separated from them as widely as heaven from earth. What makes them representatives of the petty burgeoisie is the fact that in their minds they do not go beyond the limits which the latter do not go beyond in life, that they are consequently driven theoretically to the same tasks and solutions to which material interest and social position practically drive the latter. This is in general the relationship of the *political and literary representatives* of a class to the class that they represent.[8]

Marx here rejects the simple reductionism so common among his followers. For Marx, representation was an objective relationship—one did not need to be of a class to be its representative. And, in fact, representatives and their classes did not always see eye to eye, since their different positions could lead to different perspectives. In sum, representatives are *not* typical members of their classes, and it is a mistake to attribute to the class as a whole the consciousness that parliamentary or literary representatives display.

Marx's idea of representation suggests the geneal structural links between the capitalists and those who manage the state apparatus. Marx recognized that those in the state apparatus tended to have a broader view of society than the capitalists, although their view is still far short of a general understanding of what is necessary to reproduce the social order. After all, the state managers' preoccupation with the struggle for political power distorts their understanding. This is the source of the "parliamentary cretinism" that made Louis Bonaparte a better defender of the bourgeoisie's interests than that class's own representatives. But if neither the ruling class nor its representatives know what is necessary to preserve and reproduce capitalist social relations, why then does the state tend to do just that? The answer is that such policies emerge out of the structural relationships among state managers, capitalists, and workers.

Subsidiary Structural Mechanisms

When Marxists put forward a radical critique of instrumentalist views of the state, they usually do so to justify reformist Socialist politics. When one argues that the ruling class is diffused, lacks class consciousness and political sophistication, it seems to follow that if Socialists could gain control of the levers of the existing state, they would be able to use the state to effect the transition to socialism. The logic is impeccable—if the state is not inherently a tool of the ruling class, then it can be turned into a tool of the working class. This reformist view shares with instrumentalism a personalistic reductionism—either the ruling class controls the state personally and directly or it does not control it at all, in which case the state can be used for other purposes. Neither view recognizes the structural mechanisms that make the state serve capitalist ends regardless of whether capitalists intervene directly and consciously. However, once these mechanisms are understood, it is possible to construct a critique of Socialist reformism that is far more powerful than the critiques derived from the instrumentalist tradition.

Before considering the major structural mechanisms, it is necessary to consider a number of subsidiary mechanisms. The first of these includes all the techniques by which members of the ruling class are able to influence the state apparatus directly. Even though the members of the ruling class lack class consciousness, they are acutely aware of their immediate interests as capitalists and of the impact of the state on those interests. Capitalists, individually and in groups, apply pressure on the state for certain kinds of lucrative contracts, for state spending in certain areas, for legislative action in their favor, for tax relief, for more effective action to control the labor force, and so on. Needless to say, the pursuit of these various interests does not add up to policies in the general interest of capital. Even in the area of control of the labor force, where the common interest among capitalists is strongest, the policies that the capitalists demand might not even be in their own long-term best interest. Nevertheless, capitalists attempt to assure responsiveness by the state through various means, including campaign contributions, lobbying activities, and favors to politicians and civil servants. While these techniques are primarily used for increasing the state's receptivity to the special interests of particular capitalists or groups of capitalists, the overall effect of this proliferation of influence channels is to make those who run the state more likely to reject modes of thought and behavior that conflict with the logic of capitalism.

Included in the category of influence channels is the recruitment of ruling-class members into government service, and in recent years, into participation in various private policymaking groups that have a powerful impact on the formulation of government policies. Instrumentalists tend to see such individuals as typical members of their class, and their impact on the state is viewed as the heart of capitalist class rule. In the perspective being advanced here, this direct ruling-class participation in policy formation is viewed differently. For one thing, ruling-class members who devote substantial energy to policy formation become atypical of their class, since they are forced to look at the world from the perspective of state managers. They are quite likely to diverge ideologically from politically unengaged ruling-class opinion. More important, even if there were no politically engaged ruling-class members, there is still every reason to believe that the state and policymaking groups would advance policies that are in the interests of the ruling class. Marx's formulation cited earlier makes clear that one does not need to be of the ruling class to "represent" it politically; when there are no ruling-class individuals around, individuals from other social classes will eagerly fill the role of ruling-class "representatives."

All of the techniques of ruling-class influence, including direct participation, constitute a structural mechanism of subsidiary importance. The influence channels make it less likely that state managers will formulate policies that conflict directly with the interests of capitalists. But it is a subsidiary mechanism because, even in the absence of these influence channels, other structural mechanisms make it extremely difficult for the state managers to carry through anticapitalist policies. While instrumentalists argue that influence is the core of ruling-class control of the state, it is really more like the icing on the cake of class rule.

The same cannot be said of a second subsidiary mechanism— bourgeois cultural hegemony. The relevant aspect of cultural hegemony is the widespread acceptance of certain unwritten rules about what is and what is not legitimate state activity. While these rules change over time, a government that violates the unwritten rules of a particular period would stand to lose a good deal of its popular support. This acts as a powerful constraint in discouraging certain types of state action that might conflict with the interests of capital. However, simply invoking the existence of bourgeois cultural hegemony begs the problem of explaining how that hegemony is generated. Here, too, there must be specific structural mechanisms that operate to make "the ruling ideas" consistent with class rule. However, the task of explaining these structural mechanisms is beyond the scope of this essay.

Major Structural Mechanisms

A viable structural theory of the state must do two separate things. It must elaborate the structural constraints that operate to reduce the likelihood that state managers will act against the general interests of capitalists. An understanding of these constraints is particularly important for analyzing the obstacles to reformist Socialist strategies. But a structural theory must also explain the tendency of state managers to pursue policies that are in the general interests of capital. It is not sufficient to explain why the state avoids anticapitalist policies; it is necessary to explain why the state has served to rationalize capitalism. Once one rejects the idea of ruling-class class consciousness, one needs to provide an alternative explanation of efforts at rationalization.

Both tendencies can be derived from the fact that those who manage the state apparatus—regardless of their own political ideology—are dependent on the maintenance of some reasonable level of economic activity. This is true for two reasons. First, the capacity of the state to finance itself through taxation or borrowing depends on the state of the economy. If economic activity is in decline, the state will have difficulty maintaining its revenues at an adequate level. Second, public support for a regime will decline sharply if the regime presides over a serious drop in the level of economic activity, with a parallel rise in unemployment and shortages of key goods. Such a drop in support increases the likelihood that the state managers will be removed from power one way or another. And even if the drop is not that dramatic, it will increase the challenges to the regime and decrease the regime's political ability to take effective actions.

In a capitalist economy the level of economic activity is largely determined by the private investment decisions of capitalists. This means that capitalists, in their collective role as investors, have a veto over state policies in that their failure to invest at adequate levels can create major political problems for the state managers. This discourages state managers from taking actions that might seriously decrease the rate of investment. It also means that state managers have a direct interest in using their power to facilitate investment, since their own continued power rests on a healthy economy. There will be a tendency for state agencies to orient their various programs toward the goal of facilitating and encouraging private investment. In doing so, the state managers address the problem of investment from a broader perspective than that of the individual capitalist. This increases the likelihood that such policies will be in the general interest of capital.

Constraints on State Policies

This is, of course, too simple. Both sides of the picture—constraints and rationalization—must be filled out in greater detail to make this approach convincing. One problem, in particular, stands out—if capitalists have a veto over state policies, isn't this simply another version of instrumentalism? The answer to this question lies in a more careful analysis of the determinants of investment decisions. The most useful concept is the idea of business confidence. Individual capitalists decide on their rate of investment in a particular country on the basis of a variety of specific variables such as the price of labor and the size of the market for a specific product. But there is also an intangible variable—the capitalist's evaluation of the general political/economic climate. Is the society stable; is the working class under control; are taxes likely to rise; do government agencies interfere with business freedom; will the economy grow? These kinds of considerations are critical to the investment decisions of each firm. The sum of all of these evaluations across a national economy can be termed the level of business confidence. As the level of business confidence declines, so will the rate of investment. Business confidence also has an international dimension when nations are integrated into a capitalist world economy. Multinational corporations, international bankers, and currency speculators also make judgments about a particular nation's political/economic climate that determine their willingness to invest in assets in that nation. This, in turn, will affect the internal level of business confidence and the rate of productive investment.

Business confidence is, however, very different from "ruling-class consciousness." Business confidence is based on an evaluation of the market that considers political events only as they might impinge on the market. This means that it is rooted in the narrow self-interest of the individual capitalist who is worried about profit. Business confidence, especially because of its critical international component, does not make subtle evaluations as to whether a regime is serving the long-term interests of capital. When there is political turmoil and popular mobilization, business confidence will fall, and it will rise when there is a restoration of order, no matter how brutal. It was business confidence that responded so favorably to Louis Bonaparte's coup d'état, because he promised to restore the conditions for business as usual, despite negative implications for the political rights of the bourgeoisie. The crudeness of business confidence makes capitalism peculiarly vulnerable to authoritarian regimes that are capable of acting against the general interests of capital.[9]

The dynamic of business confidence as a constraint on the managers of the state apparatus can be grasped by tracing out a scenario of what happens when left-of-center governments come to power through parliamentary means and attempt to push through major reforms. The scenario distills a number of twentienth-century experiences including that of Chile under Allende. From the moment that the left wins the election, business confidence declines. The most important manifestation of this decline is an increase in speculation against the nation's currency. Reformist governments are always under suspicion that they will pursue inflationary policies; a high rate of inflation means that the international value of the nation's currency will fall. Speculators begin to discount the currency for the expected inflation as soon as possible.

This association between reformist governments and inflation is not arbitrary. Reformist policies—higher levels of employment, redistribution of income toward the poor, improved social services—directly or indirectly lead to a shift of income from profits toward the working class. Businesses attempt to resist such a shift by raising prices so that profit levels will not be reduced. In short, price inflation in this context is a market response to policies that tend to benefit the working class. The reformist government, faced with the initial speculative assault on its currency, has two choices. It can reassure the international and domestic business community, making clear its intention to pursue orthodox economic policies. Or it can forge ahead with its reform program. If it pursues the latter course, an increased rate of inflation and an eventual international monetary crisis is likely.

The international crisis results from the combination of continued speculative pressure against the currency and several new factors. Domestic inflation is likely to affect the nation's balance of trade adversely, leading to a real deterioration in the nation's balance-of-payments account. In addition, inflation and loss of confidence in the currency leads to the flight of foreign and domestic capital and increased foreign reluctance to lend money to the afflicted nation. The initial speculative pressure against the currency could be tolerated; the eruption of an acute international monetary crisis requires some kind of dramatic response. The government may renounce its reformism or cede power to a more "responsible" administration.

But if the government is committed to defending its programs, it will have to act to insulate its economy from the pressures of the international market by imposing some combination of price controls, import controls, and exchange controls.

Escalation in the government's attempt to control the market sets off a new chain of events. These new controls involve threats to individual capitalists. Price controls mean that firms lose the ability to manipulate one of the major determinants of profit levels. Import controls mean that a firm may no longer be able to import goods critical to its business. Exchange controls mean that firms and individuals no longer are able to move their assets freely to secure international havens. The fact that assets are locked into a rapidly inflating currency poses the possibility that large fortunes will be lost.

These are the ingredients for a sharp decline in domestic business confidence. Why should business owners continue to invest if they must operate in an environment in which the government violates the fundamental rules of a market economy?

A sharp decline in business confidence leads to a parallel economic downturn. High rates of unemployment coexist with annoying shortages of critical commodities. The popularity of the regime falls precipitously. The only alternative to capitulation—eliminating controls and initial reforms—is sharp forward movement to socialize the economy. The government could put people back to work and relieve the shortages by taking over private firms. However, the political basis for this kind of action does not exist, even where the leaders of the government are rhetorically committed to the goal of socialism. Generally, the reformist government has not prepared its electoral supporters for extreme action; its entire program has been based on the promise of a gradual transition. Further, the government leaders themselves become immersed in the political culture of the state apparatus, militating against a sharp break with the status quo.

The outcome of this impasse is tragically familiar. The government either falls from power through standard parliamentary means—loss of an election, defection of some of its parliamentary support—or it is removed militarily. Military actions that violate constitutionality meet formidable obstacles in liberal capitalist nations, but when economic chaos severely diminishes the legitimacy of a regime, the chances of a military coup are enhanced. When the militay intervenes, it does not do so as a tool of the ruling class. It acts according to its own ideas of the need to restore political order and in its own interests. Naturally the removal of the reformist government leads to a rapid revival of business confidence simply because order has been restored. However, it should be stressed that this revival of business confidence might not be sustained, since there can be substantial conflicts between the interests of the military and the capitalists.

The key point in elaborating this scenario is that the chain of events can unfold without any members of the ruling class consciously deciding to act "politically" against the regime in power. Of course, such a scenario is usually filled out with a great deal of editorializing against the regime in the bourgeois press, much grumbling among the upper classes, and even some conspiratorial activity. But the point is that conspiracies to destabilize the regime are basically supefluous, since decisions made by individual capitalists according to their own narrow economic rationality are sufficient to paralyze the regime, creating a situation where the regime's fall is the only possibility.

Rationalization

The dynamic of business confidence helps explain why governments are constrained from pursuing anticapitalist policies. It remains to be explained why governments tend to act in the general interests of capital. Part of the answer has already been suggested. Since state managers are so dependent upon the workings of the investment accumulation process, it is natural that they will use whatever resources are available to aid that process. In administering a welfare program, for example, they will organize it to aid the accumulation process, perhaps by ensuring certain industries a supply of cheap labor. Unlike the individual capitalist, the state managers do not have to operate on the basis of a narrow profit-maximizing rationality. They are capable of intervening in the economy on the basis of a more general rationality. In short, their structural position gives the state managers both the interest and the capacity to aid the investment accumulation process.

There is one major difficulty in this formulation—the problem of explaining the dynamic through which reforms that increase the rationality of capitalism come about. Almost all of these reforms involve an extension of the state's role in the economy and society, either in a regulatory capacity or in the provision of services. The difficulty is that business confidence has been depicted as so shortsighted that it is likely to decline in the face of most efforts to extend the state's role domestically, since such efforts threaten to restrict the freedom of individual capitalists and/or increase the tax burden on capitalists. If the state is unwilling to risk a decline in business confidence, how is it then that the state's role has expanded inexorably throughout the twentieth century?

Most theorists escape this problem by rejecting the idea that the

capitalists are as shortsighted as the idea of business confidence suggests. Even if many members of the class share the retrograde notions
implicit in the idea of business confidence, there is supposed to be a
substantial segment of the class that is forward-looking and recognizes
the value of extending the state's power. Theorists of corporate liberalism
have attempted to trace many of the major extensions of state power in
twentieth-century America to the influence of such forward-looking
members of the ruling class. However, the position of these theorists
ultimately requires an attribution of a high level of consciousness and
understanding to the ruling class or a segment of it, and assumes an
instrumental view of the state where state policies can be reduced to the
input of certain ruling-class factions.[10]

There is, however, an alternative line of argument, consistent with
the view of the ruling class and the state that has been advanced in this
paper. It depends on the existence of another structural mechanism—
class struggle. Whatever the role of class struggle in advancing the
development of revolutionary consciousness, class struggle between
proletariat and ruling class in Marx's view has another important function. It pushes forward the development of capitalism—speeding the
process by which capitalism advances the development of the productive
forces. This is conservative in the short term, but progressive in the long
term; it brings closer the time when capitalism will exhaust its capacity to
develop the productive forces and will be ripe for overthrow. Class
struggle produces this result most clearly in conflict over wages. When
workers are able to win wage gains, they increase the pressure on the
capitalists to find ways to substitute machines for people. As Marx
described the cycle, wage gains are followed by an intense period of
mechanization as employers attempt to increase the rate of exploitation;
the consequence is an increase in the size of the industrial reserve army,
as machines replace workers. This, in turn, diminishes the capacity of
workers to win wage gains, until the economic boom again creates a labor
shortage. While this description applies particularly to competitive capitalism, the point is that workers' struggles—in Marx's theory—play an
important role in speeding the pace of technological innovations. *Class
struggle is responsible for much of the economic dynamism of capitalism.*

This pattern goes beyond the struggle over wages. From the beginning of capitalism, workers have struggled to improve their living conditions, which also means upgrading their potential as a labor force. For
example, unbridled early capitalism, through child labor and horren-
dously long working days, threatened to destroy the capacity of the
working class to reproduce itself—an outcome not in the long-term
interests of capitalists. So working people's struggles against child labor,

against incredibly low standards of public health and housing, and for the shorter day, made it possible for the class to reproduce itself, providing capitalism a new generation of laborers. In each historical period, the working class struggles to reproduce itself at a higher level of existence. Workers have played an important role, for example, in demanding increased public education. Public education, in turn, helped create the educated labor pool that developing capitalism required. Obviously, not every working-class demand contributes to the advance of capitalism, but it is foolish to ignore this dimension of class struggle.

In its struggles to protect itself from the ravages of a market economy, the working class has played a key role in the steady expansion of the state's role in capitalist societies. Pressures from the working class have contributed to the expansion of the state's role in the regulation of the economy and in the provision of services. The working class has not been the only force behind the expansion of the state's role in these areas. Examples can be cited of capitalists who have supported an expansion of the state's role into a certain area either because of narrow self-interest— access to government contracts, or because government regulation would hamper competitors—or because of some farsighted recognition of the need to coopt the working class. However, the major impetus for the extension of the state's role has come from the working class and from the managers of the state apparatus, whose own powers expand with a growing state.

Once working-class pressures succeed in extending the state's role, another dynamic begins to work. Those who manage the state apparatus have an interest in using the state's resources to facilitate a smooth flow of investment. There will be a tendency to use the state's extended role for the same ends. The capacity of the state to impose greater rationality on capitalism is extended into new areas as a result of working-class pressures. Working-class pressures, for example, might lead to an expansion of educational resources available for the working class, but there is every likelihood that the content of the education will be geared to the needs of accumulation—the production of a docile work force at an appropriate level of skill. Or similarly, working-class pressures might force the government to intervene in the free market to produce higher levels of employment, but the government will use its expanded powers of intervention to aid the accumulation process more generally.

This pattern is not a smoothly working functional process, always producing the same result. First, working-class movements have often been aware of the danger of making demands that will ultimately strengthen a state they perceive as hostile. For precisely this reason, Socialist movements have often demanded that expanded social services be placed under working-class control. However, working-class demands are rarely granted in their original form. Often, the more radical elements of the movement are repressed at the same time that concessions are made. Second, there can be a serious time lag between granting concessions to the working class and discovering ways that the extension of the state's power can be used to aid the accumulation process. There might, in fact, be continuing tensions in a government program between its integrative intent and its role in the accumulation process. Finally, some concessions to working-class pressure might have no potential benefits for accumulation and might simply place strains on the private economy. If these strains are immediate, one could expect serious efforts to revoke or neutralize the reforms. If the strains occur over the long term, then capitalism faces severe problems because it becomes increasingly difficult to roll back concessions that have stood for some time.[11]

These points suggest that the tendency for class struggle to rationalize capitalism occurs with a great deal of friction and with the continuous possibility of other outcomes. Nevertheless, the tendency does exist because of the particular interests of the state managers. Where there is strong popular pressure for an expansion of social services or increased regulation of markets, the state managers must weigh three factors. First, they do not want to damage business confidence, which generally responds unfavorably to an expansion of the government's role in providing social services or in regulating the market. Second, they do not want class antagonisms to escalate to a level that would endanger their own rule. Third, they recognize that their own power and resources will grow if the state's role is expanded. If the state managers decide to respond to pressure with concessions,[12] they are likely to shape their concessions in a manner that will least offend business confidence and will most expand their own power. These two constraints increase the likelihood that the concessions will ultimately serve to rationalize capitalism.

Major Reforms

This argument suggests that while some concessions will be made to the working class, the threat of a decline in business confidence will block major efforts to rationalize capitalism. Since business confidence is shortsighted, it will oppose even procapitalist reform programs if such programs promise a major increase in taxes or a major increase in the government's capacity to regulate markets. This leaves the problem of explaining the dramatic increases in the state's role that have occurred in all developed capitalist nations during the course of this century. The explanation is that there are certain periods—during wartime, major depressions, and periods of postwar reconstruction—in which the decline of business confidence as a veto on government policies doesn't work. These are the periods in which dramatic increases in the state's role have occurred.

In wars that require major mobilizations, business confidence loses its sting for several reasons. First, international business confidence becomes less important, since international capital flows tend to be placed under government control. Second, private investment becomes secondary to military production in maintaining high levels of economic activity. Third, in the general patriotic climate, it would be dangerous for the business community to disrupt the economy through negative actions.[13] The result is that state managers have the opportunity to expand their own power with the unassailable justification that such actions are necessary for the war effort. Some of these wartime measures will be rolled back once peace returns, but some will become part of the landscape.

In serious depressions and postwar reconstruction periods, the dynamics are somewhat different. Low levels of economic activity mean that the threat of declining business confidence loses its power, at the same time that popular demands for economic revival are strong. In such periods, the state managers can pay less attention to business opinion and can concentrate on responding to the popular pressure, while acting to expand their own power. However, there are still constraints on the state managers. Their continued rule depends on their capacity to revive the economy. As government actions prove effective in reducing unemployment, redistributing income, or expanding output, the political balance shifts. Pressure from below is likely to diminish; business confidence reemerges as a force once economic recovery begins. In short, successful reforms will tilt the balance of power back to a point where capitalists regain their veto over extensions of the state's role.

The increased capacity of state managers to intervene in the economy during these periods does not automatically rationalize capitalism. State managers can make all kinds of mistakes, including excessive concessions to the working class. State managers have no special knowledge of what is necessary to make capitalism more rational; they grope toward effective action as best they can within existing political constraints and with available economic theories.[14] The point is simply that rationalization can emerge as a by-product of state managers' dual interest in expanding their own power and in assuring a reasonable level of economic activity. The more power the state possesses to intervene in the capitalist economy, the greater the likelihood that effective actions can be taken to facilitate investment.

Not every extension of state power will survive beyond those periods in which state managers have special opportunities to expand the state's role. After a war, depression, or period of reconstruction, the business community is likely to campaign for a restoration of the *status quo ante*. State managers in these new periods will be forced to make some concessions to the business community in order to avert a decline in business confidence. However, the state managers also want to avoid the elimination of certain reforms important for the stabilization of the economy and the integration of the working class. Self-interest also leads them to resist a complete elimination of the state's expanded powers. The consequence is a selection process by which state managers abandon certain reforms while retaining others. In this process, reforms that are most beneficial for capitalism will be retained, while those whose effects are more questionable will be eliminated.[15] Again, the ultimate outcome is determined by intense political struggle.

Conclusion

The purpose of this essay has been to argue that a viable Marxist theory of the state depends on the rejection of the idea of a conscious, politically directive ruling class. By returning to Marx's suggestions that the historical process unfolds "behind the backs" of the actors (including the ruling-class actors), it is possible to locate the structural mechanisms that shape the workings of the capitalist state. These mechanisms operate independently of any political consciousness on the part of the ruling class. Instead, capitalist rationality emerges out of the three-sided relationship among capitalists, workers, and state managers. The structural position of state managers forces them to achieve some consciousness of what is necessary to maintain the viability of the social order. It is this consciousness that explains both the reluctance of state managers to offend business confidence, and their capacity to rationalize a capitalist society. However, the fact of consciousness does not imply control over the historical process. State managers are able to act only in the terrain that is marked out by the intersection of two factors—the intensity of class struggle and the level of economic activity.

This framework has implications for a wide range of theoretical and political questions. One of the most critical of these concerns capitalism's capacity to overcome its current economic difficulties. Analysts on the left have predicted that the forward-looking segment of the American ruling class will favor a further extension of the state's role in regulating the economy as a means to solve the problems of stagflation.[16] This perspective exaggerates the capacity of capitalism to reform itself in "normal" periods, and is unable to account, for example, for the inability of British capitalism to rationalize itself during the long period of decline since the nineteen-fifties. The framework developed here predicts that while the working class and the state managers themselves might favor an expansion of state intervention, business confidence will effectively veto such changes. It is therefore quite possible that the American economy will continue in its present state of crisis for many years to come.

4

Cooperation and Conflict
in the Capitalist World Economy

Two interpretations have long dominated Marxist, and much non-Marxist, discussion of the world capitalist system. According to the first, developed with special force by Karl Kautsky, the growing interpenetration of capital creates the possibility of an "ultraimperialism"—a stable and cooperative organization of relations based on a convergence of interests among the dominant capitalists of the major powers. According to the second, developed in its most politically influential form by V.I. Lenin, any period of cooperation simply indicates a truce in a perpetual war since, sooner or later, capitalists in one or more countries will grow dissatisfied with their share of the world markets, investment opportunities, and access to raw materials.[1] These dissatisfied capitalists will pressure their government to push for a revision of the system of international cooperation. Demands for revision are likely to meet resistance, and the dissatisfied power will use more and more aggressive tactics that will lead to sharpened economic conflict and increase the possibility of interimperialist war.

In stark form neither interpretation proves satisfactory today, and adherents of both have attempted various refinements and combinations. Even during the period of the Communist-Social Democrat fight, the Russian Revolution, and the apparent bourgeois stabilization that followed World War I, the two interpretations necessarily talked past

This essay is reprinted from *Marxist Perspectives*, spring 1979, pp. 78–88. Reprinted by permission of the *Socialist Review*.

each other. The one could always treat a period of international capitalist cooperation as evidence of permanent stability, whereas the other could always treat it as a prelude to new hostilities. When the hostilities came, the one could always treat them as a moment of bloody aberration, the other as proof of imperialism's fundamental instability.

The argument continues apace, for no objective methodological criterion satisfies adherents of both sides. Increasingly, however, it risks irrelevance. Lenin assumed that instability and hostility had to result in world war, but many Leninists today drop the assumption in the light of the political consequences attendant upon the rise of the Soviet Union to world power and the threat of nuclear destruction. Short of world war, however, competition and hostility can be interpreted either as evidence of international capitalist cooperation or of undiminished rivalry in new form. Clearly, nothing will be gained by continuing the debate in these now sterile terms, for the problem must be recast as one of new forms of a contradictory process of cooperation and rivalry.

Marxist writers, nevertheless, continue to interpret contemporary developments through a ritualistic invocation of either the Kautskian or Leninist position and have thereby seriously weakened their analyses. A review of some recent interpretations of the Carter administration's foreign economic policies indicates the partial and one-dimensional quality of the interpretations that rely too much on the classical formulations. Neo-Kautskian interpretations have exaggerated the impact of Trilateralism on the Carter administration, while neo-Leninists have once again warned of escalating trade wars without considering the factors militating against increasing interimperialist conflict.

The Trilateral Mystique and the Decline of the Dollar

In recent years some observers, including Marxists of a neo-Kautskian bent, have insisted upon the emergence of an international ruling class based in the 300 to 500 leading multinational corporations, including banks.[2] Ostensibly, a few giant firms, some based in the United States, some in the European Economic Community (EEC), and some in Japan, now dominate the world economy. The competition among these firms cuts across national boundaries. Firms based in different parts of the world are linked together through thousands of cooperative arrangements—licensing agreements, partnerships, bank consortiums. Their common interests in a stable organization of the world economy far outweigh their competitive conflicts. Hence, the small groups of people who own and manage these firms constitute an increasingly cohesive class. Initially brought into contact with each other through business dealings, they increasingly develop social and political ties, especially through organizations designed to bring together economic leaders from all the relevant nations to develop common perspectives on critical issues.

By far the most well known of these groups is the Trilateral Commission, which since 1973 has brought together prominent capitalists and politicians from the Trilateral powers—the United States, the EEC, and Japan.[3] It consistently has defended liberal economic principles against any tend toward neomercantilism, and it has advocated increased economic coordination as a countermeasure against both internal and Third World threats to liberal economic principles. The Trilateral Commission's notorious study that complains of an excess of democracy in the developed capitalist nations grew out of a concern that parliamentary institutions were making it difficult for political leaders to adhere to liberal economic principles in domestic and international economic policy.[4]

The Trilateral Commission emerged in public view when the Carter administration took office in 1977. Almost all the principal figures of the new administration had been active in the Trilateral Commission's deliberations: the President, Vice-President, National Security Adviser, and Secretaries of State, Defense, and Treasury, as well as other high-ranking members of the administration. The sudden appearance of so many Trilaterialists in the executive branch of the government seemed to provide powerful evidence of the validity of the "international ruling class" hypothesis.

But despite the strength of the Trilateral connection, the actual policies of the Carter administration have strayed far from the principles of Trilateralism. In fact, the Carter administration has presided over the most sustained deterioration of U.S.–Japanese and U.S.–Western European relations of the post–World War II period. On a series of interrelated issues—foreign steel imports, the Japanese trade surplus with the United States, the rate of economic expansion in Germany and Japan, and the declining value of the dollar—Carter administration policies have increased the level of tension with the other Trilateral powers. In some cases, such as the reference-pricing system for steel imports, the violation of Trilateralist principles has been blatant. In other cases the United States has violated the spirit of Trilateralism by attempting to exercise its power unilaterally, rather than engaging in the desired process of Trilateral consultation and compromise.

The gap between the Carter administration's Trilateral origins and its actual policies has led one Washington observer to write, "The Trilateral idea . . . appears to have hit the floor soon after the administration took office." This observer goes on to quote a foreign policy official as saying, "The Trilateral idea is dead. It was just rhetoric."[5] The irony is that a number of Marxist writers whose perceptions have been shaped by neo-Kautskian theories have been unable to distinguish rhetoric from reality.

Analysts in the neo-Leninist tradition have not been taken in by the Trilateral mystique. They have tended instead to minimize the importance of Trilateralism except as a device to coordinate imperialist policies toward the Third World.[6] But this stance creates its own problems. Neo-Leninists tend to assume that the corporate Trilateralists are insincere in their expressed support for higher levels of international cooperation, and that instead they favor more aggressive governmental policies designed to improve the position of U.S. capitalists at the expense of their Trilateral competitors. Sweezy and Magdoff, for example, argue that the decline of the dollar in the period from July 1977 to the beginning of 1978 was part of a deliberate policy designed to gain a competitive edge for U.S. capitalists in international trade.[7] They imply that the policy reflected the interests of the most powerful U.S. capitalists.

If so, they would be correct to foresee an intensifying trade war between the United States and the other Trilateral powers, for Japanese and Western European capitalists would be almost certain to demand compensatory actions by their own governments. These compensatory actions would necessarily lead to further escalation by the United States, and a full-scale trade war would ensue. However, Sweezy and Magdoff's implication that big capital in the United States favored a competitive depreciation of the dollar remains unproven and dubious. There is no evidence in the business press during 1977–1978 of any significant business support for a reduction in the value of the dollar. On the contrary, the business press expressed continuing anxiety over the dollar's fall. At least a part of this anxiety can be traced to the interests of many U.S.-based multinationals that stand to lose from a declining dollar. Since these firms tend to service foreign markets through foreign-based production, rather than through exports, their actual sales would be only marginally influenced by a cheaper dollar. More important, they stand to lose significant sums of money in currency transactions when the foreign exchange markets are thrown into turmoil by a declining dollar. The large U.S. banks also stand to lose significantly as declining international confidence in the dollar leads investors to shift their assets to banks in stronger currency countries.

A more plausible explanation of the dollar decline during 1977–1978 centers on the motivations of the Carter administration, which has been determined to sustain an economic expansion that would bring unemployment rates down from the potentially explosive levels reached during the Ford administration. Pursuit of expansionary economic policies in 1977–1978, with the rest of the world economy stagnant, created a substantial trade deficit. Throughout 1977 the Carter administration sought to reduce the size of the deficit by convincing Germany and Japan to expand their economies more rapidly. The administration argued that with all three "locomotive" economies—the American, Japanese, and West German—expanding rapidly, business activity would pick up in the rest of the world economy. With a global economic revival the United States could expand without a devastating trade deficit because foreign demand would boost U.S. exports.

The Germans and Japanese refused to cooperate and allowed their economies to grow only slowly through 1977 and most of 1978.[8] Since German and Japanese demand for imported goods remained depressed, the rest of the world economy stagnated, and the U.S. trade deficit reached record levels. The Carter administration continued its expansionary policies on the theory that any decline in the value of the dollar resulting from the growing trade deficit would act as an additional pressure on West Germany and Japan to step up their economic growth. The threat that German and Japanese goods might be priced out of certain markets by a declining dollar was designed to convince the other Trilateral powers that faster economic expansion would be the lesser of two evils. All pressures pointed in the same direction, since, if Germany and Japan sought to forestall the dollar's decline through massive interventions in the foreign exchange markets, they would risk inflationary growth in their domestic money supplies as their central banks accumulated huge quantities of unwanted dollars.[9]

In Sweezy and Magdoff's view the depreciation of the dollar was designed to give U.S. firms a competitive advantage in a stagnant world economy. I am suggesting instead that the dollar's decline was an undesired consequence of the administration's pursuit of domestic economic objectives. A secondary gain from the dollar's decline was, however, the increased pressure on Germany and Japan. If those two nations had succumbed to the pressure, U.S. policymakers believed that the U.S. deficit would have been sharply reduced and the dollar's decline reversed.

In this context it is possible to understand the decision of Germany and Japan not to take strong retaliatory actions. Despite their dissatisfaction with a declining dollar, they could hardly be enthusiastic about most of the available remedies to reduce the size of the U.S. deficit. In particular, if the United States attempted to reduce the deficit by pushing its economy back into recession, it would have closed off any prospects for a world wide economic recovery that would revive the German and Japanese economies. The most the Germans and Japanese could do was resist American pressures to reflate their own economies and hope that the United States would moderate the speed of its expansion, enact measures to reduce its oil imports, and increase its interventions on the foreign exchange markets to slow the dollar's decline. In light of these goals, sharp retaliatory actions hardly seemed to make sense.[10]

The State and Interimperialist Relations

This explanation acknowledges some divergence between the interests of state managers and the interests of dominant capitalists. The Carter administration pursued expansionary policies despite the negative consequences for U.S.-based multinationals occasioned by the decline of the dollar and the international currency instability. Neither the neo-Kautskian nor the neo-Leninist analyses allows for such a divergence. Both err by relying on an instrumentalist view of the state.[11] For the one, the dominant capitalists who are part of an emergent ruling class directly prevail on the state to pursue policies designed to increase interimperialist cooperation. For the other, the dominant capitalists direct the state to follow policies that bring it into conflict with other powers. In neither do other social classes or state managers play a significant role in determining policy. Both result in either/or positions—either there will be international economic cooperation or there will be international economic conflict. In reality, however, pressures for conflict and cooperation coexist with sufficient force to generate an indefinite stalemate.

A division of labor exists in contemporary capitalist societies between accumulators and state managers, and this division gives rise to differences in interests and ideology.[12] It occurs within a structural framework that operates so that the pursuit of self-interests by state managers tends to serve the long-term interests of capital. The self-interest of state managers—their capacity to continue their own rule—depends on the maintenance of reasonable levels of economic activity because economic downturns make likely a change in administration or even in regime. Hence, to serve their own interests, state managers have to act to assure reasonable levels of investment. This concern with the investment level provides a powerful disincentive against taking anti-capitalist actions and provides a strong incentive for measures to improve the investment climate—measures usually in the long-term interests of capital.

If we recognize that state managers are concerned with preserving and expanding their own power, then it follows that they will be preoccupied with three interrelated goals: 1. to protect their nation's position within the international state system since those who preside over a decline in their nation's political, economic, or military strength are likely to find their own power reduced as their nation's freedom to maneuver internationally declines; 2. to maintain or restore reasonable levels of economic activity;[13] 3. to build or preserve a political base of support that extends into the subordinate classes.

Frequently, these goals are mutually exclusive. The defense of a nation's position in the competitive state system might require substantial diversion of resources toward military spending that could undermine domestic prosperity and weaken the administration's base. And the incompatibility of the second and third goals has been analyzed at length as a conflict between accumulation and legitimation.[14] State managers have to juggle these often contradictory goals as best they can, changing the trade-offs in accord with changes in international and domestic circumstances. Typically, different parts of the state apparatus specialize in one or another of these goals, and the struggle for priority takes the form of interagency conflicts over policy directions. Those at the top of the state apparatus will attempt to mediate these conflicts, but their final decisions might well be strongly influenced by the particular balance of bureaucratic forces. In this context we can understand the Carter administration's relationship to Trilateralism. No matter how strong Carter's commitment and that of his leading aides to the principles of Trilateralism when they took over the reins of national power, their self-interest as state managers dictated another direction.

The reference-pricing of steel reflects a similar conflict, for all imports of certain steel products have to be priced above a minimal level. This blatant form of protectionism restricts the possible price competitiveness of imports. The Carter administration was subject to a number of pressures before it responded with this policy initiative. The major steel firms, agitating for some kind of protection against Japanese imports, used various tactics—intensified lobbying, legal procedures against alleged Japanese dumping, and the closing of a number of older steelworks. And union pressure for protection intensified as large numbers of workers were being thrown out of work by present and expected plant closings.

Despite the intensity of the immediate pressure, the Carter administration apparently made its concessions to protectionism on the basis of two related long-run considerations. It feared that the plant closings in Youngstown and Lackawanna would be followed by others if the steel industry did not receive protection. Both industry and administration knew that the next five to ten years would bring substantial increases in steel production in various low-wage parts of the underdeveloped world. These potential imports, as much as current Japanese and European imports, threatened a major decline in domestic steel production if free trade prevailed. The combination of the unemployment and the impact on national security of such a dramatic decline in the domestic steel industry forced the administration's hand. Obviously, the closing of additional steel plants would have worsened the already serious problems of unemployment in the Northeast and Middle West. But national security considerations were at least as important, for the prospects of substantial dependence on imported steel would leave the United States without assured access to an essential component in the production of armaments for conventional warfare.[15] In this case the first and third goal—protecting the nation's international position and maintaining a domestic political base—forced another lapse from liberal economic principles.

Yet the state clearly confronts limits on its capacity to pursue neomercantilist economic solutions. If it did not, the fabric of international economic relations would long since have broken down in trade wars and worse. No one country, not even a superpower like the United States, can dictate to all others. Neomercantilist policies provoke countermeasures, which can raise the stakes dramatically. Thus, a government must calculate the effect of its policies on the nation's international standing and domestic prosperity, and every government must understand that effective countermeasures depend largely upon its position within the competitive state system. Japan, for example, could not afford, politically or economically, to take strong measures against the American reference-pricing actions on steel. It had to be content with such lower-level responses as continuing to withhold liberalization of certain regulations on American investment in the Japanese economy. Yet in other instances even weak powers can exert effective pressure to force a strong power to abandon or modify a neomercantilist initiative.

The action of other states imposes only a partial restraint on state managers, for a combination of differential power and imperfect information can drive neomercantilist initiatives to the point where they could lead to significant escalation of economic conflict. Here, the perceptions of the internationally oriented segments of the domestic business community come into play. These segments, while not unified, generally maintain some variant of a Trilateralist ideology since their interests depend on the smooth working of the world economy, and they tend to be acutely conscious of the fragility of the international economy. Members of these segments, when their own particularistic interests are at stake, rarely hesitate to pressure the state to violate liberal economic principles.[16] But when they act as a group, their general interest in maintaining the fabric of international economic cooperation exerts itself in the form of continuing support for liberal economic principles.

The perceptions of these segments are likely to become a significant factor when an administration has moved in a strongly neomercantilist direction in an effort to resolve domestic contradictions at the expense of foreigners. Even when other nations cannot adopt effective countermeasures, the internationally oriented business community is likely to exert itself as a "peace interest" and agitate for a reduction in tension.[17] It will use various types of political influence, including the threat of a decline in business confidence, which could well result in a drop in stock market prices and in new domestic investment. In short, these segments can fulfill their own prophecy by precipitating a domestic recession if the adminstration refuses to reverse its policies.

A version of this scenario with more subtle forms of business pressure seems to have been enacted in 1971 when John Connally, President Nixon's Secretary of the Treasury, was acting aggressively to force Japan and Germany to agree to substantial revaluations of their currencies. Even though Germany and Japan had few effective countertactics, America's internationally oriented business community began exerting pressure for a modification of the administration's policies.[18] The administration did retreat substantially and reached a settlement with Germany and Japan. Connally's tenure as Secretary of the Treasury did not last much longer; he was replaced by George Schultz in May 1972.

Similarly, the Carter administration's no-action policy during 1977 and early 1978 has resulted in increasing dissatisfaction in the internationally oriented business community. Editorials in the business press have insisted that the Germans and Japanese are probably right to resist pressures for faster economic growth.[19] They have also insisted, with the Germans and Japanese, that the problem arose from the Carter administration's attempt to sustain too strong an economic expansion. This pressure from business circles did not force an immediate change in administration policy, but it did weaken the government's bargaining position with Germany and Japan. Also, business pressure apparently made an important contribution to the Carter administration's decision in April 1978 to bolster the dollar by auctioning some 300,000 ounces of gold—a measure that the administration had long resisted.[20]

Thus, when state managers are pursuing neomercantilist policies and the internationally oriented business community is exerting itself as a "peace interest" and urging greater international cooperation, it often remains unclear which group's policies are the more enlightened—the more sensitive to the long-term interests of capitalism. Neither group is acting on the basis of the needs of capitalism as a system; each is acting on its own short-term and long-term interests. The state managers are pursuing policies they regard as necessary for their continued exercise of political power, while the internationally oriented business interests are acting to insure their direct stake in an international economic climate in which they can make money.

Often, faulty perceptions by business of the fragility of the international economy lead to overreactions against neomercantilist policy initiatives. More important, in opposing neomercantilist initiatives, internationally oriented business opts for costly domestic policies—slowing down the domestic economy, cutting government spending, and allowing more workers to be displaced by imports. The pursuit of such alternative policies endangers social peace and makes it more difficult to reproduce capitalist social relations. But even though state managers might be more rational in avoiding such costly domestic policies, the costs of intensified international economic conflicts are also potentially enormous. The danger exists that neomercantilist policies can lead to an escalating conflict that would seriously damage the international trading and financial system and lead to a global depression—hardly an attractive alternative to a temporary slowdown of the domestic economy. In sum, it is not as though one side or the other has a monopoly on rationality; rather, both state managers and business are caught in a continuing contradiction between the needs of the national political economy and the needs of capitalism as a world system.

Left there, the argument appears to find little merit in the Leninist insistence on the probability of intensifying interimperialist conflict. The appearance is deceptive. Under normal circumstances internationally oriented business successfully exerts itself as a peace interest, but its success can by no means be taken for granted. In a variety of circumstances state managers continue to pursue conflicting policies regardless of the pressures of business "peace interests." State managers must respond to domestic political challenges, either of the Left or Right. Such challenges can convince state managers that the costs of retreating from neomercantilist initiatives might include a political revolution or at least a severe disruption. In such a case, ignoring the pressures of the internationally oriented business community would appear to be the lesser of two dangers.

The business community can also, under certain circumstances, lose its most effective weapons against state managers. If, for example, the level of economic activity is already low, then the threat of a loss of business confidence loses much of its force. But even when economic activity remains vigorous, state control over the economy may reach a point at which capitalists fear to risk an investment slowdown and cannot transfer large quantities of capital abroad. State managers are then freer to pursue a foreign policy that might lead to intensified interimperialist conflict.[21]

Since none of these special circumstances yet exists in the major Trilateral powers, it is reasonable to expect an intensification of neomercantilism moderated by pressures toward greater cooperation. In other words, we can expect a succession of incidents in which the great capitalist powers move toward the brink of intensified conflict and then draw back as internationally oriented business interests exert counterpressures. But if the world economy remains mired in stagnation during the next five to ten years, those special circumstances could develop in one or another Trilateral power, with unbridled interimperialist conflict once more a historical reality.

5

Beyond Relative Autonomy: State Managers as Historical Subjects

Neo-Marxist analyses of the state and politics now center on the vexed question of the "specificity of the political." What is the degree to which politics and the state have independent determining effects on historical outcomes? Can the state or the people who direct the state apparatus act as historical subjects? The questions are critical because without a clear set of answers, it is impossible to develop a consistent theory of the state.

In an interview done only months before his death, Nicos Poulantzas insisted that these questions had been answered through the idea of the relative autonomy of the state. Poulantzas' remarks are worth quoting at length:

> Interviewer: Much of your writing has been directed towards questions of the state and of politics, based upon the concept of "relative autonomy." What is your assessment of the capacity of a theory based on a concept of "relative autonomy" to grapple with the problems of the specificity of the state and politics?
> Poulantzas: I will answer this question very simply because we could discuss it for years. It is very simple. One must know whether one remains within a Marxist framework or not; and if one does, one accepts the determinant role of the

This essay is reprinted from *The Socialist Register* 1980, pp. 227–240. Reprinted by permission of The Merlin Press, Ltd.

economic in the very complex sense; not the determination of forces of production but of relations of production and the social division of labor. In this sense, if we remain within this conceptual framework, I think that the most that one can do for the specificity of politics is what I have done. I am sorry to have to speak like that.

I am not absolutely sure myself that I am right to be Marxist; one is never sure. But if one is Marxist, the determinant role of relations of production, in the very complex sense, must mean something; and if it does, one can only speak of "relative autonomy"—this is the only solution. There is, of course, another solution, which is not to speak of the determinant role of the economic at all. The conceptual framework of Marxism has to do with this very annoying thing which is called "relations of production" and the determinant role of relations of production. If we abandon it then, of course, we can speak of the autonomy of politics and of other types of relations between politics and economics.[1]

Poulantzas' comments constitute a direct challenge to those in the Neo-Marxist tradition who would argue for greater recognition of the specificity of the state and politics than is possible within the relative autonomy formulation.[2] The challenge does not rest ultimately on a dogmatic assertion about what is and what is not Marxism. Rather, implicit in Poulantzas' formulation is the warning that those who proceed beyond the relative autonomy formulation risk losing what is most valuable in Marxism—the analytic power of the framework. The clear danger is slipping into a form of theorising in which everything influences everything else, so that it becomes impossible to grasp the basic dynamics of a particular social formation.

The present paper is intended as a provisional attempt to take up this challenge. My argument is that the relative autonomy formulation is too limiting and that it is possible to construct an alternative framework that goes further in recognizing the specificity of the state, while still acknowledging the "determinant role of relations of production." In a brief essay, I can only outline such an alternative formulation, but I hope to demonstrate its analytic power by comparing the interpretations of the present conjuncture that flow from the two competing frameworks.

The Limits of Relative Autonomy

The major thrust of recent Marxist work on the capitalist state has been to view the state "as a system of political domination with specific effects on the class struggle."[3] The relative autonomy formulation has played an important role in this development by making clear that the state is not subject to direct and immediate control by the capitalist class, but that it has a degree of autonomy from such control. This insight makes clear that not all state actions can be explained as responses to the interests of particular fractions of the capitalist class, but rather many actions can be understood as flowing from the state's function as the *"factor of cohesion"* in the social formation.[4] Yet in fulfilling these functions, the state is acting in the interests of the capitalist class as a whole—hence the autonomy of the state is relative and limited.

The central problem with this formulation is the difficulty of specifying the limits of "relative autonomy." The phrase suggests that if the state managers were to exceed certain limits, the capitalist class—or factions thereof—would act to bring the state back into line. But such disciplinary action would appear to depend on the degree of consciousness, consensus, and political capacity of the capitalist class or its most important factions. But if the argument is formulated in this way, it is possible to imagine historical circumstances in which capitalists are unable to keep the state from achieving full autonomy. Alternatively, if the argument is that there are structural limits on the degree of state autonomy, then it should be possible to identify concrete structural mechanisms that prevent the state from exceeding its normal authority. Thus far, there has been little said about what those structural mechanisms might be.

Another important problem is that the relative autonomy formulation preserves the tendency in orthodox Marxism to explain all major state initiatives as the products of specific class interests. Hence, theorists of relative autonomy, no less than earlier Marxist theorists, explain Roosevelt's New Deal or Hitler's policies as reflections of specific class interests. This approach requires locating the relevant fraction of capital whose policies were being pursued even when there is little historical evidence that such fractions existed.[5] The result is such anomalies as the claim that both the National Socialist regime and the German Federal Republic were rooted in German heavy industry and finance capital.

These difficulties suggest that the relative autonomy formulations might not be, as Poulantzas suggests, the final destination of the Marxist theory of the state. It appears rather as a cosmetic modification of Marxism's tendency to reduce state power to class power. This reduction does not occur in the relative autonomy formulation as quickly as it does in orthodox Marxist formulations that center on the state as executive committee of the ruling class. But the reduction does ultimately occur because state power is still conceived as entirely a product of class relations. In Poulantzas' phrase, the state is the "condensation of class relations."[6] A condensation cannot exercise power.

An Alternative View: State Power in a Class Context

The starting point of an alternative formulation is the acknowledgment that state power is *sui generis*, not reducible to class power. As Weber insisted, the heart of that power is the monopoly over the means of violence, which is the basis on which the managers of the state apparatus are able to force compliance with their wishes. But the exercise of state power occurs within particular class contexts,[7] which shape and limit the exercise of that power. These class contexts in turn are the products of particular relations of production. To put it in other terms—each social formation determines the particular ways in which state power will be exercised within that society and social formations will vary in the degree to which the exercise of state power is constrained by class power.[8]

This formulation assumes that state managers[9] collectively are self-interested maximizers, interested in maximizing their power, prestige, and wealth. But any set of political institutions will set limits on the kind of maximization normally pursued. For example, within a parliamentary system, where control of the executive branch alternates between two parties, it is generally foolish for a particular group of state managers to take excessive actions to preserve their power in the short term if these actions might jeopardize their party's future chances for electoral victory. In short, state managers will tend to maximize within particular political "rules of the game." Beyond these rules lie particular patterns of class relations that reinforce the limits on state managers' pursuit of their collective self-interest. Yet it must be stressed that all of these limits are contingent and not absolute. Within particular historical circumstances, state managers might pursue their self-interest in ways that violate both the existing political rules and the normal constraints of class relations.

This possibility means that state managers pose a potential threat to other classes, particularly those classes that control substantial resources. The possibility exists that state managers, to improve their own position, will seek to expropriate, or at the least, place severe restrictions on the property of dominant classes. This threat is the root of the emphasis in bourgeois ideology on the need to prevent the emergence of a Leviathan state that swallows civil society. Yet since the bourgeoisie or other propertied classes cannot survive without a state, those classes have little choice but to seek a *modus vivendi* with the state managers. In social formations dominated by the capitalist mode of production, the dominant historical pattern has been the development of a *modus vivendi* that is highly favorable to the owners of capital. Not only have state managers been generally restrained from attacking the property rights of capitalists, but the exercise of state power has largely been used in ways that strengthen the capitalist accumulation process. This *modus vivendi* is rooted in the class context created by capitalism.[10]

The Capitalist Context

One key dimension of the context is capitalism's existence as a world system. One need not accept all of Wallerstein's formulations to acknowledge that capitalism operates on a world scale. The components of this world system are a world market and a competitive state system. Although the competitive state system predated the rise of capitalism, it became a critical component of the global workings of capitalism. The self-interest of state managers, particularly within the more developed nations of the capitalist world system,[11] leads directly to a concern with their nation's relative standing within the world economy and state system. Both military defeat and declining international competitiveness raise the specter of fewer resources available internally and effective challenges by outside or inside forces to the state manager's control over the state apparatus. These dangers can be reduced if state managers pursue actions to strengthen the accumulation process. An expanding economy provides the resources for an effective military and the means to buy off potential challenges for state power.

The pressures of the competitive state system also give state managers an additional impetus to reduce internal conflicts, even when those do not pose an immediate threat to state power. If significant groupings in the society such as racial, ethnic, national, or class groups are strongly discontented, they create possibilities for an internal "fifth column" for a rival power or, at the least, of noncooperation in the event of war, significantly weakening the nation's military posture. While pressure to conciliate such groups increases with the likelihood of war, the pressure is present at other times since war is a constant possibility within a competitive state system.[12]

These aspects of the international context interact with a number of key aspects of the domestic class context in shaping the exercise of state power. The first and most important of these domestic factors is the reality of capitalist control over the investment process. State managers are dependent upon maintenance of rates of investment that will assure a high level of economic activity. As noted above, economic strength is a critical component of military preparedness. Further, declining rates of economic activity make it more difficult for state managers to finance the state budget. Finally, declining rates of economic activity tend to lead to increasing discontent and political attacks on the existing order. Hence, state managers have a strong interest in persuading businesses—both domestic and foreign—to invest at rates that will assure high levels of economic activity. Further, there is a strong disincentive against taking actions that will damage business confidence and lead to an investment slowdown.[13]

The second internal contextual factor is the disproportionate control of the capitalist class over wealth of all types. This means that capitalists tend to own the most effective means of persuasion such as the mass media, and the capitalists, more than any other group, have the resources to bribe state managers. This can occur through simple payoffs, through promises of lucrative jobs after individuals leave political office, and through the bankrolling of election campaigns. The weight of these factors can be attenuated through state control over certain mass media, state financing of elections, and strict codes of ethics. Yet the basic pattern of disproportionate control of resources by a single class remains.[14]

A third factor is that the capitalist mode of production generates a set of interrelated contradictions. The operation of a market economy, as Polanyi insisted,[15] if left to its own devices would destroy society, as capitalists in search of profits would deplete both the labor force and the physical environment. Further, a market economy creates periodic economic crises, resulting from the "anarchy of production." These contradictions threaten social dislocation and social rebellion, so that state managers are impelled to act to regulate the market both to protect society and to protect their own rule. Yet in regulating the market, state managers act to save capitalism from itself, reforming and modifying the system in ways that tend to increase its viability.

When these contextual elements are taken together, one can see how the exercise of state power has generally served the needs of the capitalist accumulation process. On the one hand, state managers are reluctant to disrupt the accumulation process, but on the other hand, they face pressures to intervene to ameliorate the economic and social strains that capitalism produces.[16] Yet it must be emphasized that these interventions still involve conflict between capitalists and state managers. In order to conciliate subordinate social groups, protect society from the market, prevent severe economic crises, and maintain national defenses, state managers have had to pursue policies that impinge on the property rights of the capitalist class. Taxation and various forms of state regulation represent challenges to capitalist property rights, and have often been perceived as such. The consequence is that many of the state actions that have served to strengthen capitalism have been opposed by large sections of the capitalist class because they are seen as threats to class privilege and as steps towa-d the Leviathan state.

One can even speak of a modal process of social reform, where state managers extend their regulation of the market or their provision of services when faced with pressures from subordinate groups or the threat of social disorganization. Such actions are often opposed by many capitalists, but once the reforms are institutionalized, they are used by state managers in ways that contribute to the accumulation process and to the maintenance of social control.[17] Hence, for example, the extension of educational opportunities might result from working-class pressure, but the expanded schools are used to prepare pliant workers and good citizens.

But given the power held by capitalists, such reforms are ordinarily likely to occur only at the margins of the system. If state managers pursue policies that large sections of the capitalist class see as posing serious challenges to their property rights, the results are likely to be a collapse of domestic and international business confidence, leading to high levels of unemployment and an international payments crisis. Even when motivated by a desire to break with the capitalist mode of production, state managers are likely to respond to such a collapse of business confidence by retreating from their proposals for reform.

Exceptional Periods: War, Depression, Reconstruction

There are, however, certain historical periods in which the capitalist context changes, allowing state managers more freedom of action in relation to capitalists. In the twentieth century, periods of war, depression, and postwar reconstruction have been marked by the use of various forms of economic controls that tend to weaken the links between a national economy and the world market. With such controls in place, the loss of international business confidence ceases to be as critical an element because the controls impede the flight of capital. At the same time, the role of domestic business confidence also declines significantly. In depressions, when economic activity has already been sharply reduced, the threat of a further loss of business confidence loses its urgency since the negative consequences are already present. In periods of wartime and of postwar reconstruction, the business threat is less compelling for the opposite reason—fueled by government efforts or by pent-up demand—the economy is so strong that business has little freedom to withhold investment. There is also an ideological dimension, particularly during wartime, because the withholding of investment would appear unpatriotic.

It is hardly surprising therefore, that such periods have seen the most dramatic qualitative growth in state activity and the most serious efforts to rationalize capitalism. State managers take advantage of the changes in the structural context to expand their own power and to pursue policies that they perceive as necessary to strengthen the nation's position in the world system and to preserve internal order. Yet even in these circumstances, the capitalist context continues to place certain limits on the exercise of state power. First, state managers still depend upon the capacity of capitalists to produce an economic surplus from the direct producers. Second, such exceptional periods are generally of limited duration and state managers know that they will soon return to their earlier dependence on capitalist cooperation. In depression periods, for example, if state managers succeed in restoring reasonable levels of business activity, they are vulnerable to capitalist pressure, since another economic downturn would be likely to have devastating political consequences. Third, capitalists do retain other weapons, such as their control over the media and often over an opposition party, and these weapons place further constraints on state managers' freedom of action.

But there has been at least one historical case where state managers have taken advantage of the dynamics of an exceptional period to free themselves of constraints imposed by the capitalists. This was the case in Nazi Germany after 1936.[18] Depression conditions and the system of exchange controls imposed during the Mark crisis in 1931 gave Hitler a good deal of freedom of action in the period from 1933 to 1936. He used this freedom to destroy the parliamentary system and to increase vastly the state's role in the economy. Given the seriousness of the social and economic crisis, these actions were generally accepted, if not applauded, by German capitalists. However, the manner in which the Nazi economic programs were implemented placed German capitalists in a position of growing dependence on the National Socialist regime. Because of the vastly expanded economic role of the state, capitalist firms depended on the state for government contracts, for access to raw materials, and for export and import permits. In the years after 1936, the Nazis used this dependence to discourage capitalist resistance while pursuing policies that were no longer in the interests of German capital. An investment strike became impossible because too many of the major firms feared that noncooperation with the regime would lead to severe economic penalties. Furthermore, the authoritarian nature of the regime stripped capitalists of their normal access to the media or opposition parties, and since even the capitalists lived in fear of the Gestapo, there was no effective capitalist response.

To be sure, the capitalists generally remained in control of their property, and many profited handsomely from such services of the Nazi regime as the provision of slave labor for their factories. Nevertheless, the capitalists had been reduced to the role of highly paid functionaries of a state whose direction they did not control. They had little leverage to resist the orders that came from the state about the direction of their own firms, and they could not halt the the regime's irrational march toward self-destruction.

The Tipping Point, Late Capitalism, and the Left

This interpretation of the Nazi experience suggests the idea that the growth of the state's role in the economy can reach a tipping point past which capitalists lose their capacity to resist further state intervention, leading ultimately to the Leviathan state. Obviously, where parliamentary forms still exist, the capitalists will have more room to maneuver, but if the state's economic weapons are powerful enough, they can be used to discourage a variety of different forms of resistance including legal political opposition. The essence of the tipping point is that increased state intervention in the economy means that state managers will be making decisions with serious consequences for the profitability of most of the major firms. Through withholding licenses or contracts or credit or a variety of other regulatory or legal actions, the state managers can threaten key firms with retaliation if they withhold cooperation with other government policies. If these threats work, and the state managers are able to augment their economic powers even further, then at the next stage, the costs of resistance by capitalists will be even higher, and ultimately, state managers would succeed in depriving capitalists of the freedom to withhold investment, so that they become, as in the Nazi period, mere functionaries.

While this tipping point has not yet been reached in any of the developed capitalist nations, a number of developments have brought it closer. Most obviously, the expansion in the state's regulatory role and in the state's purchases of goods and services have drastically increased its leverage.[19] Moreover, the concentration of capital—to the point that a few hundred firms control the vast majority of capital investment—increases the vulnerability of capital, since there is a high likelihood that most of those firms can be seriously hurt by a hostile state. This vulnerability is suggested by a number of recent developments in the United States. The Nixon administration, at a number of junctures, threatened or did use its regulatory and legal powers to punish corporate opponents and to gain campaign contributions from otherwise reluctant firms. More recently, the Carter administration sought to back up its "voluntary" program of wage and price controls by denying contracts to offending firms. While these incidents fall far short of the systematic use of state economic power to assure capitalist compliance, they do suggest that these powers represent a growing temptation for state managers.

While the Socialist left has generally supported or acquiesced in the growth of state regulatory powers *vis-à-vis* capital, the left can take little comfort from the prospect that the tipping point might soon be reached. One problem is that there is little prospect that the left could take advantage of the tipping point as a means to launch a transition to socialism. In fact, the closeness of the tipping point makes the parliamentary road to socialism even more problematic than it was previously. Nevertheless, a variant of the tipping point argument has been used to defend the practicality of the electoral road to socialism, most recently in reference to the strategy of the Communist–Socialist alliance in France in the period in which an electoral victory seemed imminent. The argument was that because of the enormous powers of the French state including a large nationalized sector and a strong tradition of economic controls, a left government would have the means to counter effectively the inevitable capitalist offensive against the new government. By using this power effectively, the new government would block capital flight and keep investment at some reasonable levels during a transition period in which popular support was gradually rallied for additional series of reforms that would ultimately end with the expropriation of the remaining centers of private capital.[20]

The flaw in this argument is that the tipping point mechanism can only work in a situation where capital is caught off guard because it is dealing with a group of state managers who appear committed to the maintenance of private property. As long as businesses have some advance warning that they face a threat—as they would with the election of a left government—they will be able to launch a capital strike and an outflow of capital. Not even the most draconian controls can be assured of restoring economic stability once such a capitalist offensive has begun, and the chances are great that the resort to such draconian controls would fatally weaken the electoral base of a parliamentary left regime. Since the prospect of a left electoral victory in France occurred in a period when capital was already preoccupied with the tipping point, it was a certainty that the new regime would have had no breathing space at all before the capitalist offensive began.

Another problem for the left is that the scenarios in which the state passes the tipping point all suggest the emergence of a dangerously authoritarian regime. The point is that such a regime, whatever its rhetoric, would still depend heavily on the capacity of the capitalists to control the labor force, since continuity in production would remain essential. Yet through its fusion of economic and political power, this state capitalist regime would have far more formidable weapons for destroying labor and political resistance than exist in liberal capitalism. State managers, with relatively little difficulty, could deprive dissidents of a livelihood providing a powerful disincentive against political action. Furthermore, since parliamentary forms and civil liberties would no longer serve vital needs of the capitalist class, their elimination would encounter less resistance.

Moreover, the authoritarian outcome is made more likely by the prospect that such a regime would be unable to solve the underlying problems of the capitalist economy. To be sure, there might be an initial period in which controls are effective and the elimination of certain forms of waste could strengthen the economy. But soon the familiar problems that plague Soviet planners would emerge as a source of contradiction. Once one has relegated to secondary importance the forms of accounting based on corporate profits, how does one make the basic decisions about what to produce, how much to produce, how to produce, and so on? Further, because the contradictions of the late capitalist economy require fundamental forms of reorganization of energy resources, of land use, of transportation patterns, and so forth, what are the chances that state planners will choose optimal directions for restructuring? The strong commitment of state planners in both East and West to nuclear energy is an indicator of how easy it is to make the wrong choices, even in a situation where private interests are a negligible consideration. But since wrong choices can be very costly, the likelihood is that problems of slow growth and inflation will persist, forcing the state capitalist regime in a more repressive direction.[21]

Analyzing the Present Conjuncture

While the tipping point argument raises the specter of authoritarian state capitalism, it also points in a more hopeful direction. To see this direction requires a further analysis of the present conjuncture of state-capital relations. This can best be done througha critique of the analyses that flow from the relative autonomy framework.

Theorists of the relative autonomy framework tend to view the present period as one in which there is a drift toward corporatism and more authoritarian forms of rule. It is generally accepted that a capitalist offensive began in the early seventies throughout the developed capitalist world that was designed to erode working-class living standards by reducing wage gains, increasing "normal" levels of unemployment, and cutting state-provided services. In this view, capital, faced with mounting economic difficulties, has chosen to sacrifice a part of the state's legitimacy in order to make changes that would strengthen accumulation. Theorists of relative autonomy acknowledge, in short, that some of that autonomy has been temporarily abandoned, as capitalists have reverted to more direct forms of control over the state in order to use the state as a weapon in a more intense period of class conflict.[22]

While this account has a good deal of plausibility, especially in regard to the state's role in labor relations, it fails to penetrate beneath the level of appearances. Its major single flaw is its failure to account for the absence of corporatist institutional innovations. One would expect, if this analysis were correct, to see forms like the NRA of the early New Deal in which corporations and government worked together to limit inflationary pressures. But instead of such institutional innovations, we see such anomalous behavior as the American corporate elite opposing the corporatist government bail out of Chrysler as an interference with the free market. The latter incident makes little sense within the perspective of a drift towards corporatism.

The underlying problem with this argument is its failure to recognize that the core of the capitalist offensive has been an attack on the state itself. Capitalists realized that with the mounting problems of stagflation, there would be powerful pressures for a further extension of the state's role in the economy. But they also realized that such an increase in state power might well push the state past the tipping point, depriving them of their leverage over the state managers. To prevent this outcome, an offensive was launched to blame state intervention for the economy's difficulties and to propose reductions in taxes, state spending, and government regulation as the solutions to stagflation. At the same time, efforts were redoubled to use business channels of influence on the political system to block expanded state regulation and to pressure for a rollback of certain forms of state activity.[23] Of course, the capitalist offensive has also been characterized by attempts to use state power to weaken the bargaining power of the union movement.

This offensive has been remarkably successful in reversing a drift toward more *dirigiste* economic policies and in bringing conservative politicians to power, but it suffers from a major weakness—the lack of a coherent solution to the problems of stagflation. The recycling of traditional free market ideology with its emphasis on monetary restraint and balanced budgets was more a useful ideology to attack the state than a serious set of policy proposals. It is hardly surprising, therefore, that the efforts to implement those proposals have proven ineffective. It is hardly worth repeating the explanations of why such policies cannot succeed; suffice it to say that the solutions to the underlying problems that generate stagflation require serious forms of restructuring, including direct challenges to some of the major corporate actors in the "free market."

Yet, if "free market" solutions do not work, the basic contradiction that generated the capitalist offensive remains. As long as stagflation persists, the danger is acute that opportunistic state managers, under pressure from subordinate groups, will attempt to resolve the economy's problems with dramatic increases in the state's role, including the imposition of controls over wages, prices, credit allocation, and investment. Capitalists must maintain constant vigilance to prevent this outcome: they must maintain at a high level their efforts to use channels of persuasion and bribery to keep state managers in line. And they must also be careful to avoid inadvertently giving state managers more leverage over them. This is the reason why there have been few corporatist innovations, since such forms of corporate–government cooperation require, at the very least, a surrender of vital information to government officials.[24]

My argument is that under the surface of recent corporate successes in shaping state policies lies a sharpening contradiction between the interests of capital and the fundamental interests of state managers. While this contradiction has thus far been contained, the continuation of economic difficulties is likely to bring it to the surface. The reasons for this are clear from the earlier discussions of the pressures on state managers. Stagflation undermines a nation's position in the world market and in the competitive state system because it makes high levels of defense spending politically and economically more problematic. Furthermore, stagflation threatens to weaken the political base of any particular administration and it undermines the legitimacy of the entire political regime. This means that it is increasingly in the interests of state managers to attempt to solve the problems of stagflation through a further extension of state power. Even without any grand design to pass the tipping point, state managers will be pulled by objective economic circumstances to pursue more statist policies.

Capitalists will continue to attempt to counter this pull through the use of various forms of persuasion and by the threat to withhold investment. But it is reasonable to expect that over time, as the political costs of inaction by state managers rise, and the "free market" solutions become discredited through failure, the contradictions will surface in the form of more direct conflict between state managers and capitalists. One possibility might be that state managers take advantage of a sharp economic downturn to impose certain types of economic controls when capital's threat to withhold investment is less potent, and that capitalists will respond with other types of economic sabotage such as the creation of artificial shortages. Yet because the two parties to the conflict are relatively evenly matched, it is unlikely that a clear resolution would be reached quickly. State managers are unlikely in the short term to pass the tipping point, nor are capitalists likely to succeed in persuading state managers to abandon their interventionist ambitions. It is more likely that there will be a prolonged period of conflict, attenuated only by the fact that there remain certain areas in which the antagonists still need to cooperate. Yet as the conflict intensifies, even shared interests will not suffice to heal the divisions.

While the notion of an underlying contradiction between capitalists and state managers appears counter-intuitive in the present period, it is already implicit in recent discussions of the internationalization of capital and of the fiscal crisis of the state. The process of global optimization of profits by international corporations creates serious problems for the "home" countries of those firms. The most obvious problem centers on the export of jobs to other parts of the world, leaving structural unemployment in what had been the industrial heartlands of the developed nations. Similarly, the pattern of collusion between the international oil majors and the OPEC nations forces the developed nations to adjust to rapidly rising oil prices, at a time when the power of oil firms had suppressed energy alternatives. In each case, it is state managers who are forced to handle the resulting problems, as short-term political problems that threaten their own political base, and as larger structural problems that weaken the entire political economy.[25]

Similarly, the fiscal crisis of the state thesis also suggests growing strains between capitalists and state managers. In O'Connor's framework,[26] there is mounting pressure for increased state expenditures to maintain the military, to manage the surplus populations, and to provide forms of social investment necessary for continuing capital accumulation. Under optimal circumstances, these expenditures could be financed by the state taking a constant share of a growing economic pie. Yet in late capitalism, this proves impossible, since the pie is expanding too slowly. The state can only cover its expenses by expanding its percentage share of total resources. But this leads, in turn, to inflation, as both workers and capitalists attempt to avoid any reduction in their shares of the total economic product. It also leads, as we have seen, to efforts to reduce the inflationary pressures by restricting state expenditures. The point is that state managers are caught in a contradictory position. On the one hand, they have the responsibility to carry out those state expenditures that are necessary to make a capitalist economy work, but on the other hand, that economy does not generate the economic growth needed to finance those expenditures. This contradictory position is bound to produce strains between capitalists and state managers.

Conclusion

To assess the meaning of a contradiction between state managers and capitalists, an historical analogy is useful. In her recent study of the French, Chinese, and Russian revolutions, Theda Skocpol argues that those revolutions grew out of a structural crisis in the old regime—a conflict between the pressures that the international state system placed on state managers and the limited productiveness of the existing system of agricultural social relations.[27] The problem, in brief, was that state managers needed expanded revenues to defend their nation's position in the state system, but there were structural obstacles to any significant increase in agricultural revenues. State efforts to raise more money through increased taxes generated fierce resistance from the dominant landed classes, who saw this as a fundamentl threat to their own privileges. The resulting political conflict between the state apparatus and the landed classes produced political paralysis and a breakdown in the machinery of social control. As a result, other social groups were able to mobilize and carry out a revolution against the old state apparatus and the old landed classes.

An analogous structural crisis emerges in late capitalism. Neither the state nor capital are willing or able to carry out the forms of reorganization needed to release new productive forces that could overcome the economy's weaknesses. Instead, the contradictions and conflicts between capitalists and state managers grow deeper as neither statist nor "free market" solutions are capable of solving the underlying problems. The result is likely to be political paralysis and an accelerating erosion of bourgeois ideological hegemony. In the context of deepening state–capital conflicts, new opportunities would exist for oppositional social forces determined to eliminate the oppressive power of both capital and the state. Hence, we might well be at the beginning of a period in which the contradictions between state and capital dramatically shift the balance of forces in favor of those who envision an emancipatory form of socialism. Yet circumstances will not by themselves create a new society, and the failure to seize this possible opportunity redoubles the likelihood of new forms of barbarism.

Part II

6

New Productive Forces and the Contradictions of Contemporary Capitalism: A Postindustrial Perspective

with LARRY HIRSCHHORN

No social order ever perishes before all the productive forces for which there is room in it have developed; and new, higher relations of production never appear before the material conditions of their existence have matured in the womb of the old society itself.[1]

This familiar but enigmatic sentence appears in Marx's extremely condensed statement of his world view in the Preface to the *Contribution to a Critique of Political Economy*. The entire brief passage has been subject to textual quotations and close analysis by writers attempting to find support for one or another interpretation of Marx's meaning. We intend here not to make another argument about Marx's true meaning, but to show how our interpretation of this segment of Marx's writing provides a starting point for conceptualizing the contradictions of advanced capitalism.

The core of our theoretical framework is an effort to make a postindustrial argument within Neo-Marxism. With the postindustrial theorists, we argue that the most developed societies—both capitalist and

This essay is reprinted from *Theory and Society* 7 (May–June 1979): 363–390. © copyright Martinus Nijhoff Publishers, Dordrecht, Holland.

state Socialist—face a transition from industrial society, organized around the production of goods, to postindustrial society, organized around the provision of services and advanced technologies that release labor from direct production.[2] But while most postindustrial writing sees this transition occurring through a process of gradual evolution, we argue that the transition to a postindustrial society creates a profound social crisis: contemporary capitalism is ripe for a transition to postindustrial society, but existing social relations block the release of new productive forces, creating social and economic stalemate.

In developing this line of argument, we are building on the body of Neo-Marxist writing of the sixties that stressed that the contradictions of advanced capitalism are radically different from those of early or competitive capitalism.[3] Such writers as Mallet, Gorz, Nicolaus, Sklar, and others pointed to the inadequacy of orthodox Marxism for understanding an advanced capitalism that had successfully improved the standard of living of the working class. They stressed that within advanced capitalism, new contradictions and new social forces would become the basis for emancipatory social possibilities, as capitalism created new needs that could not be satisfied within it. But despite the insights of these writers, their ideas have generally been neglected in recent years largely because of their failure to anticipate capitalism's growing economic difficulties in the seventies.

We think, however, that the idea of postindustrial crisis provides a framework for integrating the insights of the Neo-Marxists with an understanding of advanced capitalism's economic problems. In short, we are attempting to revise and reformulate the Neo-Marxist analysis in order to develop a theory of advanced capitalism that joins the critique of capitalist culture with the critique of political economy. This synthesis is critical to avoid the twin pitfalls of contemporary Marxism—an economistic stance that tends to ignore issues of culture and an idealistic cultural critique that is oblivious to political economy.[4] In the present paper, we are not able to develop the political implications of our analysis, but we are convinced that an emancipatory politics in the present period requires such a theoretical synthesis.

Productive Forces and Social Relations

Prior to the opening quote from Marx, he develops the distinction between material productive forces and the relations of production, arguing that at a certain stage in the development of material productive forces, the relations of production become a fetter. Further development of the productive forces can come about only with a social revolution that transforms the relations of production. All of this is familiar; one immediately thinks of capitalism developing in the interstices of feudal society up to a certain point, beyond which capitalist productive forces cannot be further developed without a social revolution that dismantles feudal social relations. Two problems remain, however; first, what Marx means by material forces of production and relations of production is not clear, and, hence, it becomes difficult to see how to use this conceptual framework for analyzing the transition from capitalism to socialism. Second, there is an inescapable element of tautology, particularly in the sentence quoted above, because it is difficult to determine both how severe the contradiction between forces and relations is, and whether room remains in a particular social order for other productive forces to develop.

The latter problem is central and inescapable. Marx was trying to develop a conceptual framework that would allow one to comprehend the most fundamental types of social transformations. Necessarily, one could not prove to a skeptic in 1800, or even in 1840, that industrial capitalism, a whole new social order, was emerging out of the old social relations. All that one could do was develop a conceptual framework that both argued that a new social order can emerge in the womb of the old, and showed how such a process occurs. This framework still provides guidelines for constructing a compelling argument that a particular historical period is just such a turning point, but there is no royal road to truthful predictions.

Marx's framework is violated by attempts to operationalize or measure the contradiction between forces and relations. Rather, the amorphousness of Marx's concepts such as forces and relations indicates that he was more interested in creating a heuristic, totalistic framework than in developing a model that could be interpreted in terms of dependent and independent variables. In this light, both "material forces of production" and "relations of production" can be understood as concepts that relate not to specific aspects of society, but to the totality of society as seen from different perspectives. "Material forces of production" comprehend the totality of social relations in society as they shape the capacity of the society to produce wealth. "Relations of production" comprehend the ensemble of social arrangements seen from the point of view of the society's reproduction of itself. In every mode of production there will be a time when the fit between these production and reproduction arrangements is extremely tight as, for example, when the organization of property reinforces the system of production and vice versa. But the development of the material productive forces can lead to the emergence of "new productive forces" that are not compatible with the existing patterns of social relations. It is the development of these new productive forces that poses the issue of social transformation. For a period, these new productive forces might develop fairly smoothly, but over a time, they will come into greater conflict with the existing relations of production. A period of crisis will ensue in which the old productive forces cease to function effectively, even though the new forces have not yet broken through the fetters that constrain them.

Karl Polanyi describes such a crisis period in the development of capitalism in Great Britain in his account of the impact of different types of poor law measures.[5] At the end of the eighteenth century, the emergence of the factory and the transformation of agriculture placed tremendous pressure on the organization of labor in rural areas. In particular, industrial capitalists demanded that displaced peasants be ready to move anywhere in search of work. Yet the old landed classes resisted the push for "free" mobility, understanding well that this would destroy their political and social base by depopulating many rural areas. For some forty odd years, from 1795 to 1835, the result was an explosive stalemate. The shift toward capital-intensive agriculture permanently displaced countless numbers of peasants by 1800, while subjecting others to the vagaries of price fluctuations, falling income, and near starvation. The traditional landed interests responded by introducing an expanded welfare system to cope with the impoverished rural population, while also taking actions to limit the mobility of these displaced people.

Polanyi argues that the consequence of these measures was to throw the displaced peasants on the scrapheap of dysfunctionality. They lost all sense of workmanship and could not even be hired by rural authority as laborers because they were so unproductive. The costs of the welfare system began to eat into the economic base of the rural areas. But the existing social relations had also stalemated the development of machine capitalism since the welfare measures interfered with the proletarianization of the displaced rural population. In the process, the economic viability of both the farm areas (which were faced with labor surplus) and the cities (which were faced with labor shortage) were threatened. The passage of the Poor Law Reforms of 1834 finally broke the stalemate. The welfare system was destroyed, "free mobility" was forced upon the displaced rural population, and a modern labor market was created. Industrial capitalism, based on the new productive forces of "free labor," measured labor time, and the factory was now able to take off.

We argue that in advanced capitalism, a similar process occurs as new productive forces develop partially and haltingly within the constraints of capitalist social relations. These new productive forces both undermine the existing system of production, and create the potential for a reorganization of social relations that would vastly expand society's capacity to produce wealth. As these new productive forces mature within the womb of capitalism, they create the material conditions for the development of higher relations of production. While Marx's impatience for Socialist revolution led him to alter his formulations on this issue, our argument is consistent with the position he lays out in the *Grundrisse*. There, he suggests that capitalism collapses only when the development of technology has progressed to a point where "labour, in its direct form, has ceased to be the main source of wealth."[6] In other words, socialism becomes a real possibility only when the new productive forces are almost fully developed within the womb of capitalist society.

The *Grundrisse* is also useful in clarifying the nature of the new productive forces. Marx writes that with technological advance,

what appears as the mainstay of production and wealth is neither the immediate labor performed by the worker, nor the time that he works—but the appropriation by man of his own general productive force, his understanding of nature and the mastery of it; in a word, the development of the social individual.[7]

The productive forces of industrial capitalism are based on the direct labor of workers, measured and exploited in terms of labor time. The new productive forces, in contrast, are based on the capacity of people to learn. In other words, as the new productive forces advance, this capacity becomes increasingly important and labor time ceases to be an effective standard or measure of productivity or wealth.

The surplus labor of the masses has ceased to be a condition for the development of wealth in general; in the same way that the non-labor of the few has ceased to be a condition for the development of the general powers of the human mind. Production based on exchange value therefore falls apart.[8]

The new productive forces cannot be reduced to the existence of particular types of technology or of particular types of workers. In fact, new productive forces exist in both latent and developed forms. The displaced peasantry in Britain before the Poor Law Reforms were as much a part of the new productive forces of industrial capitalism as were the early factories; they existed in a latent form only because they remained fettered by the old social relations. Similarly, in advanced capitalism, latent new productive forces exist where the capacity of individuals to learn is not utilized productively. Capitalism therefore develops the new productive forces in two ways. First, it appropriates science and technology, by expanding the role in production of "the appropriation by man of his own general productive force,"[9] that is, by increasing the use of learning in the production process. Second, as a result of these technological changes, more and more human labor is released from participating in simple direct labor. This means for the society as a whole a qualitative increase in the amount of time in which individuals contribute to productivity by learning. Under these conditions, both the distinctions between work and learning, and between work and nonwork break down. "To economise on labour time means to increase the amount of free time, i.e. time for the complete development of the individual, *which again reacts as the greatest productive force of labor*" (our underlining, FB and LH).[10] To be sure, this last step, the development of the individual as a learner, as the basis for the development of the productive forces, emerges only partially because capitalist social relations place fetters on the new productive forces.

The Emergence of the New Productive Forces Historically

Clearly, knowledge, science, and technology have always played a role in the production process in capitalism. But in these passages in the *Grundrisse*, Marx suggests that there is a turning point at which a change in degree becomes a change in kind. After a certain point, the old productive forces based on direct labor and measured labor time cease to be as important for productivity advance as are the new productive forces. There is considerable evidence that such a turning point occurred in the development of American capitalism during the twenties. Martin Sklar made this argument in his seminal article on disaccumulation.[11] Sklar argued, in brief, that up to World War I the labor force involved in direct industrial production always expanded, though with cyclical ups and downs. In the twenties, however, industrial production increased sixty-five percent while the amount of labor time in manufacturing fell. The industrial economy was no longer accumulating labor power; it had begun to disaccumulate labor power. Sklar argued that this transition from accumulationist to disaccumulationist capitalism created profound new contradictions because capitalists had to repress or contain the emancipatory possibilites inherent in the disaccumulation process.

While we draw heavily on Sklar's argument, our emphasis differs. In our view, the key factor in the twenties was not that necessary labor time in manufacturing fell. That resulted from a more fundamental change, the qualitative shift in the importance of the new productive forces that occurred during the decade. Here it is critical that output expanded while *both* labor and capital inputs remained constant or declined. Total person hours of work in manufacturing rose from 11.3 billion in 1889 to 20.4 billion in 1909, but person years rose only four billion more to 24.3 billion in 1929, and there was no increase at all during the twenties.[12] Similarly, the amount of capital required to produce a unit of output (in dollar terms) rose from 1889 to 1919, but fell 12 percent from 1919 to 1929 and has continued to fall ever since.[13] In sum, during the twenties, the inputs of measured labor time, both living and dead (variable capital and constant capital), declined in significance in the production equation. The expansion of production, independent of an expansion in labor or capital inputs, indicates that the role played by the new productive forces had qualitatively changed.[14]

The new productive forces manifested themselves in the twenties in the growing importance of such "background" factors as information, new modes of management, technological advances, and the expansion of services, such as education, welfare, and medical care. Each of these background factors increased the impact of knowledge and learning on the production process. Even Taylorism, introduced widely in the twenties, partly appropriated the new productive forces since production was reorganized by systematically applying human intelligence. To be sure, within the framework of capitalist social relations this reduces the conceptual skills of the direct producers, but it still represents a quantum change in the extent to which conscious intervention shapes and reshapes production.

As the example of Taylorism suggests, capitalism first appropriates the new productive forces naturally, as a consequence of the accumulation process. On the one hand, capitalists appropriate new productive forces in response to competitive pressure from other capitalists, domestic and foreign. As they try to retain or improve market position they can introduce a new technology, spend funds on research and development, and pressure the state to expand its programs for producing various forms of educated labor. On the other hand, the struggle between labor and capital provides an interrelated set of motivations to appropriate new productive forces. Capitalists introduce new technologies to undermine the position of labor and resort to Taylorism to break the power exercised by skilled workers.[15]

Yet the apparent ease with which capitalists appropriate new productive forces, at first, should not blind us to the contradictions that emerge as those new productive forces are no longer just auxiliaries to the old productive forces of capital and simple labor. The more new productive forces develop, the more they tend to undermine the set of social relations organized around the older, industrial productive forces. Here, again, the twenties were critical. The contradictions emerged both at a level of macroeconomics and at the level of sensibilities.

The new productive forces created economic strains centered on the classical problems of overproduction and underconsumption. But the declining relative importance of the old productive forces—capital and labor—dramatically changed the context in which these problems emerged. In brief, the tremendous growth of production during the decade of the twenties, with the relative stagnation in the size of the paid labor force, created the conditions for overproduction/underconsumption. Industrial real wages rose dramatically during the decade, but not enough to generate the necessary demand. The outcome was, of course, the economic crash and a prolonged depression. But the Great Depression was most significant because, though wages, prices, and interest rates fell, business investment did not expand as it had in earlier cycles. We believe this happened because the productivity of industrial workers in both consumer and capital goods sectors increased dramatically. The normal business upturn happens spontaneously because consumer demand expands. As people are hired back, consumer spending grows, leading capitalists to expand their facilities, which, in turn, leads to further increases in hiring. But in the thirties, this dynamic broke down because the increment to consumer demand that resulted from each additional worker hired was too small relative to the increase in the quantity of goods produced as a result of that worker's labor.[16]

The same point can be stated in other terms. Once the new productive forces emerged as a significant component of productivity advances, the system of distributing income shares that was based on measured labor time no longer served as an adequate basis for generating sufficient demand to keep the economy at a high level of economic activity. It was in this context that Keynesian measures emerged to resolve these problems. Keynesian policies respond to these contradictions in two ways. On the one hand, Keynesian policies try to alleviate the demand problem by slowing the society's appropriation of new productive forces; that is, by assuring that a substantial portion of the society's wealth is used wastefully or unproductively. On the other hand, Keynesian policies develop new mechanisms for distributing income shares and claims on the total product, so that demand will expand.

The contradictions in the realm of sensibilities that emerged in the twenties are far less dramatic than the crash and the Great Depression, but they are equally important. Here, again, Sklar's arguments are very useful. He argued that the coming of disaccumulation—the reduction in simple direct labor time—produced a profound rebellion against the values of accumulationist capitalism. In particular, the Protestant values of self-sacrifice, self-discipline, and the redemptive nature of hard work were broadly challenged by new sensibilities that stressed the importance of personal psychology, the legitimacy of pleasure-seeking, the need for artistic expression, and the idea that the development of the individual was an end in itself.[17]

The manifestations of this development were many and varied; the rise of the "new intellectuals," the new sexual freedoms, the emergence of taste management and cultivation through advertising, the spread of the psychological perspective into the helping professions. These were all signs that a new sensibility expressed in the desire for personal development, leisure, and the consumption of life-styles was replacing older ethics based on saving, achievement, and the disciplined and repressed family. To be sure, such tendencies emerged in an ambivalent and conflict-ridden way—sometimes appearing to be antagonistic to capitalism and sometimes appearing to strengthen it. But these tendencies anticipated the new contradictions, the new antimonies of a postindustrial epoch. Taken as a whole, they signified the turning away from the historical patterns of cultural integration under an accumulationist capitalism.[18]

In short, we argue that the growing importance of new productive forces creates contradictions for capitalism. These contradictions first emerged significantly in the twenties, but capitalism found ways to handle them. Keynesian economic policies, implemented in the period after World War II, resolved the problem of overproduction/underconsumption. Similarly, the new sensibilities were contained in the privatistic, consumer-oriented, suburban life-style that became dominant after World War II. *But these were and are temporary and partial solutions.* New productive forces continue to develop, even as a result of measures designed to contain them, and they continue to erode the social relations of accumulationist capitalism. Hence, both the economic crisis of contemporary capitalism and the profound social crisis can be understood as consequences of the development of new productive forces that come into conflict with capitalist social relations.

The theory is, therefore, a two-sided one. It is a theory of *decay,* a theory of the gradual dissolution of the patterns of organizing work, labor markets, and social life that developed out of accumulationist capitalism. But it is also a theory of *development,* a theory of the potential emergence of a new work system that is no longer based on the capitalist labor market. The theory posits that new productive forces, new sources of productivity, are emerging in capitalist society, that are not consistent with the capitalist organization of work or with the capitalist organization of social life. But because of these capitalist social relations the new productive forces emerge only piecemeal. Consequently, the disorganizing impact of these forces dominates their potential reorganizing effects. The system decays. Yet, and this is crucial, it decays within a developmental setting, which means that the theory of new productive forces is not a theory of stagnation or permanent depression. Rather, it is a theory of development in which stagnation predominates to the degree that the social relations stifle the developmental forces.

New Productive Forces and Contemporary Crises

In the next two sections of this essay we show the ways in which the further development of new productive forces have undermined the patterns of social and economic life that emerged in the aftermath of the twenties and thirties. We argue that the new productive forces create the process of decay as well as the potential for reorganization. The negative moment, the process of disorganization and dislocation, is always dominant, but we stress equally the positive moment, the potentialities for an emancipatory social reorganization. Our central point, however, is that the positive and negative moments are completely intertwined and that we can make the positive moment dominant only through conscious collective action.

As we suggested earlier, the further emergence of the new productive forces in the period since the twenties involves two elements. First, capitalism continues to appropriate the new productive forces *directly* by developing new technologies, expanding research and development, employing educated labor, upgrading the skills of sectors of the labor force, and expanding services that produce people with higher capacities for learning. The continuing decline of the capital-output ratio testifies to the ongoing impact of these new productive forces on productivity. Second, capitalism develops the new productive forces *indirectly*, by continuing to release people from direct production. For example, the excessive expansion of higher education (excessive from the point of view of job opportunities for graduates) has been used as a Keynesian measure to expand demand—through the building of campuses and the hiring of teachers—while removing many young people from the labor market. But this expansion has also accelerated the development of new productive forces in the form of highly educated people who nevertheless cannot find jobs commensurate with their capacities to learn.

The direct and indirect emergence of the new productive forces thus have the same effect: they both disrupt and undermine the previously existing patterns of social life. As the new productive forces emerge indirectly, they create feelings of superfluity and dysfunctionality. People feel within themselves the capacity to be useful and productive but the jobs that they have do not engage their faculties and capacities. As the new productive forces emerge directly, people who work in new postindustrial settings find that their basic unconscious assumptions about how they organize their lives become problematic. As the new productive forces break down the distinctions between work and learning, between work and nonwork, people are forced to rethink their relationship to work and family life. Consequently, a fundamental crisis of social life emerges as people experience a growing tension between their own expectations for stability and change and the workings of social institutions. In the coming section we analyze this crisis in depth.

New Productive Forces and the Crisis of Social Life

The patterns of social life consolidated in this country after the twenties and thirties continued to organize people's lives around measured labor time, the basis of the old productive forces. This was linked with the establishment of a progressively linear life course in which the stable institutions of the job and family dictated a fixed schedule of progression through life. A man grew up, got his job, got married, formed his own household, had children, lived with his wife after the children left, died. A woman might work briefly before marrying but then would settle into a lifetime of domesticity. For both, there were no sanctioned reversals such as divorce, career switching, or going back to school. These happened, but the overwhelming cultural pressure was toward uniformity around the linear life course.[19]

The job, whether white collar or blue collar, left little scope for learning or personal development. A person learned a set of skills at the beginning of a work career, and this set was supposed to carry him or her through an entire work-life, with only minor variations. This work-life dominated the individual's adulthood; entrance into the work force was early and retirement, if it happened at all, occurred very late. Vacation time and leisure time were relatively brief, so that the sexual division of labor that made women predominantly responsible for child-rearing was reinforced by the pressure of work.

All aspects of this organization of social life have been undermined by the progressive emergence of new productive forces over the course of the past fifty years.[20] The linear life course, and the family arrangements associated with it, have broken down while the earlier patterns of work organization are also in crisis. We will trace out this process of decay first, and then examine the potential for reorganization that lies in the present situation. We will examine three different but interrelated sources of decay, all of which are rooted in the way in which the new productive forces release individuals from simple or direct labor.

The first source of decay is the actual displacement of individuals from work, as the economy's need for labor time fails to keep pace with the growth of the labor force. The decline of the old productive forces means that the economy cannot provide the millions of unskilled, entry-level jobs that are needed to absorb the available labor power. The result is that millions of people, particularly inner-city minority residents, become a surplus population with little prospect for even minimal economic security. But now, with employment declining in many traditional industrial sectors of the economy, "structural unemployment" threatens many industrial workers of all races.[21] The impact of structural unemployment on family patterns is well known. Unemployment can undermine people's sense of self-worth, and the resulting self-denigration can threaten the equilibrium of the family unit, leading to higher levels of marital breakup.[22]

But the declining need for labor time has an impact far beyond those who experience long-term unemployment. For all sectors of the working population, the actual weight of work on the life course has diminished. The median age at entry into the labor force has risen over the past fifty years, and the median age at retirement has fallem, particularly since World War II.[23] Even though the length of the work week has remained relatively constant since the thirties for full-time workers, the amount of vacation time has risen.[24] The consequence of these trends is that work ceases to be synonymous with adulthood and the linear life course begins to be undermined. The more time people spend outside of the paid labor force before, after, and during a work career, the more they find that work is no longer a sufficient focus for organizing their lives. This is seen most graphically in the case of retirees who face problems of psychological adjustment, unless they reorder their personal lives and change family patterns. Retirement counseling has emerged to warn prospective retirees that the linear adult life course has come to an end.

Women who work at home are also finding that this form of work no longer structures adult life. For reasons that cannot all be traced to the emergence of new productive forces, lifetime domesticity has ceased to organize a woman's adult life effectively. The reduction in family size, the introduction of labor-saving machinery in the home, and the weakening of multigenerational family ties means that only during the relatively brief period when a woman is raising small children can housework be a full-time occupation. To be sure, many women use their leisure time for a variety of volunteer and creative tasks that can be quite satisfying. But many others have responded by rejecting lifetime domesticity, either by entering the paid labor force after child-rearing is completed or by pursuing careers during or instead of child-rearing.[25]

The resultant accelerating increase in labor force participation for married women undermines the linear life course and related family patterns in still other ways. First, working wives are less economically dependent on their husbands, so that the power relations within the family are changed fundamentally. Women are in a better position to press emotional demands on their husbands, and they can much more easily contemplate living on their own. Men, in turn, are likely to respond to these new emotional demands with a combination of flight and anger.[26] Consequently, marriages become more unstable. Second, as women move in and out of the labor force in relation to child-rearing and shift back and fourth between full-time and part-time work, a much more fluid life course emerges that is not determined by the demands of paid or unpaid work alone. Finally, when mothers of small children continue to work, the husband faces strong pressure to reduce his own work commitment in order to play more of a role in child-rearing. Even if he proves unable or unwilling to respond to these pressures, he is likely to experience strain between family and work commitments.

A second source of decay is the problem of underemployment. While we argued earlier that Taylorism represented a partial appropriation of the new productive forces because human learning was used to shape and reshape the work process, Taylorism itself becomes a fetter on the further development of new productive forces. It is a fetter because it reduces workers' conceptual knowledge to a minimum, thus eliminating any significant possibility that their capacity to learn will be used in the production process. Nevertheless, Taylorism remains an attractive form of work organization in both blue-collar and white-collar settings because it vastly simplifies the problem of controlling the work force. A work force stripped of conceptual skills is easily replaceable, hence cheaper, and is unable to use its knowledge as a lever against management.[27]

As capitalists retain and expand Taylorist forms of work organization underemployment increases under two different conditions: where the educational level and set of capacities of the labor force is rising, and where new technologies release workers from the tasks of direct production. In both situations, the worker is likely to feel that work does not engage his or her energies and capacities. As with unemployment, this experience of underemployment can undermine an individual's sense of self-worth, with the same negative impact on family life. More commonly, workers respond to underemployment with a deep sense of boredom with work and a heightened desire to escape from it. This is reflected in rising absenteeism rates, frequent job-switching, and pressure for early retirement options.[28] All of these suggest that underemployment tends to break up the linear life course, since the individual is decreasingly likely to organize his or her life strictly around work.

A number of recent studies have suggested that underemployment rooted in rising educational levels is epidemic in this society.[29] Ivar Berg's book, *Education and Jobs*, provides evidence that the use of a college or high school degree as a prerequisite for certain jobs has no basis in the relative capacities of people with different levels of schooling or in the actual requirements of the job.[30] Hence, in many settings where a high school degree is a minimum criterion, there is evidence that those without such a degree can do the job as effectively; college diplomas are often similarly unnecessary. This suggests that the skill level of many jobs could be upgraded without placing any serious strains on the capacities of present jobholders. Yet while such a broad upgrading would vastly expand the productivity of the economy, it is blocked by Taylorist work organization and the present patterns of stratification within the labor force. As Berg suggests, the cost of the *status quo* is a high level of job dissatisfaction among those who are overeducated relative to the demands of their jobs.

While the type of underemployment that Berg describes seems pervasive in white-collar settings, the other type of underemployment seems increasingly common in blue-collar settings. It is rooted in technological changes that shift the worker from a direct producer to someone who stands outside of the production process, performing such tasks as supervision, maintenance, and regulation.[31] This happens most clearly in the movement from assembly line production to continuous process; on the assembly line the worker handles the product directly, while in continuous process, machinery mediates the worker's relation to the product and tasks are generally intermittent. The same shift occurs less dramatically when, for example, certain parts of an assembly line process are automated. This shift is significant because, though assembly line work is oppressive, the worker is continually engaged by the production process. While the worker is engaged only physically, repeating over and over again certain mechanical motions, his or her mind can wander. In this context the worker can establish a physical rhythm that while tiring can be satisfying, since the worker's mind is left free for fantasy and daydreaming.[32]

In contrast, as production shifts to automation or continuous process technology the worker has less opportunity to establish this kind of rhythm. Typically, a worker will have to remain alert to make corrective adjustments in the productive process, but will not intervene in any normal rhythm. Hence, a worker might sit watching a dial with long periods between any physical activity. The consequence can be a level of boredom and frustration far greater than anything experienced on the assembly line.[33] Even in less extreme cases than the dial watcher workers are likely to experience a job that requires continuous alertness yet intermittent activity as deeply irritating and unsatisfying. Because they have been released from the drudgery of direct production, but their work continues to be organized on Taylorist lines, their capacities have not been redirected into any substantial set of new skills. The opportunity for expanded learning created by the release from direct production is not pursued, and the workers experience a debilitating sense of underemployment instead.

The third and final source of decay ironically is rooted in those work settings that have moved beyond Taylorist work organization. Particularly at the higher levels of the occupational structure—in managerial and professional settings—but increasingly at lower levels as well, managers are experimenting with a variety of post-Taylorist forms of organization.[34] These experiments are motivated by a desire to raise the productiveness of workers by taking advantage of new productive forces—the capacity of worker to learn—but concretely the process is complex. First, managers must motivate and mollify workers who are increasingly discontent with Taylorist forms of work organization, often because of their feelings of underemployment. Second, in white-collar settings, skills are becoming quickly obsolescent within a turbulent business environment. Management has to develop new organizational techniques for motivating employees to upgrade their skills continuously as well as new ways of training managers who will be able to learn to cope with new and different circumstances.[35] Finally, as the psychological component—the capacity to communicate with subordinates, superiors, colleagues, and clients without distortion—becomes more important in the effective functioning of organizations, managers have to develop techniques for increasing the psychological learning of their employees.[36]

These post-Taylorist experiments cover a vast range from the introduction of transactional analysis training sessions to the replacing of bureaucratic hierarchies with egalitarian work groups. Yet all such experiments create a fundamental tension, as management tries to expand the learning of workers without losing its control over the direction of the organization. Professionals in an organization might experience strong pressure to upgrade their job skills, for fear of losing their jobs or becoming more marginal within the organization. In response to this pressure, individuals might go out and take refresher courses, get new degrees, or explore new fields. As a person does this, however, he or she has no guarantee that the employer will be able to use his or her new expanded skills. If his or her new skills are unrewarded, the individual is likely to attempt a job or career switch in the hope of finding a setting where there will be rewards. But the consequence of this process is that the individual is forced to abandon the idea of a linear life course; he or she is forced to accept the idea of periods of retraining and a more fluid relation to the job structure.

Similarly, as these experiments stimulate psychological selfawareness, the individual's tolerance for stable work commitments diminishes. The idea of "burn-out" has emerged in social servce settings where workers are pushed to have some level of psychological awareness.[37] However, because they cannot change the work setting, increased psychological awareness leads workers to recognize the psychological costs of the work they are doing. And as the idea of burn-out suggests, workers develop a more flexible relation to the job structure since a person might have to quit for a while or find a less taxing job.

In sum, where capitalism appropriates new productive forces by developing non-Taylorist forms of work organization, people find it difficult to cling to the security of the linear life course and the associated family life patterns. They are pressured to accept a more fluid life course that in turn disrupts family life. Finally, people begin to question their basic commitments to a particular set of job and family arrangements as the experience of fluidity itself leads to greater self-awareness.

It is in the nature of our argument that both lack of work and work, both Taylorist and post-Taylorist forms of work organization, can contribute to the decay of the old social patterns. Arguing that things and their opposites can produce similar results is not an attempt to develop a nonfalsifiable theory. Rather, the new productive forces emerge dialectically. On the one side the breakdown of the distinction between work and nonwork as a negative moment of development creates unemployment, underemployment, and feelings of superfluity and worthlessness. On the other side, the breakdown of the distinction between work and nonwork as a positive moment of development, reflected in the integration of work and learning, creates new stresses and uncertainties as people reshape their lives and commitments in work environments that force them to develop but over which they have little control. The new productive forces change the relationship of people to work across much of the society. This changed relationship to work, in turn, has profound effects on the patterns of social life, since a particular type of relationship of individuals to work has been the lynchpin of industrial society.

The Positive Moment

As we argued earlier, the decay of old social patterns occurs in a developmental setting. This means, in short, that the forms of social reorganization are prefigured in some of the ways in which people respond to the process of decay. Again, we emphasize that an emancipatory social reorganization can occur only through some form of conscious, collective praxis. But the basis for collective reorganization must lie in the efforts of individuals and groups to respond to decay in developmental ways. Before examining some of these prefigurative responses, however, we must outline as best we can, some of the dimensions of social reorganization that would realize the potentialities of the new productive forces. Our effort is necessarily tentative because we face the twin dangers of projecting a future that is utopian, that stands outside of any human history, and of projecting as major tendencies patterns in the present that are merely epiphenomenal.

Our central concept is a fluid flexible life course built around work that provides continuous opportunities for learning. Elements of this form of work organization are already evident in managerial, technical, and scientific settings. Middle managers in advanced corporations must consistently expand their knowledge of corporate affairs if they are to prove productive. The companies in turn organize career ladders to maximize the chances that managers will learn. Learning and working become synonymous. Similarly, the work of scientists and researchers cannot be gauged by any simple measure of "time at work." A team of researchers facing theoretical obstacles may stop their work to give free rein to unconscious processes that might produce new avenues of attack. Work stoppage can become the precondition for future productive work. The distinction between work and nonwork breaks down. Finally, the extraordinary growth in adult education over the last decade suggest that periods of learning, nonwork, have become essential to the continuing productivity of many technical and professional workers throughout the public and private sector. Social agencies support large training efforts to increase the professional and interpersonal competence of their employees while many skilled machinists return to school to learn to manipulate and repair computer-controlled machine tools. There is, in other words, evidence that work and learning institutions are becoming increasingly intertwined as learning and the capacity to learn become increasing sources of productivity for production, management, and organizational development. In turn, work itself appears as a more fluid experience as people move between working and learning settings. To be sure, these trends are prefigured largely at the middle and top of the occupational hierarchy. But we suggest that in a society organized around the new productive forces this same mix of work and nonwork, of work and learning, will characterize the work of increasing numbers of people.

The integration of work and learning is both shaped by and shapes the fluid, flexible life course. As the phenomenology of learning shapes work, people become more attuned to their own developmental needs and rhythms. In the linear life course the path of individual development was fixed by social institutions. But as learning shapes work, people begin to experience the ways in which they can overcome their own past frames of reference and ways of being in the world. Learning itself is a developmental process. Consequently they can begin to separate their own developmental rhythms from those imposed by social schedules.

To be sure, this is not a stress-free, nor conflict-free process. While the margin of economic insecurity can be reduced (we are writing in a semi-utopian frame here), the level of psychological insecurity and stress can rise. As people discover their own rhythms of growth they might discover that their rhythms are inconsistent with those of the people that they work or live with. Husbands, wives, children, employees, and employers may have to more continuously reinvent the settings that hold them together.

We call the fluid life course the positive moment because ultimately it allows individuals to grow and change so that they do not narrow their lives to the confines of a restricted institutional life. They must live in and through institutions, to be sure, but with a knowledge of their own developmental needs, they can also learn to shape institutional life to fit their requirements.

We write this semi-utopian digression to show why we see certain current patterns as positive and prefigurative. The breakup of the linear life course is positive, insofar as individuals take responsibility for their own movement through life, independent of institutional schedules. Similarly the decline of the prototypical intact nuclear family in which the husband works and the wife stays at home with the children, reflected in a recent estimate that only 7 percent of all households fit that pattern,[38] is positive insofar as individuals construct new living arrangements that provide them with greater flexibility and greater opportunities for personal development. The rise in part-time work, career switching, and career ladders that involve people jumping from institution to institution also suggests that people are increasingly shaping their work commitments to their own needs. And even the reduction in the weight of measured labor time on people's lives can be seen as prefiguring the new relationship between work and learning that would characterize a society organized around the new productive forces.

Positive and Negative Together

In reality, the positive and negative moments are completely intertwined. The breakup of existing family patterns, for example, creates both dangers and possibilities. The danger is that as people find it increasingly difficult to stay together in families, the vast reaches of people's emotional lives find no structured outlet, no forum in the organization of social life. Instead, their needs find expression in the anomic settings of swinging sex, the cult of pornography, and various forms of addiction. As the linear life course decays, emotional energies are let loose on a vast plane of disordered mass impulses. But possibilities also emerge for a much richer range of nondestructive forms of expression. Sexual minorities that had been directly repressed by the tyranny of the linear life course have greater freedom, and men and women have the opportunity to rebuild family life on a more solid foundation than female subordination and male dominance.

The issue of dangers and possibilities is precisely mirrored in the ambiguities of contemporary sensibilities. On the one hand, social scientists of all political persuasions denounce the "new narcissism"[39] by which they mean that the individual pursuit of pleasure has reached obsessive and destructive proportions in contemporary society. They argue that since pleasure is defined in strictly individualistic terms, its obsessive pursuit has a corrosive effect on social bonds. The tendency to place paramount importance on one's own needs makes genuine commitment to others impossible and tends to undermine the family and other social groupings. These theorists go on to argue that social life and political life become progressively more difficult to organize when everyone is committed to doing his or her "own thing." Various commentators agree that this individualistic pursuit of pleasure is self-defeating, and they deplore the fact that individuals respond to the inherent frustrations by intensifying their pursuit. The consequence is new excesses in hedonism and an expanding clientele for a variety of gurus and therapies that only serve to confirm the individual in his or her self-centeredness.

On the other hand, the current period has also been dominated by a positive reception to the new sensibilities associated with the revival of feminism. Central to these sensibilities is the idea that women must not allow their own potentialities and their own emotional lives to be dictated and distorted by the demands of social institutions. Women must not sacrifice their ambition for meaningful work simply because of the demands of family life, nor should they be blocked from career mobility by institutional patterns of sex role segregation. But the impact of these values has now extended beyond women, creating a broader cultural imperative that the free expression of the individual should not be constrained by existing institutional patterns. This value is the basis on which sexual minorities struggle against the established sexual morality and on which many men resist the paralyzing constraints of the society's dominant image of maleness. But even more broadly, the demand for free personal development becomes the basis for a more general individual resistance to the imperatives of social institutions. This is reflected in such diverse examples as the blue-collar worker who justifies his absenteeism on the grounds that his work is not fulfilling, the disabled who are escalating their struggles for equal rights, and the corporate executive who quits a job rather than move his family for the fifth time in five years.

The strength of the value of personal development is reflected in the current popularity of the idea of the adult life cycle. Gail Sheehy's bestseller, *Passages*, indicates that interest in these ideas extends well beyond academic social science. The idea of the adult life cycle is significant because it implies that individuals must be able to distinguish their own needs from the demands of work and family life. Earlier, these demands were so taken for granted that they defined the central core of the adult life cycle. Now, however, the heightened concern with the individual's own emotional development makes the tension between personal development and the demands of work and family painfully obvious. Much of the substance of Sheehy's book consists of stories of people who allowed their own personal development to be put off track by their failure to resist the pressures of career or family. The consequence is a deep crisis that can be resolved only by returning to their personal developmental tasks, regardless of the consequences for their work and family commitments.

Quite obviously, the sensibilities associated with feminism and the adult life cycle concept are part of the phenomenon against which the theorists of the new narcissism have been polemicizing. Once again, positive and negative moments are tightly intertwined. The positive moment is that the expanded concern with personal development prefigures the full development of individual capacities that can be achieved in a society organized around the new productive forces. The negative moment is that these new sensibilities pull people away from developing social ties by reducing people's capacities to become intimate with and make genuine commitments to others. But few people can stand alone, and the narcissistic pursuit can paradoxically lead to collective behaviors of social regression. While the negative moment is bound to appear dominant in a period such as the present, in which constructive responses to social crises are weak, it is important not to lose sight of the positive moment.

Economic Crises and New Productive Forces

The same methodology of analyzing decay in a developmental setting and locating negative and positive moments can be used to understand the economic crisis of the American economy. But our argument is not simply an "economic" one; social relations and social reorganization are central to our analysis of economic crisis. While we incorporate into our framework a number of arguments that have become a familiar part of Marxist poltitical economy, we focus on social life to provide a broader understanding of the "economic" contradictions of advanced capitalism.

There has been considerable convergence in Marxist circles in recent years around an analysis of the economic difficulties of the American economy in the seventies. This analysis centers on the contradictions and limitations of the Keynesian responses to the Great Depression of the thirties. In brief, the core of this analysis is that Keynesian measures such as dramatic increases in military spending, federal underwriting of suburban growth through subsidized mortgages and the highway program, the development of a variety of transfer payments that served to maintain demand, and the rapid growth of credit, all helped to solve the problem of demand in the aftermath of World War II, and created a period of sustained economic growth from the late forties to the late sixties. By the late sixties, however, the very measures that had served to stimulate economic growth became obstacles to further economic expansion.[40]

One important example of this pattern has been the growth of state spending. While this growth had been a key factor in stimulating expansion, state spending grew faster than the economy as a whole by the late sixties, and became an obstacle to economic expansion. This growth of state spending created strong inflationary pressures in the economy, resulting in higher interest rates and greater economic uncertainty. Uncertainty and high interest rates discouraged new business investment, leading to a slackening of demand. Similarly, the rapid growth of credit in the post–World War II era fueled economic expansion, but again, by the late sixties, the rising debt/equity ratios of corporations became a drag on further expansion. Firms with high levels of debt were extremely vulnerable to economic downturns. They became increasingly cautious about accumulating new debt, and hence reluctant to embark on new investment projects.[41] In these and other ways, the older Keynesian measures contributed to stagflation—the simultaneous existence of strong inflationary pressures and economic stagnation. By discouraging vigorous new investment, the Keynesian measures blocked the type of dynamic economic expansion that would be necessary to ease the inflationary pressures in the economy.

We believe that these contradictions of Keynesian policies were there from the start, since Keynesianism has an ambiguous relationship to the development of new productive forces. On the one hand, Keynesian policies developed new mechanisms for distributing claims on the total economic product so that the capacity to consume would not be restricted by market-determined wage levels. On the other hand, Keynesianism developed forms of waste designed to slow the appropriation of new productive forces. Since in the United States the first dimension of Keynesianism minimized planning and relied heavily on market forces, much of the positive developmental component of Keynesianism was lost.[42] The market-oriented Keynesian measures for expanding demand became exhausted at the same time that the costs of the wasteful element of Keynesianism (particularly military spending) began to weigh more heavily on the economy.[43] The investment component of demand consequently faltered while inflationary pressures accelerated.

Capitalists respond to stagflation by trying to reduce the share of state spending that goes to social programs and to reduce real wage levels. They reason that this would boost profits, and that higher profits would stimulate expanded investment, creating the conditions for a new period of dynamic growth. But the nature of the structural impasses makes capital's program contradictory.[44] Even though capitalists have had some success in rolling back the gains won by the poor and the working class in the sixties and in reducing real wages, these measures do not have their intended effect. Slowing the growth of state employment and reducing the population's purchasing power only reinforces the weakness of demand in the economy, and further discourages new investment. Hence, Marxists, as well as some bourgeois economists, increasingly realize that escaping from stagflation requires more than raising profit levels. The growing interest in Kondratieff's theory of the long wave (40–50 years) reflects an awareness that, at the very least, more basic institutional changes are a precondition for a new period of dynamic capitalist expansion. While little has been done to clarify the nature of these necessary institutional changes, there is every reason to believe that new practices and policies would differ from existing ones in the same degree that Keynesian measures differed from the political economic arrangements of the pre–1929 period.

However, we do not want to describe the types of institutional changes necessary for a new wave of capitalist expansion here.[45] Rather, we want to deepen the above analysis of economic crisis by examining some of the ways in which the social decay resulting from the partial emergence of the new productive forces undermines present economic arrangements. We will focus on three particular impediments to the accumulation process—obstacles to productivity increase, the rising cost of reproducing the labor force, and the problems of generating new domestic markets. In each of these factors, the economic dimension cannot be separated from the social dimension. We intend this since we argue that the economic crisis is a social crisis and cannot be solved through economic rearrangement alone.

Productivity

We argued earlier that productivity gains can best be achieved in advanced capitalism by appropriating the new productive forces. However, because the new productive forces are based on new patterns of labor organization, capitalists face risk and uncertainty in developing them. Many managers in both the private and public sectors have demonstrated a clear preference for exploiting the older productive forces even more intensely, rather than taking risks associated with new ones. The "runaway shop" phenomenon can be understood in this context. Rather than taking risks to develop a more technologically advanced production process in the United States, firms take existing technology to a low-wage country where there are few obstacles to exploiting industrial productive forces.[46] Similar patterns exist within the American economy, as managers attempt to take advantage of various marginal labor pools—blacks, Chicanos, Puerto Ricans, rural Southerners, "illegal" immigrants, women—by exploiting people who are grateful for any type of employment.

There are, however, limits to this process. Not all production processes can be conveniently moved to low-wage countries, and if the deindustrialization of the American economy proceeds too rapidly, it will generate dangerous instabilities. Furthermore, workers from marginal groups tend to gain greater self-confidence over time, and they are more likely to resist intensified exploitation. All this means that in order to achieve substantial results, the intensified exploitation of older productive forces has to be generalized across much of the economy. There has been evidence of this in recent years in many sectors, as reduced work forces are expected to match or exceed the productivity of earlier, larger work forces.[47] But as the relationship between work and the life course decays, such attempts to increase productivity quickly meet their limits.

As we discussed earlier, the partial emergence of new productive forces has led to a widespread flight from work, as individuals feel that less and less of their personal identity is bound up in the work process. This has resulted in increases in absenteeism, job switching, and the subjective sense of dissatisfaction with work. In this context, attempts to increase productivity through forms of speed-up can be counterproductive. People respond to the increased exploitation by intensifying their psychic flight from work, reducing even further their commitment to the job. While this only occasionally leads to self-conscious collective struggles against management, even individualistic forms of response interfere with management's objectives. For example, there is evidence of a substantial rise in the work force's awareness of medical problems, reflected in dramatic increases in disability payments[48] and medically sanctioned absences. While this rise has a variety of roots, it seems logical to explain a part of it as a consequence of the intersection of declining commitment to work with attempted speed-up. The result is that time lost for medical reasons, and the rising costs of medical insurance coverage for the work force, cut sharply into any actual productivity gains that management ekes out.

In short, while managers in both private and public sectors respond to profit squeezes and fiscal crises by intensifying the exploitation of labor time, the economy's overall problems of profitability and productivity remain unsolved. On the contrary, such efforts further undermine the labor force's commitment to work, while creating additional costs such as higher medical expenses and expenditures for supervision and security against employee sabotage and pilferage. Efforts to intensify the exploitation of older productive forces lead, in sum, to a further decay of the social relations that developed with them.

Reproduction Costs[49]

Reproduction costs are the expenses of maintaining and reproducing the labor force and various surplus populations. This includes much of the society's expenditures for health care, for education, and transfer payments to the unemployed, the disabled, the welfare population, and the aged. Part of the rise of reproduction costs is due directly to the process of social decay. As work life and family life become disorganized, the population's physical and mental health deteriorates. Expenditures for medical and therapeutic services consequently rise. When efforts are made to reverse this trend through simple austerity measures, these rising costs are transferred to other institutions such as the criminal justice system.

But there is an even more important process that drives reproduction costs up. The appropriation of new productive forces has expanded the size of the surplus population. Keynesian measures are thus required to put purchasing power in the hands of the unemployed, the disabled, the retired, and the welfare population through government transfer programs. But the emergence of new productive forces has also served to blur the boundary line between work and nonwork, reducing the legitimacy of substantial income penalties on those who are not working. Hence, members of the various surplus populations are able to press for higher levels of economic support, so that they will not have to live in abysmal poverty. Welfare mothers organize for welfare rights and the older people mobilize for substantial increases in Social Security benefits. While these groups do not get everything they want, they have succeeded in gaining support for the idea that they have a right to a decent standard of living with benefits that roughly keep pace with inflation. This has resulted in rapid increases in various transfer expenditures. The growth of these expenditures has been a major component of the fiscal crisis of the state, limiting the state's capacity to use an expanding share of its revenues for direct subsidies for private sector investment.

However, reversing this trend, once it has been set in motion, presents contradictions for capitalism. First, for example, attempts to make a serious reduction in Social Security benefits would place more of the burden of financial support of the aged on their children. This increased economic burden on individuals in the 35–50-year-old age range would cut into discretionary expenditures that are a critical component of consumer demand. Second, victimizing the aged through direct efforts to reduce their living standard would seriously demoralize all employees over fifty who are relying on Social Security for their retirement income. This demoralization could decrease productivity and increase resistance to pressures for retirement, exacerbating in turn the problem of youthful unemployment.

Finally, decent levels of economic support for the unemployed, the disabled, and the retired provide a valuable safety valve for discontent resulting from structural unemployment. If the victims of a plant closing, for example, suffered an even more dramatic decline in income in addition to the dislocation of lost employment, pressure would mount for state intervention to prevent such plant closings. For capitalist firms, serious state intervention in their decision to disinvest (or even more so in their decision to displace large numbers of workers through a new process) is far less desirable than buying off displaced workers with relatively generous benefits. In sum, rising reproduction costs, particularly for the various surplus populations, is integrally related to the process through which individuals are increasingly displaced from stable jobs.

The Disorganization of Markets

But even assuming that a program of austerity could succeed in raising profits through productivity gains, reductions in real wages, and falling reproduction costs, the central question is whether substantial new waves of investment would be forthcoming, especially since the reduction in wages would place a damper on demand. Such a new wave of investment requires that new markets based on new patterns of consumption emerge. Yet the decay of social life itself is a major impediment to the emergence of those new markets.

The partial emergence of the new productive forces breaks down the modal life course, and this means that the household structure of urban areas becomes more variable and more unstable. Consequently, markets for the development and sale of new consumer products become harder to delineate and maintain. While particular goods can be marketed purely on the basis of limited advertising campaigns and the manipulation of images, a general self-sustaining pattern of consumption can emerge only on the basis of a well-defined pattern of social life. The post–World War II consumption boom, for example, was fueled by a variety of forces, but it was sustained because the resultant package of consumer goods— the automobile, the single-family house, appliances—fit with a broader reorganization of social life based on suburbanization and the spread of the nuclear family to the ethnic working class. A sustained pattern of consumption that has its own momentum, creating its own new needs independent of advertising, requires an underlying unity and coherence to social life.

Not only does social life currently lack the potential for that coherence and unity, but it has also become more difficult for the state to develop the appropriate social infrastructure to encourage a new package of consumption.[50] On the one hand, state planners lack the rationale and direction drawn from a specific conception of social life that they had to guide them in the period after World War II. On the other hand, the development of state policy to encourage new investment in such areas as communication, transportation, energy, and leisure activities encounters such a morass of conflicting corporate and public interests that it becomes impossible to discern what types of infrastructural investment would actually be productive. Hence, as social life unravels, the general marketing climate becomes more uncertain and contingent, as it becomes more difficult to predict the likely consequences of investment either in infrastructure or in a particular product line. Regardless of the rate of profit, the chances for the emergence of self-sustaining new markets seem slight.[51]

Decay and Development

Thus far we have focused on the elements of decay in the economic crisis. This is essential for two reasons. First, it is important to show that the economic crisis is part of a larger social crisis, and cannot be solved through simple economic alterations. Second, it is critical to recognize that an economic crisis rooted in capitalism's difficulties in appropriating the new productive forces intensifies older forms of exploitation—industrial speed-up, a squeeze on real wages, cutbacks in social services, and attacks on the standard of living of the surplus populations. Yet we have also tried to show that there are real constraints that make it irrational for capitalism to try to solve its problems with extreme austerity policies.

Finally, austerity policies are limited in their rationality because, despite the economic crisis, the new productive forces continue to emerge. The new productive forces are not appropriated fast enough to tap all the latent potentials in the economy and society, nor do they emerge quickly enough to solve the overall productivity problem. But firms, particularly in the leading sectors, are actively developing new technologies and experimenting with new ways of organizing work that expands the learning component of jobs. At the same time, various government and private sector agencies are developing new services or modifying old services in ways that provide support for the appropriation of new productive forces. Universities, for example, might be developing new programs to increase the number of people they supply to business that understand the management of systems in which people are encouraged to learn.

If policies of austerity are carried out across the board, then these forms of development would be seriously slowed. The supportive services necessary for the appropriation of new productive forces could not emerge in the context of generalized austerity. Similarly, generalized austerity with the resulting decline in the physical and mental health of the population would undermine the capacity of organizations to expand the learning component of jobs.

This helps to explain the peculiar unevenness of the current economic situation. Some social services are cut back because of fiscal crisis, at the same time that new services are emerging and expanding. Similarly, some economic regions appear to be booming, while others are in obvious decline.[52] Development is occurring in the context of generalized decay, and while limited austerity is a product of decay, a generalized pattern of austerity would serve only to block the development that is occurring. The crucial point remains—a pattern of economic growth that is rapid enough to eliminate the need for austerity requires the accelerated appropriation of new productive forces. Such an accelerated appropriation of new productive forces appears to us unlikely unless social life is reorganized along the lines that we earlier described—the institutionalization, with social supports, of the flexible life course, and the widespread utilization of non-Taylorist forms of work organization. Social reorganization along these lines would both unlock substantial productivity gains and provide a firm basis for new patterns of consumption rooted in genuine needs.[53]

Conclusion

The analysis that we have put forward is necessarily incomplete without developing its implications for political practice. However, considerations of space prevent us from elaborating on this aspect of our argument here. It is also the case that our ideas on politics are less coherent and developed than the theoretical perspective that we have outlined. This seems inevitable, since political thinking must be a collective project; political programs written by isolated individuals always sound hollow and abstract.

Yet there are a few broad political implications of our analysis that are important to state here. The first is that any emancipatory politics in the present must begin with the realities of contemporary society, rather than from Marxist categories that have been rendered obsolete by the passing of accumulationist capitalism. While this point might seem obvious, it bears restating since so much current Marxist writing fails to grasp this idea. Second, while some might read our argument as an optimistic alternative to those theorists (Piccone, Lasch, Jacoby) who despair of the existence of emancipatory possibilities in the present, that is not our intention. For us, optimism and pessimism are not the important categories. In fact, our analysis incorporates the most pessimistic possible scenarios, since continued social stalemate in the face of postindustrial transition can unleash awesomely powerful pressures for individual and social regression. The point is rather that we have sought to develop an analysis that is genuinely dialectical—recognizing in this historical moment the interlocking processes of decay and development.

7

The Myth of Reindustrialization

One of the most important legacies of the 1980 election has been the rightward shift in the society's social and political discourse. Even though the right has been largely frustrated in many of its central objectives, it has succeeded in shifting the entire terrain of political discussion. This is most evident in the restrained rhetoric of the major Democratic Party presidential hopefuls, but the Socialist left itself has not been immune to this rightward drift. In subtle ways the left has accommodated itself to certain assumptions fundamental to mainstream discourse. The danger in this accommodation is that where those assumptions prove to be false, the left is unable to propose real political alternatives. This process is particularly clear in the case of the left's attempts to use the idea of "reindustrialization."

The idea of "reindustrialization" emerged in the late seventies as a political code word designed to reconcile two conflicting pressures within the American political economy. The first pressure is created by increased international competition both in traditional industrial goods and in high-technology products. Increased competition makes it imperative that the nation's industrial plant be modernized, and such modernization will entail the elimination of manufacturing jobs in older industrial sectors. The second pressure is to respond to the needs of industrial workers displaced by imports and modernization, as well as the millions of others in the economy who are unemployed or underemployed. Since the term reindustrialization evokes simultaneously the

This essay is reprinted from *Socialist Review* 73 (Jan.–Feb., 1984): 59–74. Reprinted by permission of the *Socialist Review*.

revitalization of older industries, the more rapid growth of new industries, and a general expansion of industrial employment, the term obscures the tension between industrial modernization and the displacement of labor. Reindustrialization appears to offer something for everyone, so it is hardly surprising that the slogan was ultimately used by both Jimmy Carter and Ronald Reagan.

A number of analysts on the left have sought to capitalize on the broad appeal of reindustrialization by devising plans for "rational reindustrialization"—the development of strong, internationally competitive new industries that would provide jobs for those displaced from declining industries.[1] But despite the ingenuity of their specific proposals, left advocates of reindustrialization serve to reinforce the implicit promise of the slogan—that some kind of policy mix will produce a sharp upturn in the number of manufacturing jobs, thus dramatically alleviating high unemployment. While this promise is rarely stated explicitly, it doesn't have to be. The very term invokes the image of a return to the glory days of industrialism when factory gates allegedly welcomed all of those who were willing to work.

And even when the term is not used, the idea of significant employment growth in manufacturing undergirds most contemporary economic policy-making. Even before its recent shift toward more conservative economic policies, the administration of François Mitterrand shared with that of Ronald Reagan a belief in the need to commit more resources to investment in manufacturing in order to produce faster economic growth and more jobs. While Reagan sought to do this by shifting wealth to the rich, who would them presumably have more resources and incentives for investment, Mitterrand sought to achieve the same goal by nationalizing key firms, particularly in high-technology industries. In both cases, it was assumed that such increased investment in manufacturing would lead to a virtuous cycle of more employment, more demand, and even higher investment.

Leftists in the United States have not always shared this faith in employment growth in manufacturing. In fact, some twenty years ago a group of left intellectuals that included Michael Harrington, Irving Howe, and Tom Hayden signed a document entitled the "Triple Revolution."[2] The document's thesis was that American society was being transformed by three fundamental processes—the rise of the civil rights movement, the development of more advanced weapons systems, and the automation of industry. Automation, it was argued, meant that manufacturing employment would steadily decline as agricultural employment had during the nineteenth century. The Triple Revolution proclaimed that the epoch of industrialism had come to an end and that without fundamental political and economic changes, American society would suffer from chronically high unemployment and economic stagnation.

In the short term, the predictions of the Ad Hoc Committee on the Triple Revolution were clearly wrong. In the second half of the sixties, manufacturing employment in the United States rose dramatically, and those who had dismissed the automation scare as seriously mistaken were completely vindicated. But the predictions may have been simply premature. The large and clumsy computers of the 1960s suggested the promise of industrial automation, but it required a series of technological advances that miniaturized and cheapened computers to make widespread industrial automation a practical possibility.

If the Triple Revolution theorists were actually premature in their predictions, then manufacturing employment might well fall regardless of the level of new investment in manufacturing, revealing that the core assumptions behind the economic policies of both Reagan and Mitterrand are mistaken. Moreover, it would also be apparent that discussion of reindustrialization misses the point that only more fundamental changes in the American political economy would reduce the level of unemployment and create the conditions for economic growth and equity.

This is precisely the argument I want to make. An examination of actual trends in manufacturing employment in the United States, France, and West Germany—up to the onset of the 1980–1983 recession—indicates that there is little prospect for manufacturing employment to expand in the foreseeable future. On the contrary, the evidence strongly suggests that we will see sharp declines in the amount of manufacturing employment, not just as a percentage of the labor force, but in absolute terms. While various policy initiatives might influence the rate of decline, they are unlikely to eliminate the fact of decline. Such predictions are contested today, just as they were twenty years ago, particularly by mainstream economists who insist that new industries will emerge to create jobs to balance those that are lost in declining industries. While there is no sure way to settle such competing predictions about the future, it is possible to examine in detail what has happened in the recent past. Certainly, if new technologies are going to dramatically transform the economy's need for labor, there should already be indications of those changes in recent trends. Conversely, if the rise of microelectronics is going to create vast quantities of employment in new sectors, there should be some evidence of that as well.

Jobless Growth in Manufacturing

One difficulty with most discussions of employment trends is that they focus on the number of *jobs*. This is a problem because of the growing importance of part-time work and because the content of a job in hours of work can change dramatically with shorter work weeks and increased paid vacations. If we are interested primarily in the economy's total requirement for manufacturing labor, then we need to look at the total number of hours of work provided. The question of how these hours are distributed among a greater or lesser number of workers is secondary. Fortunately, such data are available because government statistical offices make a serious effort to track changes in aggregate hours of manufacturing employment for their relevance to the measurement of productivity.

Tables 7–1 and 7–2 present a summary of recent trends in aggregate manufacturing hours for the United States, France, and West Germany. These figures all represent estimates of the total hours actually worked in manufacturing, so that time spent on paid leave for vacation, medical, and other purposes is not included. Both the American and the European data are derived from periodic surveys of establishments.

As one would expect, these figures are strongly influenced by the business cycle. In the United States, the total production worker-hours in a year at the peak of the business cycle such as 1973 are more than 14 percent higher than in a recession year such as 1975. Similarly, some of the European decline between 1972 and 1975 can be attributed to the post–oil-shock recession. But what is striking for the United States is the relative stability between business cycle peaks. Total manufacturing hours grew by only 1.5 percent between the 1969 and 1979 peaks. Yet total manufacturing output grew by close to 40 percent in the same period.

In this context, it is important to recognize how marginal the impact of military spending has become. Department of Defense estimates are that at 1982 levels of spending, defense procurement accounted for 2.2 million industrial jobs, or roughly 4.4 billion worker-hours. They estimate that the extraordinary military buildup over the next five years— from $190.5 billion to $346.6 billion—will bring this to 3.4 million industrial jobs, or a gain of only 2.4 billion worker-hours.[3] When these figures are seen against the overall size of manufacturing employment, it becomes clear that defense spending's impact on overall employment has become increasingly marginal. As has frequently been noted, the explanation for this is the increasing weight in military procurement of

Table 7-1. Aggregate Hours of Manufacturing Work United States (billions of hours)

Year	I Total Manufacturing	II Production Workers
1960	32.56	23.91
1961	31.71	22.99
1962	33.14	24.22
1963	33.44	24.38
1964	34.15	24.92
1965	35.98	26.39
1966	38.47	28.32
1967	38.37	27.77
1968	38.85	28.07
1969	39.47	28.49
1970	36.94	26.33
1971	35.42	25.34
1972	36.90	26.63
1973	38.98	28.30
1974	38.18	27.40
1975	34.50	24.12
1976	36.14	25.55
1977	37.57	26.55
1978	39.25	27.75
1979	40.08	28.28

Sources: The figures in column 1 are from United States Department of Commerce, *U.S. National Income and Product Accounts.* Column 11 has been calculated by determining the Commerce Department's adjustment for paid leave and then applying that adjustment to Bureau of Labor Statistics figures on total manufacturing production hours, calculated from U.S. Department of Labor, *Employment and Earnings.*

Table 7-2. Aggregate Hours of Manufacturing Work France and West Germany (billions of hours)

Year	FRANCE		WEST GERMANY	
	Total Manufacturing	Manual	Total Manufacturing	Manual
1972	9.29	6.51	14.25	10.22
1975	9.01	6.09	12.03	8.24
1978	8.27	5.47	12.70	8.63

Source: Statistical Office of the European Community, *Labour Costs in Industry.* Note that the survey from which these data are derived excludes firms with fewer than ten employees.

high-technology goods that are built with advanced capital goods and relatively small amounts of human labor.

For Western Europe, the trend in manufacturing worker-hours is sharply downward. While the patterns are slightly different between France and Germany, it is clear that the decline between 1972 and 1975 was not just a cyclical phenomenon. The year 1978 was one of expansion and recovery, but in France total hours were even lower than in 1975 and in Germany, only slightly higher. Between 1972 and 1978, the index of industrial production increased from 99 to 113 in France and from 100.7 to 112.9 in Germany (1975 = 100), so this decline cannot be attributed simply to the absence of economic growth.

These data give some surface credibility to the claim that we have entered a period where expanding manufacturing output can be produced with a constant or declining labor input. But there are a number of counterclaims that need to be examined. The first is the argument that the manufacturing employment has moved overseas either to Japan or to the underdeveloped world. If Japanese exports are taking over markets in the United States and Europe and if American and European multinationals have moved large quantities of low-wage work to the Third World, then one would expect a decline in demand for manufacturing labor in the United States, France, and Germany. Yet data that Japan provides to the International Labor Organization (ILO) indicate that Japanese manufacturing has also been experiencing a decline in worker-hours. The index of total manufacturing worker-hours declined from 100 in 1970 to 83.0 in 1979.[4] Moreover, the promise of "lifetime employment" for some workers has led to disguised unemployment in Japan's manufacturing where employees are kept on doing trivial tasks such as polishing cars.[5] In short, Japan has also been producing more with less manufacturing labor.

In the Third World, manufacturing employment has been rising at a 4.7 percent rate from 1967 to 1978, although most of the gains have been concentrated in a handful of countries such as South Korea, Taiwan, Brazil, and Singapore.[6] But since the total amount of manufacturing employment was still so low in 1967, this growth is small relative to the numbers employed in the developed countries. For example, a Commerce Department survey of all United States manufacturing subsidiaries and affiliates in the Third World in 1977 reported a total of 1.4 million employees, of whom many had been on the books for years.[7] Even if we assume that these employees averaged sixty hours a week, fifty weeks a year, the total comes to 4.2 billion worker-hours, hardly enough to account for the failure of manufacturing worker-hours to rise in the developed nations. Moreover, there is strong evidence that one of the major areas of growth in Third-World manufacturing jobs during the seventies—assembly of parts for the electronics and computer industries—has already begun to decline as firms substitute automated equipment for female detail laborers.[8] Finally, it must be stressed that the factories established in the Third World are also highly capital-intensive by any historical standard. A contemporary textile factory in Brazil makes it possible for an individual worker in a day's work to produce a thousand, perhaps ten thousand, times the amount of cloth produced by an individual worker in a textile plant in industrializing New England a century earlier.[9] The capital intensity reduces the amount of labor employed as the industrialization process goes forward.

A second counterclaim is that the failure of manufacturing worker-hours to grow during the seventies is simply a result of worldwide economic problems in that decade. Had economic growth been faster—that is, closer to the levels of the fifties and sixties—then increases in manufacturing hours would have taken place. Yet the data show that the *nongrowth* of manufacturing worker-hours has been the dominant trend for some time with only a handful of exceptions for periods of war and postwar reconstruction. Figure 7-1 shows that for the United States, production worker-hours actually declined during the twenties despite the rapid growth in output. Similarly, between 1948 and 1964 production worker-hours failed to increase despite rapid growth in demand and output. The only significant exceptions to this pattern in the United States were the buildups associated with the Second World War (1941–1945) and the Vietnam War (1965–1969). Comparable data are not available for France and Germany, but estimates can be constructed from the available data. In the period of rapid economic expansion from 1958 to 1972, manufacturing employment in Germany grew by 9.7 percent, but

Figure 7-1. Worker-Hours in Manufacturing, United States 1967 = 100

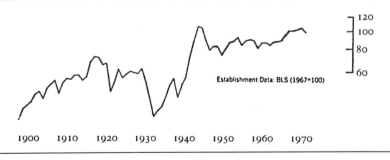

Source: United States Department of Commerce, *Long-Term Economic Growth, 1860–1970,* p. 25.

the average annual hours per employee fell by 17 percent, producing a net drop in total manufacturing hours. In France during the same period, manufacturing employment grew by 13.8 percent, while average hours declined by 8 percent. This produced a small increase in aggregate hours—a gain of 0.5 billion hours over a fourteen-year period.[10]

If neither the job flight nor slow growth can explain away the lack of growth in manufacturing worker-hours in the seventies, an explanation for the pattern is still necessary. Since there have been periods of economic development where the number of worker-hours in manufacturing within particular countries rose substantially, there must be an explanation for why this has happened in the United States only in periods of wartime.

The Technological Factor

Two basic factors shape the path of manufacturing employment—demand and the productivity of labor. Employers are constantly seeking ways to cut costs and increase productivity, so that manufacturing employment in a particular industry will tend to remain constant or decline unless demand is growing faster than productivity. In theory, in a world where most people have enormous unmet needs, aggregate demand for manufactured goods could grow at a rapid rate—faster than 10 percent a year—for many years before there was any threat of satiation. But income is distributed unevenly across countries and within countries, so that those most in need are unable to contribute significantly to overall demand. The reality is that even in periods of dynamic international economic growth, aggregate demand for American or Western European manufactured goods is unlikely to grow more than 3 or 4 percent a year. However, certain growth industries will experience even more rapid expansion in demand. But these growth industries have tended to be those that are capital-intensive and most able to achieve very high levels of productivity growth. For example, a particular industry might be able to meet a 12 percent annual growth in demand with very small increases in employment because productivity is rising at 9 percent a year. While some sectors grow significantly faster than total manufacturing demand, other sectors grow more slowly or experience an actual decline in demand. These will tend to be sectors in which it takes more workers to produce a unit of output than in the growth industries, in which each reduction in output will displace proportionally more workers. In short, dynamic growth sectors of the economy tend to add new workers more slowly than they are displaced from declining sectors.

Before the twenties, the differentials in productivity across sectors were not that important, but the new industries of the period—chemicals, auto, and electrical goods—relied more heavily on technological advances. This meant that it was possible for these industries to grow rapidly while adding fewer new employee hours than were being displaced from the older, less productive industries. This is what made possible the rapid growth in output with an actual decline in manufacturing production worker-hours. A similar pattern can be seen today.

The leading growth sector of today's world economy—the electronics industry—has grown explosively with only minor increases in manufacturing employment. This has happened because the application of its own new technologies has made possible another dramatic upward shift in labor productivity. As with the new industries of the twenties, there is again a significant gap between the amount of labor required to produce a dollar amount of value in the electronics industry and traditional industries. Some of these productivity gains come from the automating of production processes. One recent innovation—the development of automated bonding equipment—allows one worker to replace thirty, dramatically reducing the industry's need for cheap, foreign labor.[11] Furthermore, the traditional argument that new jobs will be created in the industries that produce such machines is belied by the development of highly automated, robotized factories for the production of industrial robots. At the same time, the incorporation of microelectronics into products simplifies them and reduces the labor time necessary for production. An electronic cash register requires only a quarter of the labor time needed to produce an electromechanical one because of the reduction in moving parts.

Over time, both types of innovation will have a growing impact on employment needs throughout the economy.

But the changes are already well under way in the electronics industry. An OECD survey of major electronic firms in the United States, Europe, and Japan found a general pattern of declining employment during the course of the seventies.[12] Increased demand was met by higher productivity and a decreasing global labor force. In Germany between 1970 and 1979, production of office and data processing machines grew by 74.5 percent. During the same period, hourly productivity rose by a staggering 117.9 percent and hours of employment dropped by 19.9 percent.[13] In the United States manufacture of electronic components, office machines, and computers by all firms grew by only 266,900 jobs between 1970 and 1979, of which roughly half were production jobs.[14] In contrast, in 1980 alone, 300,000 were laid off in the automobile industry, with many of those jobs expected to be permanently lost.[15] The decade-long expansion of the electronics industry might barely be able to offset the decline in only one of the older industries.

This suggests two further points. First, the United States is unlikely to regain the manufacturing worker-hour peak of 1979 (Table 7–1) even when the current slump ends. Between 1975 and 1979, worker-hours in some of the older industries such as auto were still rising; this was a kind of Indian summer period when the downward adjustment in these industries was temporarily postponed. Hence, when the adjustments came during 1980, they were particularly sharp, and there is every reason to believe that much of that adjustment will be permanent. Second, the weight of the declining industries remains far greater than that of the dynamic ones. A rough calculation indicates that the five manufacturing subsectors that are generally acknowledged to be in decline—primary metal, fabricated metal parts, motor vehicles and equipment, textiles, and apparel—still accounted for 29 percent of all United States manufacturing employment in 1979. In contrast, even a generous estimate of the dynamic, growing sectors would not put their contribution at more than 10 percent of total manufacturing employment—electronics accounted for only 4.4 percent of all manufacturing employment in 1979. This suggests that even with the end of recession, in the eighties the United States may well follow the West European pattern of sharp declines in total manufacturing worker-hours.

Problems with Economic Orthodoxy

As long as employers continue to have strong incentives to produce goods more cheaply, it seems highly unlikely that any program of rein-dustrialization will increase manufacturing worker-hours. The choice of particular policies—protection of older industries vs support for high-technology firms—is likely to influence only the rate at which manufacturing employment declines. Hence, it would be best to dispense altogether with the term "reindustrialization." An active industrial policy designed to remove obstacles to productivity growth and to encourage the use of new technologies would only accelerate the trend to produce more with less human labor. It would not reindustrialize, but would rather continue the process of deindustrialization of the labor force.

But these employment trends call into question not just reindustrialization but the broader economic growth model that informs current economic policies. This orthodox model holds that the route to faster economic growth is to increase investment and worker discipline. The combination of higher investment and greater worker effort will be expanded output and increased employment. The increased employment will, in turn, expand demand and encourage even greater investment. Since the onset of slower growth in the early seventies, this model dictates the imposition of austerity policies because only by holding the line on wages, welfare, and social-service spending can the rate of profit be increased and resources be freed for higher levels of investment. With a higher profit rate as an incentive, the likelihood is increased that the newly freed resources will be invested productively. Moreover, austerity, temporarily including higher unemployment, also has the positive effect of reinforcing work discipline, thus accelerating productivity gains.

If, however, there is not necessarily a positive relationship between expanded manufacturing output and employment, then it is not clear how growth can be self-sustaining. Even when economic recovery is under way, few additional employees will be added to the manufacturing employment rolls, and total demand will continue to stagnate. In such a context, corporations and the rich have little incentive to invest in expanding industrial capacity.

But this is only one of four problematic assumptions in the orthodox growth model. A second problem is that it is no longer clear that faster growth requires an increase in aggregate investment. Many of the new technologies based on microelectronics are capital-saving as well as labor-saving. A new high-technology machine tool, for example, might be twice as efficient as the machine tool it replaces without being more expensive. Hence, a constant or even declining quantity of investment dollars could assure continued increases in manufacturing output, even while the labor input declines. This implies that there is no need to sacrifice consumption in the name of investment. Third, worker insecurity, rather than contributing to productivity growth by reinforcing labor discipline, might, in fact, undermine productivity gains. Workers who live in fear of technological displacement are likely to resist technological innovations and slow the pace of their effective utilization. Moreover, there is increasing evidence that even in many blue-collar settings, increased worker learning is the key to productivity gains.[16] But insecure workers are unlikely to be good learners; they are more likely to cling ritualistically to the traditional ways of doing the job.

Finally, the orthodox model fails to address the central question of the fit between expanded output and social need. In certain sectors, such as the automobile industry, there is already more productive capacity than is needed because of shifting patterns of demand. In other sectors, such as electrical power and petroleum, it is far from clear that we will be better off with more production as opposed to more efficient use of existing supplies. In still other sectors, standardized products have given way to a multitude of diverse products for different market segments, so that the problem of coordinating supply with demand is a more vexing problem for the firm than simply expanding production.[17] In each of these cases, the market mechanisms are either too slow, too clumsy, or too ineffective to assure a fit between output and social need. Genuine economic growth—as opposed to a paper increase in GNP—requires more than investment; it requires improved institutions of social decisionmaking to assure that additional output is both needed and socially useful.

At each point, the orthodox growth model naïvely insists that more of the same—more investment, more growth, more worker discipline—will suffice to solve economic problems. But while it is somewhat plausible that economic growth was accelerated one hundred years ago by getting workers to apply themselves more energetically, such a claim is unconvincing today. Increased worker productivity does not depend so much on increased physical effort but on the social and technological environment in which the worker operates. Hence, the core issue becomes institutional rather than quantitative—how does one create new organizational contexts in which human beings can be more productive?

Toward an Alternative Growth Model

When it is recognized that the problems are institutional, it becomes apparent that we need an alternative growth model to conceptualize the positive linkages that are potential in the current situation. The actual implementation of such an alternative growth model remains a formidable political task involving dramatic shifts in popular political discourse and the creation of new political coalitions. But even the tentative outlining of such an alternative model can be useful in clarifying problems of political strategy.

The alternative model starts with the assumption that the appropriation of new technologies[18] makes rapid growth in real output possible while reducing the need for labor in manufacturing.[19] But while such rapid growth is possible, it cannot be realized without two different sets of facilitative institutional changes—macroeconomic changes and changes in decisionmaking structures. At the macroeconomic level, it is necessary to respond to the problem of employee insecurity that is aggravated by chronically high unemployment. As long as workers perceive themselves as threatened by technological change, they will find ways to resist technological change. Even when such resistance is unable to halt the introduction of new technologies, it still has serious consequences, since the technologies can be used to the fullest only when employees perceive the technology as benign and operating in their own interests. To overcome this obstacle, it is necessary to pursue policies that expand employee security. Such employee security policies would have five dimensions.

First, through changes in tax and labor laws, strong incentives would be created for firms (private, public, and nonprofit) to find new tasks for redundant employees with compensation and responsibilties comparable or better than those they had before. This redeployment of people would reduce the resort to layoffs. Second, there would have to be a resumption in the historic trend to reduce average working time by rapidly moving toward the thirty-hour week. This would make possible some lowering of current unemployment by redistributing the workload and would further reduce the need for layoffs. To avoid a reduction in standards of living, the government would have to provide some income support in the interim but employees would trade off some future wage gains for shorter hours.[20] Third, an "educare" system would be established through which people would be entitled to financial support for pursuing education or retraining at different stages of their lives.[21] Presumably, there would be some limit on the number of years that any particular individual might be entitled to full-time support, but the level would be fixed high enough so that people in mid-life would have the option to take several years off in order to retool for new careers. Fourth, a system of guaranteed income at reasonable levels would be established as a final cushion for those who were displaced and either ineligible or uninterested in additional schooling. Finally, substantial programs to provide loans and technical support to small businesses and cooperatives would give displaced employees the opportunities to start their own businesses either in manufacturing or the service sector. Taken together, these five measures could help create a new climate in which tehnological change was perceived as opening up options rather than threatening livelihoods.

Some of the same measures would serve double duty in responding to the second macroeconomic problem. This is the familiar problem of demand—as technology displaces people, consumer purchasing power is diminished and overall growth becomes sluggish. The "educare" system and the guaranteed income would play an important role in sustaining consumer demand even as the private sector's demand for labor is contracting. In addition, policies would be pursued to reorganize and expand the public sector to create new jobs, particularly in the provision of human services. Finally, institutional forms would be created to make possible a sustained transfer of goods and services to the

Third World in ways that are supportive of indigenous cultures and development efforts. Reparations to the Third World, in short, could help simultaneously to reduce global inequalities and to sustain the developed economy's capacity for rapid growth.

As for changes in structures of decisionmaking, it is clear that even with greater employee job security, employees will not contribute to their fullest as long as firms remain authoritarian and hierarchical. Here, some of the trends that are apparent particularly in certain high-technology firms must be extended and deepened. These include the development of post-Taylorist forms of work organization in which employee work teams are granted substantial autonomy and have an input into broader decisions that affect them. Increased recognition of the employees' stake in the firm can be achieved through schemes that provide employees with a share of the profits and with a voice in the firms's overall direction. Both of these developments could be universalized through government policies that sought to alter the outmoded structures of corporate governance.

The final set of institutional changes is the most difficult to discuss because there are as yet few models. But without new mechanisms for making decisions about what is to be produced, sustained economic growth is improbable. While there are many cases where the market operates reasonably well, a subtantial part of the economy is now devoted to the production of social infrastructure—energy, transportation, communications, and housing. In these and other arenas, it is apparent that market mechanisms are seriously deficient. In order to make reasonable decisions about production and consumption in these areas, it is necessary to have greater citizen input and to develop new forms of coordination among management, employees, consumers, and various levels of government. The elaboration of such new decisionmaking instruments would help to avoid such disasters as the overinvestment in nuclear energy and could provide a planning context for the revitalization of metropolitan areas.

The different elements that make up this alternative growth model fit together to form a number of virtuous cycles. The progressive shortening of work time would serve to make employees more productive by expanding their time for learning and by reducing the present stresses of coordinating work and family life. Moreover, some of this free time would make possible greater participation in the new forms of social decisionmaking, both at the workplace and in the community. The growth and reorganization of public-sector employment would lead to real improvements in the quality of schooling, health care, and other services that contribute to the productiveness of the labor force. In sum, these kinds of benign interactions would help make the growth of social productivity self-sustaining.

To be sure, such a program of reform would have significant start-up costs. At the beginning resources would have to be freed from military spending and from other wasteful uses to phase in some of these changes. But the idea is that if the institutional changes were successful, a continuation of the reforms could be financed out of the resulting expansion of social wealth.

While the set of reforms embodied in the alternative growth model do not challenge private ownership of the means of production, they do speak directly to the historic demands of the left for democracy, equality, and improved social welfare.[22] The problem, however, is that in the current circumstances, even a reform proposal that is not anticapitalist appears hopelessly utopian. Yet this is a paradox. While it is true that pursuit of the alternative model requires political courage and a leap of social imagination, the reality is that it is the orthodox growth model that is actually utopian in the literal sense. The political-economic conditions that underlay the past successes of the orthodox model no longer exist; it has become an anachronism. When the left trims its sails to develop programs that fit the orthodox model, it becomes as practical and realistic as Reaganomics. In the new situation created by the exhaustion of the old model, we have little choice but to exercise our social imagination.

8

Postindustrial Development and the Obsolescence of Economic Categories

For at least the past ten years, political economic discourse in the United States has been dominated by images of a shortfall in the society's capacity to produce goods and services. In the second half of the seventies, the key issue was the slowdown in the rate of productivity growth. This slowdown was seen as evidence of fundamental problems of government policy, and it provided a powerful justification for a shift to "supply-side" policies that were supposed to lead to more rapid growth rates of both productivity and total product. In the eighties, the central issue has become the federal government budget deficits, which are generally seen as proof that the society cannot afford both guns and butter. While some argue for fewer guns and others for less butter, the shared consensus is that government spending is simply too high relative to existing levels of output.[1] With both the productivity and the deficit crises, the central problem is what to do when the economy's capacity to produce grows more slowly than the demands for output.

While this rhetoric has become totally familiar, it does represent a break with an earlier economic discourse. During the Great Depression of the thirties, conservatives also analyzed the economic problem as one of insufficient supply, and they focused on solutions, such as the raising of

This essay is reprinted from *Politics & Society* 14, no. 1 (1985): 71–99. Reprinted by permission of Geron-K, Inc.

profit levels, that would allow for increased production. The counter-discourse of Keynesianism insisted that there was nothing wrong with the economy's capacity to produce, but that the economic problem lay in the insufficiency of aggregate demand. By focusing their arguments on unused industrial capacity and unemployment, the Keynesians were able to shift the terms of economic debate toward the problem of changing the institutional mechanisms for structuring demand.

This Keynesian emphasis has now been largely discredited. The focus of policymaking has returned to the problem of inadequate levels of production. But the question remains: how do we know that current economic diagnoses are any better than the conventional, pre-Keynesian economic wisdom of the thirties? What if it turned out that now, as in the thirties, the key problem is not the nation's capacity to produce large quantities of goods and services, but rather the institutional mechanisms for shaping demand and for determining how productive resources are to be used? If, in fact, the problems are primarily institutional, then the basic terms within which current economic debate takes place are seriously mistaken.

My intention in the following is to provoke further consideration of this possibility by calling into question some of the empirical evidence that underlies the current conventional wisdom. I focus particularly on the evidence of a significant productivity slowdown during the seventies and argue that this supposed slowdown was largely an artifact of the existing system of categories used to measure national income. Structural changes in the economy that move the society in a postindustrial direction produce forms of economic growth that are not adequately measured in a national accounting scheme that was developed on the basis of industrial production.

Economic Transformation, Accounting Schemes, and the Productivity Crisis

By now, it is—or should be—a commonplace that different economic theories and economic accounting schemes necessarily contain judgments that are products of particular historical circumstances. These judgments then limit the historical or geographical generalizability of any particular accounting scheme. The physiocrats, writing in largely agricultural France, for example, developed a scheme for measuring wealth that rested on the assumption that manufacturing activity was unproductive. This scheme obviously became progressively more problematic as industrialization went forward. And in a classic essay, Simon Kuznets demonstrated the fundamental distortions that result when national income in underdeveloped countries is measured within the national income accounting framework that was created for the developed capitalist countries.[2]

Although the transition to postindustrial society has been discussed for some fifteen years, there has been little systematic analysis of the impact of this transition on the adequacy of existing economic categories and accounting systems. This is surprising in that theories of postindustrial development stress changes both in the nature of what is produced and in how it is produced. Specifically, postindustrialism is associated with the growing importance of services[3] and with the growing destandardization of production as mass markets give way to highly varied and segmented structures of consumer preferences.[4] Postindustrialism is also closely linked to the shift from fixed and rigid sytems of industrial production to more flexible, cybernetic systems.[5] Along with this shift comes the growing importance of intangibles in the production process; organization, information, and learning become as central for the production process as the traditional imputs of capital and labor.[6]

Each of these changes has profound implications for the measurement of economic activity. However, the assumptions and methods for measuring national income for the U.S. economy remain those that were put in place when the current system of national income accounting was developed during and immediately after the Second World War. While the Bureau of Economic Analysis (BEA) of the Department of Commerce, which produces these accounts, has made continuing improvements in the production of the data, there have been almost no changes in the basic conceptual framework that was first developed in the forties.[7]

The data that the BEA have produced on the growth of the Gross National Product (GNP) when measured against available data on employment produce unmistakable evidence of a productivity slowdown in the seventies as compared with the sixties. While productivity growth was slower from 1965 to 1973 than it had been from 1948 to 1965, there was an even sharper decline in the rate of productivity growth for the 1973–79 period.[8] Awareness of this productivity slowdown played a key role in debates about national economic policy. It was widely argued that a significant decline in productivity growth was an indication of insufficient rates of new investment, of insufficient discipline by the work force, or of a combination of the two.[9] Either way, the policy implications were conservative. To facilitate higher levels of investment, it would be necessary to raise profit levels and shift resources from wages and government spending to profits. To enforce greater work effort, it would be necessary to cut back on government programs that protect individuals from the discipline of the labor market, while also encouraging private managers to "get tough" with unions. All of these became ingredients in President Reagan's economic program.

It must be emphasized that some economists have voiced skepticism about the existence of any significant productivity slowdown. Some have argued that "trend labor productivity growth—the growth that would occur if all resources in the economy were fully employed at desired levels"[10]—did not actually decline. In other words, had the growth of output been as rapid in the post-1973 period as in the earlier period, there would have been no decline in the rate of productivity growth. Others have argued that the poor performance in the 1973–1979 period can be entirely attributed to one year—1974—when gross labor productivity declined sharply.[11] This position has also been advanced by William Dickens, who has argued that "productivity is permanently lost during business cycle downturns."[12]

There have also been a number of prestigious analysts who have argued that the productivity slowdown remains a mystery. Edward Denison ends his exhaustive study of slower productivity growth without a viable explanation,[13] and Joseph Pechman, Herbert Stein, and Albert Rees have expressed similar agnosticism.[14]

However, despite some diversity of opinions within the economics profession, the dominant view has been that the productivity decline was real and significant and that there was a need for a conservative policy shift to create the conditions for a revival of productivity growth. This consensus is most clearly indicated by the emergence of a neoliberal current within the Democratic Party that places great emphasis on the need to encourage new investment to make up for lagging productivity growth.

To evaluate these arguments, it is useful to have some sense of the magnitude of the productivity decline. Had productivity grown in the 1973–1979 period at the same rate as it grew from 1960 to 1966, total private GNP would have been $194.6 billion higher in 1979 (in constant dollars) than the reported level (see Table 8-1).[15] But since the 1973–1979 period was marked by the most severe recession of the postwar period— measured GNP actually declined in both 1974 and 1975—it seems probable that close to half of this productivity shortfall can be attributed to recession and slower growth.[16] The issue addressed here is whether measurement problems are significant relative to the remaining shortfall of output of roughly $100 billion.

Table 8-1. Measuring the Productivity Shortfall

Total Private GDP in Constant Dollars	1960	1966	1973	1979
Billions	624.5	835.9	1083.7	1282.0
Hours of private persons in production (millions)	115.0	125.8	137.9	153.5
Productivity ($/hour)	5.43	6.65	7.86	8.35
Percent increase		22.4		6.3

If productivity had risen at the 1960–66 rate in 1973–79, then the $/hour figure would have reached $9.62. When multiplied by the hours, this yields a total private Gross Domestic Product (GDP) of $1476.6 billion. Data are from *National Income and Product Accounts*. Hours exclude paid time away from work.

Examining the National Income Data

Assessing this issue requires a close examination of the government's data on Gross National Product. While these data have been reported for only forty years, economists are almost unanimous in accepting the government's published national income and product accounts as *the* definitive report on the state of the economy. This, in itself, must come as a surprise to the economists and statisticians who first developed the accounts. These pioneers faced many specific problems of measurement for which economic theory provided little guidance. They were forced to develop a variety of ad hoc conventions and approximations to make the accounts work. That many of these improvised solutions have remained unchanged ever since is testimony to the government's capacity to create official knowledge that takes on a privileged status.

From the start, there have been a number of well-established arguments that GNP data represent a poor indicator of the welfare of a society. GNP does not include any measures of the value of leisure time nor of the quality of the environment. It has often been pointed out that when pollution control expenditures increase along with pollution, GNP will rise. Moreover, GNP does not account for the contribution of unpaid household labor to the total supply of goods and services.

Even if one accepts these criticisms and sees GNP not as a measure of welfare but as an imperfect tool to gauge changes in total economic output, other equally serious problems remain. Some of these problems are conceptual and others are primarily problems of the quality of the available data. Both types of problems become increasingly salient with the postindustrial transformation of the economy.

Any system of national accounts represents only a snapshot of the economy taken at a particular moment. There is inevitable distortion when long-term, dynamic processes are reduced to a static image. The biggest problem comes with the distinction between consumption and investment. Consumption and investment activities are closely intertwined in the continuing processes of economic life, and a variety of expenditures clearly have elements of both. When an individual pays for a college education, it can be seen as a consumption good or as an investment good. Similarly, the purchase of an automobile might be classified in either way depending on the particular circumstances.

The drafters of the present national income and product accounts developed a set of conventions for distinguishing between investment and consumption. They decided, for example, that consumer purchases of homes would count as investment, but that purchases of consumer durables would be treated as consumption. They also established that only investment in "tangibles"—buildings and machinery—would be counted as business investment.[17] Expenditures for research and development, for training of employees, and for a variety of other services were treated as business expenses—as intermediate factors that were completely consumed in the production of final output.

These particular dividing lines were clearly arbitrary choices; one can easily develop sound arguments, based in economic theory, for very different definitions. And where one draws the dividing line can have significant consequences for the measurement of total output. This is particularly clear in the case of business expenditures because investments are counted as net additions to total output, while other business expenditures are measured only by their indirect contribution to the total supply of goods and services. Gross National Product consists of the sum of consumer purchases of goods and services, business purchases of investment goods, government purchases of goods and services, and exports minus imports. Hence, when a business buys a machine tool or purchases a new factory or office building, that contributes to total business purchases of investment goods. However, when the same business spends money on advertising or on research and development, that cost will be incorporated in the final value of consumer and investment goods. One could argue just as easily that the cost of purchasing the machine tool also shows up in the tool's contribution to the final value of goods and services. Yet the dollar value of investment goods is added to total output to reflect that investment goods make a contribution to the expansion of output over a multiyear period. A system of accounts that failed to "privilege" investments in this way would result in the unsatisfactory finding that a country that was pouring resources into the expansion of its productive capacity was actually experiencing a decline in real levels of output.

Recently, a number of empirical studies have been done on the United States economy using a concept of investment different from those in the national income and product accounts. John Kendrick operationalized an extremely broad concept of investment that included expenditures for human capital, consumer purchases of certain durables, and corporate expenditures for employee training and research and development. His study estimated a level of output in 1969 that was 34 percent higher than the official Department of Commerce figures.[18] More recently, Robert Eisner has carried forward some of Kendrick's estimates with significant modifications of his own. He calculated total investment in 1981 as $1,678 billion as compared with $475 billion in the Bureau of Economic Analysis figures, and found total GNP to be 53 percent larger than the Department of Commerce figures.[19] Hence, if one expands the notion of what expenditures contribute to production over a multiyear period, the result is higher levels of output.

Not all the significant problems with the National Income Accounts can be traced to these kinds of conceptual problems. There are also problems that result directly from the inadequacy of the data available to the Bureau of Economic Analysis of the Department of Commerce. For several reasons, the detailed data that are generated for manufacturing production are not available for many other sectors of the economy, such as finance, insurance, real estate, construction, and services.[20] First, the system for measuring manufacturing output was in place well before the national income and product accounts were developed; at that point, the weight of some of the poorly measured sectors probably did not appear great enough to justify a major expansion in the government's data-gathering efforts. Second, the relevant nonmanufacturing industries were far more decentralized than manufacturing, so that the problems of collecting adequate data were more formidable. For example, within a manufacturing industry one can sample output for most of the large firms and a representative number of smaller firms and generate a plausible estimate on total output for the whole industry, but the same procedure is far more problematic in service industries, which include thousands of relatively small producers. Finally, for many of the nonmanufacturing industries, it is difficult to find relevant units of output. Even more elaborate data-collection procedures would not totally make up for the absence of an obvious equivalent to tons of steel or dollar value of steel produced.

The data problem has particular importance for the construction of price indexes, which are critical for producing constant-dollar measures of output. Because one wants to measure changes in the level of output that are independent of the effects of inflation—or changes in the purchasing power of the dollar—one needs to find a way to separate out the impact of inflation. This is done for particular sectors of the economy by weighing together the price indexes of different components into a unified index—the deflator. By dividing current dollar GNP figures by the deflator, one arrives at estimates of constant dollar output.

While the Bureau of Labor Statistics (BLS) has developed an extremely elaborate system of price indexes for thousands of manufactured goods, the indexes for many other industries are quite primitive. Part of the reason for this is the difficulty of identifying a standard product, the price of which can be measured over time. Even in construction—an industry with an obviously physical output—price indexes are notoriously problematic because the industry does not produce a standardized product.[21] And with poor or inadequate price indexes, it is extremely difficult to track changes in real output over time.

To understand how these different problems are reflected in the accounts, it is necesary to examine how three of the principal GNP series are constructed. These are the calculation of total GNP in current dollars, the calculation of GNP in constant dollars, and the identification of GNP by a specific industry group.

GNP is a measure of the aggregate dollar value of all goods and services produced in a given year valued at market prices. Economists make a fundamental distinction between intermediate products—those used up in the production process—and final products. Only final products are counted in GNP in order to avoid the double counting that would result if one counted the dollar value both of the flour and of the bread that is made from the flour.

It is axiomatic for national income accounting that the total final product will equal the income generated in the process of production—wages and salaries, profits, interest, and depreciation. To assure the quality of its results, the Department of Commerce carries out separate calculations of the total product and the total income. But on the product side, the procedure is not, as one might assume, simply to add up the value added (final product minus intermediate products) of all industries. Rather, the calculation is done by summing the purchases of the key sectors of the economy. Total consumer purchases of goods and services and business purchases of capital goods (including residential construction) are the key components. To these are added government output (measured by wages and salaries paid), the output of households and nonprofit organizations (measured by wages and salaries and interest paid), and net income originating in the rest of the world.

To create the constant-dollar GNP series, the current-dollar GNP must be deflated by appropriate price indexes. Instead of using a broad index such as the Consumer Price Index, the Bureau of Economic Analysis attempts to deflate the figures on as disaggregated a basis as possible. However, the original GNP series is not calculated by adding together the products of each industry. Instead, BEA analysts use data from the income side of the accounts, which are disaggregated by industry, and apply specific deflators to the industry totals.[22]

For certain service industries, accurate price data are not available and a different technique is used. Constant-dollar output is extrapolated from a base year by some other available index, such as the number of people employed. In other words, since price data do not permit a direct comparison between measured output in two particular years, it is assumed that measured output bears a constant relation to some third indicator, which is sometimes an employment measure and sometimes a volume indicator, such as total receipts.

It should be emphasized that inadequate deflators or extrapolations can lead to either an understatement or an overstatement of changes in constant-dollar GNP. In contrast, errors in the construction of the third series—GNP originating by industry—cannot affect the total GNP figures, since this series is designed only to show the specific industry origins of constant-dollar GNP. This is thus a subordinate series that rests on the current and constant-dollar series. However, this series is widely used for productivity analysis precisely because it is the only source of GNP data disaggregated by industry origin.

To build this series, BEA analysts begin with the total current or constant-dollar GNP figures and then allocate the product among the different industries. Some industries—such as business services that are not even counted in the other GNP series because they produce intermediate products—are here given their due; their contribution to gross output is estimated. Many of the specific procedures are the same as those used in constructing the constant-dollar series, but certain additional adjustments are made to create a consistent framework for determining the allocation of product. But given the centrality of this series for productivity analysis, it is worth emphasizing that it represents a very indirect calculation of each industry's output.[23]

Accounting Problems and Postindustrial Trends

There are three principal ways in which these GNP series lead to progressively more serious undercounting of output: the failure to accurately measure quality change, the neglect of certain critical elements of investment, and the underestimation of service output.

Quality

The impact of quality changes on the measurement of output has confounded economists for some time. the problem is most serious with "costless" quality changes—those that occur without any increase in the quantity of measured inputs to the production process. If, for example, a technological breakthrough makes it possible to produce a qualitatively improved product with the same dollar inputs of labor, capital, and raw material, that is a costless quality improvement.[24]

Some economists have taken the position that, while such qualitative improvements clearly influence the level of welfare, they are basically irrelevant for measuring output.[25] This position rests on two arguments. The first is the empirical difficulty of translating qualitative changes into a quantitative measure. The second is a reluctance by economists to second-guess the market's evaluations of a product. Any scheme for measuring costless quality changes involves substituting another measurement scheme for market evaluations of the value of products. Such a substitution appears arbitrary to a profession accustomed to assuming that markets price products accurately. Indeed, economic theory assumes that, at equilibrium, prices will reflect the marginal costs of production. This suggests that any bias that results from costless quality changes is likely to be small and temporary.

Other economists have argued, however, that the failure to measure quality changes represents a serious problem, and that reliance on the assumptions of equilibrium theory is inadequate in this case.[26] They urge the use of "hedonic price indexes" to make adjustments for both costless quality changes and those changes that are associated with increased costs.[27] Such an index identifies quantitative measures of all the relevant characteristics of a particular product and then is constructed by gathering extensive price information on particular products that embody different combinations of those characteristics. With the use of regression analysis, it is then possible to associate particular values with each characteristic, so that an overall index can be created. This index can then be used to deflate the changes in aggregate production of the particular industry.

Thus far, both the Department of Commerce and the Department of Labor have resisted the use of "hedonic price indexes" in their official calculations. Part of the reason is that even with extensive computer resources, the construction of such indexes for thousands of different products would be a formidable undertaking. This is particularly true because one cannot decide what the critical characteristics of a product might be without some considerable knowledge of the circumstances of the product's use. Moreover, it is also unlikely that such indexes would be able to measure successfully what is often the most significant quality change—the improvement in the durability of a product. Even aside from these empirical problems, however, there appears to be a strong commitment to the theoretical rationales for accepting market prices as valid.

Current BEA and BLS procedures make no effort to adjust for costless quality changes in constructing the price indexes used to produce constant-dollar measures of output. Moreover, when electronic calculators costing $200 replaced electro-mechanical ones, costing $1000, they "were treated as a new product and linked into the price index to show no price change at the transition. If the number of new calculators produced equaled the former production volume of old calculators, this procedure would show a drop in the real output of calculators of 80 percent."[28] If this were to happen across a range of products, the result would be that an actual expansion in utility would show up as a significant decline of output.

It can be argued, of course, that these costless quality improvements have been a relatively constant feature of the U.S. economy and hence are unlikely to have had a growing effect in recent years. But there are a number of reasons for believing that the problem of costless quality change might be increasing in importance. The most important are the microelectronics revolution and the growing destandardization of production.

It is a striking coincidence that the coming of the productivity crisis in the seventies coincided with the microelectronic revolution that was begun with Intel's introduction of the microprocessor—the computer on a chip—in 1971. The microprocessor has dramatically cheapened the costs of developing "intelligent" machines. Nowhere is this more evident than in the computer industry itself where this latest stage of miniaturization has made possible huge reductions in the cost of computer power measured in calculations per second. Various sources have estimated the reduction in the actual dollar cost of computing power at between 20 and 25 percent per year.[29]

But the BLS has not even succeeded in constructing a conventional price index for the computer industry. Hence, the BEA operates on the obviously inaccurate assumption that computer prices have been relatively constant. The effect of this, as in the example of electronic calculators cited above, is to dramatically understate growth in the computer industry's output. One analyst has attempted to measure this understatement by developing several alternative price indexes for computers. In an unpublished paper, Michael McKee, a former staff economist at the Council of Economic Advisers, estimates that actual constant-dollar output of the office, computer, and accounting-machine industry would be between $38.4 and $72.7 billion higher than the reported 1979 figure of $15.8 billion reported by BEA.[30] McKee's estimates are built on the conservative assumption of a 15 percent per year decline in the price of computers. There are technical questions involved in how McKee ties his revised index to the rest of the economy,[31] but the numbers are so large that there can be no question of their impact on levels of aggregate output.

Moreover, similar recalculations need to be done for a number of related industries. Communications equipment and various forms of instruments have also been strongly affected by microelectronics and costless quality change. Here, as well, the existing price indexes are recognized to be nonexistent or inadequate.[32] Yet these two sectors together are almost three times as large as the unadjusted size of the office-machine and computer industry. (They account for $43.4 billion of manufacturing value added in 1979, as compared with $15.6 billion for office machines and computers.)[33] Even if a revised price index for these industries showed only a 5 percent per year price decline since 1973, the addition to GNP would be on the order of $15 billion.

Similar recalculations have to be extended as well to the machine-tool industry, where there has been a rapid shift toward production of numerically controlled and computer numerically controlled machines. By 1979, it was estimated that these advanced machines represented 30 percent of the value of new machines installed in metal-cutting.[34] There is considerable evidence that these new machine tools are 35 to 50 percent more productive than conventional machine tools,[35] but this increase in the machine's utility is not reflected in BEA data, unless prices are 35 to 50 percent higher than those for conventional machine tools. Yet since the critical element in numerically controlled machine tools is the controller, which has been falling in price with advances in microelectronics,[36] it seems extremely unlikely that there is not considerable cost savings in switching to these new machines.

For the period from 1957 to 1970, R. J. Gordon found that there was significant undercounting of the value of capital-goods output because of the neglect of quality change. He argues that between 1957 and 1970, the

BEA deflator for durable goods increased at an annual rate of 1.7 percent, while his alternative deflator declined by 1.2 percent per year.[37] Were Gordon's study to be replicated for the 1973–79 period, we would find the gap between an index that attempted to measure quality change and the BEA's deflators much increased. Given the magnitude of the gap for the computer industry alone, the difference between the two deflators could be quite large.

The rise of microelectronics is closely linked to destandardization of products since the use of computerized controls makes it possible to produce a variety of different products on the same production line while minimizing additional costs.[38] Destandardization has been noted in a broad variety of industries, including some with long-established reputations for standardization of product. The steel industry, for example, has seen a rapid shift in recent years toward a variety of specialty steels that are tailor-made for specific purposes, reducing the demand for a particular standardized steel product. The same trend is also important in consumer markets, where many commentators have noted the profusion of diverse subcultural markets for food, clothing, and home furnishings.

The destandardization of product markets has serious implications for the adequacy of economic data. The more destandardization progresses, the more central becomes the problem of quality measurement. When, for example, steel output shifts to specialty steels, it is likely that both quantity and dollar measures of steel output will significantly understate output. Obviously a ton of highly sophisticated specialty steel is not equal to a ton of standardized steel. At the same time, the advantage of the new technology is that it reduces the additional costs of producing a product with greater utility for the user. As long as part of this cost advantage is passed on to the customer, output in utility will increase more quickly than output measured in dollars.

Moreover, even aside from the question of costless quality changes, rapid processes of destandardization call into question the entire technique of price deflating. The price indexes used for deflating make sense only if they refer to specific products. But as the diversity of the products increases, one needs more and more price observations to construct adequate indexes. And when new products are constantly being introduced, considerable inaccuracies can be introduced in figuring out how to link them into the previous series and how to weight them into a constantly changing product mix.

In those industries where production has long been destandardized—construction, boat and ship production, aircraft—price indexes and the resulting measures of constant-dollar output have been highly questionable. As destandardization extends into more and more other industries, one can expect a general deterioration in the quality of the data. In theory, the direction of the bias in the deteriorating data would be indeterminate, but destandardization means that purchasers are in the position to demand particular characteristics that might well be costless or partly costless for the producer. Price deflators will therefore tend to underestimate output.

It is also relevant to note that the period of the "productivity slow-down" in the 1970s was also the period of the energy crisis and increased concern with environmental pollution. Again, the neglect of quality changes means that the published data make no effort to measure the increases in energy efficiency of products or the reduction in their con-tribution to pollution. However, we know that automobile fuel efficiency improved dramatically during this period and that there were also major improvements in the control of automotive emissions. Similar improve-ments were also made in a variety of other consumer and capital goods. Where these improvements lead to increased costs of production, the probability is that the actual expansion of utility was inaccurately re-flected in the data as inflation.

Finally, if measuring quality changes is difficult for manufacturing, such problems are even more formidable for the broad range of service industries. Even for these services where reasonable price indexes are used to deflate output figures, there are no adjustments for quality change. Yet in the case of many services, there is no reasonable way to distinguish a unit of output from the quality of the service. In the case of medical care, for example, consumers are not purchasing units of a physician's time or days in a hospital bed, but an improvement in their health. As advances come in medical research and medical practices, there can be significant improvements in the health care patients receive per dollar of expenditure. While there are no obvious reasons to imagine that qualitative improvements occurred more rapidly in nonmanufactur-ing industries from 1973 to 1979 as compared with earlier periods, the growing size of this part of the economy necessarily means that qualita-tive advances in it will have a progressively greater bearing on total output.

The Measurement of Investment
For GNP purposes, investment has to be in tangible capital—either machinery or physical plant. As noted earlier, some analysts have attempted to broaden the definition of investment to include investments in human capital and in research and development.[39] When such com-

putations are made, total GNP rises significantly, and the gap between official measures and the revised measures grows over time, indicating an increased importance to these other forms of investment.

But since the methodology of measuring the society's total investment in human capital is highly problematic,[40] it seems more appropriate to limit analysis to a number of forms of intangible capital that are clearly expenditures of the nonhousehold part of the economy. Three items are of particular importance here: expenditures for research and development, expenditures for employee training, and purchases of certain types of business and miscellaneous professional services.

While there seems little justification for the convention of excluding research and development expenditures from investment, the issue is of only marginal importance to the argument here because most measures show that these expenditures failed to rise in the seventies.[41] As for expenditures for employee training, Eisner estimates the constant-dollar value of training produced in the business sector as rising from $15.7 billion in 1971 to $20.6 billion in 1981.[42] This is a 31.2 percent increase as compared with the 12.1 percent increase in the decade from 1966 to 1976. While these estimates are probably too conservative, they do suggest that this is a growing category; its exclusion from investment results in a downward bias in the output data.

In fact, both research and development and employee training should be seen as special cases of a larger category, namely "service capital," a category that has not been seriously addressed by previous analysts. Service capital consists of those services produced within a firm or purchased from outside that are intended to have a multiyear impact on the firm's output.

The most dramatic instance of service capital is the case of computer software development. When a bank buys a new computer, it counts in the national income accounts as a capital investment and hence as a contribution to total final output. But when the same bank purchases a highly complex computer program, it is treated as the purchase of an intermediate service—a cost of doing business. This distinction makes little sense because the program is indispensable for the operation of the computer and will clearly make a contribution to output over a number of years. The same problem occurs with in-house production. When one division of IBM buys a computer from another division, that intrafirm transfer still shows up as an investment. However, when IBM or any other firm purchases computer programs from its own in-house programmers, the expenditure is not counted as investment.

This particular anomaly has striking implications since it is well known that software costs will play an ever-increasing role in the computer industry as hardware costs continue to decline. But if software development costs are considered simply a business expense, rather than an integral part of the society's productive investment, the distortion in investment and output figures will be considerable. According to the Census Bureau, the number of computer programmers grew by 150,000 from 1970 to 1980. If one estimates their mean earnings to have been $18,000 in 1979, then $2.7 billion represents a crude estimate of additional societal investment in software development during the seventies.[43]

While software development might represent the paradigmatic case, there are a variety of other types of service capital that should also be counted as investment. It is well known that modern production processes in both manufacturing and services are often highly complex. In many cases, management calls on the services of a variety of outside personnel for assistance in managing these processes. When these outsiders—whether management consultants, industrial engineers, or human-resource development specialists—come in, they tend to make, or facilitate the making of, decisions that are designed to improve the effective use of the human and physical resources of the organization. Such plans, when successful, tend to have an effect over multiple years, so the initial investment in these services has a payoff over time.

Similarly when management designs a new facility, it might spend considerable sums of money paying for architectural and engineering services. Since it is now recognized that the structure of the physical plant can have a considerable impact on the efficiency of production, these services cannot be considered extraneous to the construction industry. They represent forms of real investment.

To be sure, in the examples that I have cited, not all expenditures pay off; consultants often give bad advice that has no impact on output. But efficacy is not a condition for inclusion in capital investment; firms buy a great deal of physical capital that does not work out and is quickly scrapped. The test of inclusion in investment should be whether the expenditure was an immeditate cost of production or whether it is intended to produce results over a period of years.

There are no direct measures of these various forms of service capital, whether produced in-house or purchased from others. But it is possible to get some order of magnitude of service capital that is purchased from outside by looking at the business-service category. This category has grown rapidly in recent years in terms of employment. While such business services as advertising, building maintenance, and mailing and production are not relevant to our argument, there is reason to believe that others such as computer programming and software, research and development laboratories, and personnel-supply services represent a growing share of the entire sector.

The Department of Commerce's input-output studies of the U.S. economy show that purchased business services as a whole grew from $57.3 billion in 1967 to $88.2 billion in 1972, and to $162.0 billion in 1977. (All of these figures are in current dollars.) Unfortunately, we lack a price index for business services, but if we use the general deflator for all services, the growth still represents an increase from $76.5 billion in 1967 to $88.2 in 1972, and then to $115.2 billion in 1977. This represents growth of more than 6 percent per year in the 1972–77 period. This calculation probably understates the case since the deflator for services is biased upward by the rapid price rises in the health-care sector.[44]

If we extrapolate this increase to 1979, constant-dollar purchases of business services would be about $129.3 billion. This represents an increase of $35.7 billion as compared with 1973. If service capital constituted as much as a third of business services, that would represent an $11.9 billion addition to 1979 GNP.

These approximations are necessary because the GNP series that measures business services uses a faulty methodology. In the GNP originating-by-industry series, the output of business services is extrapolated on the basis of the number of persons employed in this sector in the base year—1947. In other words, the original estimate of the output of this sector in 1947 remains the basis for all subsequent calculations. It is assumed that the ratio of total output to total employment in this sector has remained constant so that changes since 1947 can be calculated by multiplying the number of employees times that ratio. This methodology assumes zero productivity growth in this sector and fails to adjust the data to the very different figures produced by the input-output studies. As we shall see, this methodological problem plagues many of the calculations of outputs for a variety of service industries.[45]

Measurement of Service Industries

There are serious measurement problems for both financial services and for most components of the specific service category that includes education, health care, legal services, entertainment, and other miscellaneous services. Some of the problems result from anomalies in the measurement of output and others from the techniques of deflation, but the overall result is that for a large portion of these sectors the GNP data are built on the assumption of zero productivity growth or worse.

One area of significant problems is the measurement of output of banks and other financial services, exclusive of real estate. In recent years, BEA has assumed that the constant-dollar value of services provided by financial intermediaries to individuals has grown in proportion to the number of full-time equivalent employees in this sector. This procedure posits zero productivity growth since the ratio of output to labor input is assumed to be constant. While this method of measurement is an improvement over previous methods that resulted in figures that showed a long-term decline in bank productivity,[46] there are still considerable problems. The Bureau of Labor Statistics has done its own calculations using a composite measure of demand transactions, loans, and fiduciary services. According to this indicator, commercial banking productivity grew by 6 percent per year between 1967 and 1980. This result seems far more consistent with the recent impact of computerization on banks than do the BEA's assumptions.

Since employment in financial services grew faster in 1973–79 (23.9 percent) than in 1960–66 (17.4 percent), more realistic productivity figures would strongly affect the relative growth of total output in the two periods. We could assume, for example, that financial-service productivity actually grew by 2 percent a year in the 1960–66 period and accelerated to a 4 percent annual rate in the 1973–79 period with increased computerization. The result of these assumptions is that this sector's net addition to GNP would be $13.6 billion.[48]

While the notion of the "output" of the financial-services industry is inherently elusive, it is clear that the society has devoted considerable resources of both labor and capital to the provision of financial services to individuals. However, it is not at all clear that the existing methods accurately measure the growth in this category of output.

Even more serious problems exist in the measurement of the specific service category. It has often been argued that measuring the output of government in terms of the wages and salaries paid to government employees is based on the assumption of close to zero productivity growth. (It is close to zero productivity growth because changes in salaries or shifts in the composition of employment will mean that the ratio of total wages and salaries to total employees will vary slightly over time.) It follows that as government employment increases as a percentage of the labor force, there will be a downward pull on the growth of overall productivity. In recognition of this problem, most analysts confine their discussions of productivity to the private economy. But a comparable problem exists with the nonprofit sector of the economy because for this sector output is also measured primarily by the sum of wages and salaries (although interest payments are also added in) with the result that close to zero productivity growth is built into these figures as well.

This sector of the economy has been expanding rapidly because of the problems involved in organizing many social services on a for-profit basis. Nonprofit employment has grown from 2.7 percent of all employment in 1948 to 5.6 percent in 1979.[49] The nonprofit sector of the economy includes most of private education, a large share of hospital care, membership organizations, and most social-service agencies. This sector has also been subject to very strong pressures for increased efficiencies since the early seventies, so it is difficult to accept the assumption of zero or negative productivity growth that is built into the BEA procedures. It is also relevant to note here that other countries use procedures for measuring the output of some of these industries that do not involve the same assumptions.[50]

In addition to nonpofit services, there are other parts of the service category where BEA methods are also highly inadequate. For miscellaneous repair services, output is extrapolated on the basis of total persons employed. For legal services, output is derived from total personal consumption expenditures, but the deflator is the average annual earnings of full-time employees in legal services. If, as is often the case, wages simply kept pace with productivity gains, this technique would show zero productivity growth. So here again, zero or negative productivity growth is assumed.

The portions of the service sector where the measurement techniques build on the assumption of zero or negative productivity growth account for close to half of total employment among those that produce for final consumption. In 1979, the total contribution of services to GNP was $178.6 billion. If we assume that 20 percent of this was accounted for by services to businesses, half of all consumer services still account for $71.4 billion. On the further assumption that productivity growth for these services rose from 0 percent a year in the 1960–66 period to a 2 percent annual growth in the 1973–79 period as both nonprofit and profit-making services faced a more threatening environment, then the net addition to GNP would be $8.6 billion.[51] While the assumptions I have made about the actual productivity growth in some of these service industries are arbitrary and unsupported by data, the same can be said of the official data. There is also a deeper point at stake. Analysis of the relative importance of services to the American economy often comes back to the issue of their overall contribution to GNP. For this, analysts often rely on the GNP originating-by-industry figures to show the relative contribution of services to overall output. Yet when one looks carefully at these data, it becomes clear that something very strange is going on. As Table 8-2 indicates, the service category as a percentage of total GNP has remained basically unchanged since 1948, while finance, insur-

Table 8-2. Trends in GNP Originating and Employment for Selected Sectors

	PERCENTAGES			
	GNP Originating		*Employment*	
Sector	*1948*	*1979*	*1948*	*1979*
Services	13.64	13.93	14.13	22.43
Finance, Insurance and Real Estate	13.43	17.75	3.33	6.39
Manufacturing	28.80	28.71	28.00	26.57
Agriculture	6.69	3.09	16.86	5.08
Trade	18.48	19.36	22.24	24.56
Others	18.96	17.20	15.44	14.98

Data are percentages of total private GNP originating by industry in constant dollars and percentages of total private hours of persons engaged in production. *National Income and Products Accounts.* Others include mining, construction, transportation, and public utilities.

ance, and real estate has seen only a relatively small increase. In both cases, the trends in output contrast sharply with the shifts in these sectors' contribution to total private employment.

But these astonishing figures are readily explicable in light of the previous analysis. BEA's methods for computing output of these service industries are strongly biased to show, regardless of the reality, that service productivity has been growing far more slowly than manufacturing. These biased assumptions lead directly to the claim that the contribution of services to GNP has remained basically constant over thirty years.

The implications of this argument are quite serious. It means that we lack reasonable data on the relative contribution to total output of goods production as compared with services. Just as the physiocratic economics defined industry as unproductive, so, too, our existing conceptual apparatus understates the relative contribution of services to total output. This is particularly the case when we remember that the data on the governmental contribution to total output also assume close to zero productivity growth.

While the various estimates of measurement bias are intended to be only illustrative, they are assembled together in Table 8-3 to show that the aggregate is large relative to the size of the $100 billion productivity shortfall. It should be emphasized as well that there are a number of biases I have made no effort to quantify. Costless quality changes in

Table 8-3. Estimates of Measurement Problems in 1979 GNP (in billions of constant dollars)

1. Computers and Office Machines	38.4–72.8
2. Communications Equipment and Instruments	15.0
3. Purchased "Service Capital"	11.9
4. Finance and Insurance	13.6
5. Other Services	8.6
Total Estimate	87.5–121.9

For items 1–3, it is assumed that changes in these categories had a nominal impact in 1960–66. For items 4 and 5, estimates are of net growth over adjusted rate for the 1960–66 period.

consumer goods have largely been neglected, and no estimate of the costless quality changes in the broad capital-goods sector has been provided. Similarly, I have not attempted to measure quality changes in the service sector that could include such diverse factors as improvements in health care and shorter waiting time in stores. Yet even a partial accounting strongly suggests that the portion of the productivity shortfall of 1973–79 that cannot be attributed to slower growth resulted from the failure of the established accounting conventions to measure postindustrial changes in the economy.

It is, of course, plausible that there are also factors that cumulatively bias the data in the opposite direction—to overstate the production of utilities. For example, Kuznets writes of the "costs of participation in the complicated technical, monetary civilization of industrial countries. Payments to banks, employment agencies, unions, brokerage houses, etc. including such matters as technical education, are payments not for final goods flowing to ultimate consumers, but libations of oil on the machinery of industrial society—activities intended to eliminate friction in the productive system, not net contributions to ultimate consumption."[52] It is clear that costs like these have been steadily rising with greater social complexity, but for these costs to offset the bias that I have described, there would have to have been a serious acceleration in the rate of rise from the sixties to the seventies. There is no reason to assume such an acceleration.

Another response to assertions that GNP data might undercount certain types of output is that a significant error would likely be revealed somewhere else in the accounts. For example, if new investment is being undercounted through the neglect of service capital, then surely a higher rate of new investment should be leading to expanding rates of output. In the absence of the latter, it seems hardly credible to claim increases in investment. The difficulty with this argument is that there are interactions among different sources of error. First, much of the added output is appearing in sectors that are poorly measured: in manufacturing where there is costless quality change, in government and nonprofits where there are no independent measures of output, and in a range of other service sectors where qualitative or quantitative improvements in output are unlikely to be measured. Second, some of the missing additional output is the unmeasured new investment. The data generated by Eisner and Kendrick suggest that when intangible capital is measured, the ratio of total investment to GNP has been rising. This suggests the possibility of a cumulative distortion in both the investment and the output figures.

There are also specific ways in which errors interact in the construction of the accounts. One of the most striking of these is found in the GNP originating-by-industry series. We have already seen how this series dramatically understates the output of business services. But there is also a corresponding distortion in the measurement of manufacturing output. The measure of GNP originating in manufacturing is different from the Census Bureau's measure of manufacturing value added. The former series subtracts business purchases of business from manufacturing output on the theory that the contribution of business services to output should be reported elsewhere.[53] But the consequence of this is to show slower growth in manufacturing output. In fact, the ratio of manufacturing output in the GNP originating series to manufacturing value added as measured by the Census Bureau has declined from 86.3 percent in 1966 to 76.2 percent in 1979. And if one calculates changes in manufacturing productivity from the Census Bureau's value-added figures rather than from the GNP originating series, the decline is significantly slower.[54] The GNP originating series thus understates manufacturing output in order to accurately state the contribution of business services to overall output, but then the BEA proceeds to measure the contribution of business services to output in a way that significantly understates their contribution.

Yet even if the errors are cumulative on the product side of the accounts, a significant mismeasurement of the value of output would have consequences for the income side of the account as well. If the existing measures undercount GNP by $100 billion or more, that means a comparable shortfall in the measurement of income. While a full discussion of this issue is beyond the scope of this paper, several points can be made. First, some of the disappearing income results from the inadequacy of deflators. If the absence of quality measures means that output is greater than previously thought, it also means that the constant-dollar purchasing power of income is greater than the Consumer Price Index or the Wholesale Price Index would suggest. Second, the reallocation of certain expenditures from current expenses to capital investment has immediate effects on the income side of the ledger. The offsetting changes are an increase in profits and an increase in depreciation, since intangible capital must also be depreciated.[55] Finally, as studies of the "underground economy" have indicated, the amounts of unreported income are considerable, and it seems plausible that these amounts increased dramatically in the turbulent and inflationary period from 1973 to 1979. Indeed, a recent BEA study based on income-tax returns increased previous estimates of unreported personal income in 1977 by $57.8 billion with an overall addition to GNP of $21.8 billion.[56]

Analysis and Implications

Since most of the measurement problems I have located have previously been identified in the literature, some explanation is required for the continued willingness of economists to accept the published GNP data as definitive.[57] Economists have failed to recognize that the different measurement biases interact to produce a progressively more distorted picture of the economy. Economists have made a number of specific criticisms of what they consider to be a fundamentally sound framework, but they have generally refused to consider the possibility that there are now fundamental problems with the basic framework.

This refusal can be easily understood if we remember that modern economics is not a universal system of ideas that can be equally applied to any pattern of economic organization. On the contrary, economic theories contain an implicit concept of the production process. Our modern system of economic ideas was created to make sense of a particular social world, a world organized around industrial production, and assumptions based on the circumstances of industrial production fundamentally shape the discipline.

Anyone who has sat through an introductory economics course is familiar with discussions of widgets—the prototypical industrial product frequently used for illustrative purposes. The characteristics of this semi-comical product reveal a great deal about the assumptions that pervade economic discourse. Widgets are a standardized, manufactured good; issues of quality are irrelevant because one widget is as good as another. And the widget is a completely discrete item; it is bought off the shelf, and there are no further transactions between consumer and producer after it is purchased. The circumstances of widget production are also not terribly complicated. A labor force with relatively low skills is brought together with a stock of standardized capital goods to produce a given quantity of widgets. Problems of measurement are relatively simple because one can track precisely how many widgets each employee produces, and the contribution of capital investment is also straightforward because it is entirely embodied in the standardized machine tools.

Yet the essence of postindustrial development is that there is a movement away from all of the circumstances assumed in widget production. First, there is a shift in the very nature of what is produced with the growing quantitative importance of services and destandardized goods. With this shift, there is no longer an obvious and incontrovertible way to measure output. Furthermore, many services and destandardized goods, and even some standardized goods, are no longer sold as discrete products, but their purchase involves ongoing relations with the producer in terms of support and service. And yet we have no satisfactory way to measure the value of this ongoing provision of services by producers.

Second, there are also fundamental changes in the production process itself. In many parts of the economy, production requires substantially higher levels of skill and knowledge on the part of employees.[58] At the same time, the nature of capital investment has changed fundamentally. Capital goods themselves have become more complex and less standardized, so that measuring the value of the stock of fixed capital is becoming ever more problematic. And other forms of intangible capital, including research and development, service capital, and the actual organizational structures in which production is embedded, have become progressively more important.

When one is producing health care or social services, rather than widgets, it seems obvious that investment involves something other than the purchase of durable goods and structures. But the same argument can be made as well for modern factory production. In the widget factory, there is very little other than actual production that is significant or relevant. As long as a steady supply of raw matterials is provided, with a given stock of machines the level of output is entirely a function of the effort of the workers. But in a technologically sophisticated factory with complex production technologies and many intermediate products, output is determined by a variety of new factors.

With new production technologies that rely heavily on "intelligent" machines, one of the major determinants of output is the amount of "downtime"—the time in which the machinery is not working because of some kind of malfunction.[59] Yet two factories using the same technology might experience very different rates of downtime because of differences in the labor process and in organizational structure. Similarly, much of the excitement about Japanese managerial techniques centers on their innovations in the management of inventories and in controlling the flow of intermediate products. The use of nearby satellite producers and reduction of in-house inventories involves cost savings and the elimination of certain supply bottlenecks.[60] But here again, it is an organizational innovation outside of labor or physical capital that plays a key role in increasing productivity.

Finally, the Japanese experience has also highlighted the centrality of quality control in the production process. In the hypothetical widget factory, quality control is not an issue because all the widgets produced are good enough to go to market. Yet this is hardly a realistic assumption in contemporary manufacturing. The extreme example is the production of computer chips where current processes involve the inevitability of some defective output. The reduction of the percentage of output that is defective becomes the critical factor in determining productivity and profitability. But the same issues come up in less extreme form in almost all other manufacturing settings.[61] It is necessary to test the quality of output, to repair defective units, and to trace the sources of correctable defects. Since a wide variety of factors can influence the rate of failure, here, as well, a variety of intangible expenditures are major determinants of output.

The point is that for producing goods and services other than widgets, factors other than the amount of labor time or the amount of physical capital become increasingly central. Even the efforts by some economists to measure the "quality" of the labor input into the production process miss the point; it is not the individual characteristics of the employees, but the specific features of the institutional context, that have a determining role.[62] Again two factories might be quite similar in the "quality" of their labor forces and the nature of their capital stock, but their output might differ greatly because of institutional differences that lead in one factory to greater downtime and poorer quality control.

In sum, the economists' retention of the widget as the prototypical product means that when they confront actual production in an increasingly postindustrial economy, they are able neither to accurately assess total output nor to grasp some of its key determinants. This situation helps to explain certain anomalous economic findings. One recent study, for example, found that labor productivity in metalworking industries was negatively correlated with capital investment. "Despite significantly higher rates of capital intensity in total metalworking during the latter period [1965–73 as contrasted to 1955–65], the rate of growth of labor productivity displays a significant decrease."[63] This type of finding

could result from the combination of two factors. Because of the unevenness of quality changes, the dollar value of capital investment might be a
very poor indicator of the actual effectiveness of new equipment. At the
same time, expensive new capital goods might have low rates of output
because of the failure to adjust labor relations and the larger organizational environment to accommodate them.

But the deepest significance of the passing of widget production is
the challenge it poses to fundamental assumption of national income
accounting—that it is possible to capture the state of the economy in a
single metric. Western analysts have long mocked the Soviets' system of
economic planning for the distortions caused by one-dimensional
targets. For example, the story is often told that when the targets for the
lighting industry were set in terms of weight, Soviet factories began
turning out extremely heavy chandeliers. The irony is that Western
economists have been engaged in a similar exercise by attempting to
measure all output in terms of dollars, and when the government acts to
increase this single dollar metric, parallel distortions can occur.

The reality is that the various biases in the data that I have identified
cannot be adequately addressed simply by developing more sophisticated data sources and more complex measurement schemes. There is
ultimately no adequate way to translate the increasingly important qualitative dimension of products into quantity measures. For example, as
the production of health and educational services becomes progressively
more important, any scheme that translates the value of those products
into equivalence with the output of steel or vegetables is inherently
problematic. It would be far more useful to develop a number of sector-
specific measures that could attempt to capture both the qualitative and
quantitative measures of changes without importing dubious assumptions about the dollar value of health or education. In sum, postindustrial
development increases the urgency of substituting a whole series of
"social indicators" for any single-dimensional economic indicator of the
overall state of the economy.

Conclusion

That we have left the world of widget production also has profound
implications for economic policy that are often directly contrary to current policy directions. As was argued earlier, the discovery of the productivity crisis legitimated the idea that our economic problems are rooted in
insufficient inputs of the key factors of production—tangible capital and
labor. This leads directly to policies intended to limit the growth of

civilian spending and to limit wage gains in order to increase both the rate of profit and the total sum of profits available for reinvestment. It also leads to policies that attempt to increase labor discipline by eliminating alternative sources of support. Finally, it has contributed to even greater reliance on the market as an instrument for adjusting supply and demand through the whole economy.

All of these directions are exactly contrary to the policy initiatives that flow from an understanding of postindustrial development.[64] First, postindustrial policies would expand state spending for a number of collective goods such as education, retraining, and health care that become increasingly important with the growing centrality of the human factor in production. Second, rather than increasing market-type discipline over the work force, one would want to encourage greater cooperation between management and labor based on the foundation of greater economic security for the work force. This increased economic security is necessary to facilitate the full use of new technologies and to encourage continuous retraining of the work force. Third, rather than relying exclusively on the market, one would want to develop a whole new range of institutional mechanisms to shape decisions about production and consumption. While the price mechanism alone might suffice when one is producing widgets, for the complex and interdependent goods and services of a postindustrial economy, something more is needed.

The irony is that postindustrial development undermines the established economic categories, leading to the statistical illusion of a productivity crisis, and ultimately to the imposition of economic policies that operate to slow further postindustrial development. Escaping from this conundrum requires a fundamental rethinking of economic categories and economic theory.

At the start of this paper, I argued that if there had been no real productivity shortfall in the seventies, that would increase the plausibility of arguments that the problems of the American economy are—as they were in the 1930s—primarily the results of flawed institutional arrangements. This argument violates the established terms of debate. It is customary for those who emphasize the need for greater government regulation of markets to argue that the economy is less productive than it should be; they point to the failure of markets to produce adequate levels of output as the justification for governmental action. In contrast, advocates of unimpeded markets would seize on the discovery that the GNP data understate economic growth as proof of the vitality of the market economy.[65]

But these established terms of debate represent another conundrum for advocates of significant institutional reform of the American economy. If proponents of reform must insist on the inadequacy of current levels of output, then they have no way to resist the claims of the political right. The right will use slow productivity growth or budget deficits as proof of the need for austerity, increased incentives to the rich, and cutbacks in expensive government programs. The problem is how can one afford potentially costly reform efforts when the economy is already performing below optimal levels. This dynamic was vividly demonstrated in the period before and after the 1984 election campaign when liberal Democrats who had bemoaned the size of the Reagan administration's budget deficit found it politically impossible to propose any major new federal initiatives.

However, broader possibilities for alternative policies open up when it is demonstrated that the economy is fundamentally strong in its capacity to produce an expanding flow of goods and services. When this premise is granted, the economy's problems can be understood as existing at a different level of analysis. One major set of problems centers on the horrendous misallocation of resources—excessive military spending, underproduction of a variety of critical collective goods, and overinvestment in such industries as financial services. There is a continuing insufficiency of consumer demand that results from skewed income distribution, technological displacement of labor, and the tendency for much new job creation to be low wage. There are significant sectoral problems such as in health care, where the current institutional arrangements are inefficient in terms of both money and quality. In automobiles and other older industries, there are severe problems of international competition that result primarily from these industries' slowness to utilize new technologies and to adapt their systems of management and labor relations accordingly.

Such a catalog of institutional failures could be extended. Yet it is certainly the case that the solution to these various institutional failures would result in an economy that is substantially more productive and efficient than what we have now. The problems are not primarily problems of inadequate levels of tangible capital and labor; nor are they problems that will be readily solved by consumer belt tightening and further reductions in state-provided services. On the contrary, they are the kinds of problems that can be overcome only through a process of institutional reform that changes patterns of government regulations, changes labor-management relations, and changes patterns of income distribution. Such a process of reform depends on the exercise of social imagination and sustained political struggle. The precondition of such efforts is the recognition that we no longer live in the world of widget production.

Postscript

In December 1985, the Bureau of Economic Analysis announced that it had developed a price index for computers that would be incorporated into its revision of the historical data on the national income and product accounts. The new index relied heavily on research done at IBM and showed an average annual rate of price decline of 14 percent a year from 1972 to 1984. With the new index in place, 1984 computer output was valued at $100 billion higher than it was without the computer price index. While many questions can be raised about the adequacy of this new price index, its introduction confirms the claim of a substantial undercount of GNP that resulted from the absence of such an index for computers and other high-technology industries.

It should be noted, however, that when the BEA introduced the new price index, they also shifted the base year for prices from 1972 to 1982. This routine procedure, however, eliminated the $100 billion gain in output. This dramatic impact is a result of a problem with index numbers when measuring a sector of the economy where output has been rising rapidly while prices are falling quickly. If we start with the roughly accurate assumption that computer output grew thirty times from 1972 to 1982, it is easy to see the impact of rebasing. When one uses 1972 as the base year, the 1972 figures for computer output would be the actual dollar value of computers produced in that year, while the 1982 figure would be thirty times that. If, however, one switches to the 1982 base year, the 1982 figure will be the actual current dollar value in 1982, but the 1972 figure will be one-thirtieth of that. In short, rebasing to a more recent year dramatically diminishes the weight of computers in the economy as a whole.[66]

9

Political Choice and the Multiple "Logics" of Capital

It has become an accepted truth on the political left that the conservative economic policies of Ronald Reagan are a necessary response to the needs of the capitalist system.[1] In this argument, cuts in civilian spending and reductions in the living standards of working people and the poor conform to "the logic of capital" in a period of crisis. This position grows directly out of the theory developed in the seventies that capitalist states are torn between the conflicting imperatives of legitimation and accumulation.[2] According to this theory, when legitimation pressures force the state to go "too far" in granting concessions to subordinate groups, the accumulation process is impaired. Hence, only conservative policies that roll back these excessive concessions can reestablish the conditions for a renewal of sustained growth without high inflation and with adequate levels of profit.

This essay argues that this familiar position is wrong because it is based on incorrect assumptions about the relation between politics and economics. Moreover, I will argue that this theoretical error has been politically consequential because it has diminished the political left's capacity to resist Reaganism and to develop counterprograms of its own.

The Nature of the Economic

The legitimation versus accumulation argument is very much a mirror image of conservative arguments about interference with free markets.[3]

This essay is reprinted from *Theory and Society* 15, nos. 1–2 (1986): 175–190. © copyright Martinus Nijhoff Publishers, Dordrecht, Holland.

With growing intensity during the seventies and early eighties, economists and publicists advanced the argument that problems of high inflation and slowing productivity growth were the inevitable consequence of
excessive growth of government—too much regulation, tax rates pegged
so high as to discourage initiative, and the proliferation of social programs that insulated individuals from the discipline of the labor market.
They insisted that deregulation, tax cuts, and the reduction of social
spending were necessary to restore the integrity of the free market, so
that the conditions for stable economic growth could be restored.[4]

In fact, analysts on the left frequently cited these conservative arguments as evidence for their claim that capitalism and democracy were in
conflict.[5] They suggested that if the various forms of state regulation and
state social welfare spending that had been won through popular struggles did actually interfere with the "logic of capitalism," then this would
constitute proof of the necessity and desirablility of a transition to socialism. For adherents of this position, a transition to socialism represented
the only way to preserve the gains that had come through democratic
struggles within capitalism.

Yet the persuasiveness of both leftist and rightist arguments that
posited a conflict between democracy and state action on the one hand
and the logic of the economy on the other depended on developments in
the world economy. After all, it had been the conventional wisdom for
the previous twenty years that the "mixed economy"—a combination of
private ownership and state intervention—was the optimal institutional
form for achieving economic efficiency and social welfare. It took a series of international economic shocks to undermine this conventional
wisdom.

In the seventies with growing international economic competition,
the demise of the Bretton Woods international monetary order, and
OPEC's oil price rises, American citizens and politicians were suddenly
confronted with the reality of international economic interdependence.
The scholarly community reflected this shift by rediscovering the constraints placed on national societies by the discipline of the world economy. During the seventies, American academics elaborated both "world
system theory" and "international political economy," both of which had
at their core the analysis of the pressures placed on national societies by
the world economy.

The international economy that American academics rediscovered
had changed from the self-regulating gold standard of the nineteenth
century, but the international currency markets continued to operate as
constraints on national policymakers. If, for example, a particular country were following expansionary policies when those around it were

contracting, it would likely face a balance-of-payments crisis and severe downward pressure on its currency. Moreover, citizens in country after country were told during the seventies by politicians and business leaders that they could not afford various types of social-policy measures because of their potential damage to the country's international competitive position in a context of increased conflicts over markets. And in periods of economic contraction, such as 1974–1975 and 1980–1983, existing redistributive policies came under attack on the grounds that they prevented the readjustments that were necessary for improved performance in world markets.[6]

These pressures were highlighted by the efforts of the Mitterrand government in France to go against the tide of the world economy in the early eighties. The French Socialist government pursued redistributive and expansionary policies while the rest of the major economies were still in recession. The results were higher rates of inflation and mounting balance-of-payments difficulties for France. The currency markets forced a series of devaluations of the franc and ultimately the Mitterrand government was forced to reverse many of its policies and pursue a program of austerity.

These experiences provided persuasive support for the idea of a fundamental conflict between government policies designed to increase legitimation and the logic of capitalist accumulation. The evidence appeared overwhelming that in the context of a highly competitive capitalist world economy, there exist strict limits to the types of governmental policies that are possible in any particular country. Moreover, as competition mounts within that world economy, there are powerful pressures to reduce the level of taxes and social welfare in any particular country toward the lowest international common denominator.

To be sure, leftist and free market theorists use different concepts to describe the tension between politics and the logic of the economy. Where one would discuss "the logic of accumulation," the other would refer to "the logic of the market." Yet the difference in language conceals an analytic similarity. The two sets of theorists share two central ideas in common. The first is a rejection of optimistic, Keynesian ideas about the mixed economy in favor of the view that there is no "free lunch"—efforts to improve social welfare through government action interfere with either the logic of the market or the imperatives of accumulation.

The second common idea is that there is such a thing as an economy that is autonomous and that has a single logic. This assumption, which can be called the economistic fallacy, was sharply critiqued in a book published more than forty years ago, *The Great Transformation*.[7] In that book, Karl Polanyi challenged the idea that the economy is autonomous and obeys a single logic. While there has been increased interest in Polanyi's work in recent years, this core argument of his is worth elaborating at some length because his position has still not been assimilated by economic analysts of either the right or the left.

Polanyi develops his argument about the autonomy of the economy by directly challenging economic liberalism's account of the evolution of capitalism. Adam Smith and others argued that capitalism evolved out of an innate human desire to truck and barter. While archaic social institutions had placed limits on the market, a process began in the late Middle Ages through which the market gained increasing strength and autonomy, until political institutions finally evolved that maximized market freedom. As one would expect, this history rests on the idea of an autonomous economy that needs only to be given its freedom; the process is one of natural evolution from restrictions on the human desire to trade to a society organized around that desire.

In contrast, Polanyi highlights the unnaturalness and discontinuity in the historical changes that gave rise to capitalism. The traditional account asserts that the growth of both local and international trade in the late Middle Ages resulted naturally in the development of integrated national markets. But Polanyi insists that both local and international trade could flourish indefinitely without the creation of integrated national markets. Under mercantilism, local and international markets were subordinate to political control, so there was no natural dynamic leading to integrated markets.

Polanyi emphasizes instead the importance of political intervention for the rise of modern capitalism. The emergence of national markets was not the result of spontaneous evolution but of the deliberate political interventions of the Crown.[8] Later on, the development of a market economy also depended on action by the state. The particular example that he analyzed most extensively was the role of the English Poor Law Reform in creating a modern labor market. He described in detail the consequences of the Speenhamland Act—a system of welfare relief instituted in 1795 by rural squires to maintain order in the countryside. By providing relief in supplement to wages, the act had the effect of lowering wages and productivity in the countryside, while also discouraging migration to the urban areas. Hence, Speenhamland became a significant obstacle to the full development of capitalism. Only the imposition of the Poor Law Reform created the mobile and compelled labor force that allowed industrial capitalism to flourish.[9]

In the analysis of Speenhamland, Polanyi rejects the view that welfare policies are external or supplementary to the economy; rather, he sees them as fundamentally constitutive of the market economy. The emphasis on the importance of Crown policies in creating national markets or on the centrality of welfare policies for creating labor markets is aimed at demonstrating that the economy is not an autonomous entity but that it has always been profoundly shaped by state action.

As to the logic of the economy, Polanyi's analysis is more implicit than explicit. Polanyi did insist that the nineteenth-century ideal of a self-regulating market was utopian, in the sense of being unachievable. He argued that if markets were left to themselves, they would quickly destroy human society and the natural environment. In pursuit of short-term gains, entrepreneurs would exploit the labor force so brutally that it would not be able to reproduce itself, they would devastate the environment, and they would destroy the trust necessary for a system of contracts to survive. While longer-term considerations might lead individual capitalists to oppose such actions, the pressures of a competitive market would quickly force even the most enlightened either to engage in such destructive practices or to risk bankruptcy. The only alternative is the imposition of regulations by the state that would place legal limits binding on all entrepreneurs.[10] For Polanyi, the classical example of such regulations were the Factory Acts that were passed very soon after the Poor Law Reform.[11] The Factory Acts were the first step of what Polanyi terms the protective countermovement—the movement to preserve human society from the devastation caused by the self-regulating market.

The implicit argument is that the behaviors of economic actors do not—by themselves—aggregate into a whole that is either rational or sustainable, and it is, therefore, only state action that assures a reasonable outcome. One might say that the economy has a logic that is shaped by individual pursuit of profits, but it is a semantic error to assume that this logic produces a rational or coherent outcome at the aggregate level. For example, individual employers struggle to expand output while limiting wage increases, but the result is an expansion in output without sufficient demand and the economy slips into severe depression. Only state action can redirect these economic patterns into a coherent whole.

It must be stressed that this type of argument is not the same as classical Marxist formulations. While Marx stresses the irrationality of capitalism and its tendency toward periodic crises, he emphasizes the purifying nature of those crises, reflecting his fundamental respect for the capitalist economy's capacity to regulate itself. Even in the discussion in *Capital*[12] of the importance of the Factory Acts in placing a limit on the working day and forcing employers to shift toward technological innovation, he fails to address this critical state intervention in theoretical terms.

In brief, Marx was a product of his time in perceiving economic logic as aggregating into a coherent—albeit irrational—whole without the need for state action.[13]

Recognition that economic logics by themselves do not aggregate into coherent wholes deepens the importance of the insight that the economy is never fully autonomous. It suggests that what we generally call "the economy" is always the product of a combination of state action and the logic of individual or institutional economic actors. It follows, as well, that crises or dysfunctions in "the economy" cannot be traced solely to interference with economic logics, because those economic logics have never—by themselves—produced a coherently functioning whole. Rather, one would expect to find one root of economic crises in the particular fit between economic logics and state action. In brief, instead of assuming, as does the conservative wisdom, that the problem is too much state intervention, this Polanyian view suggests that the issue is the specific structure of state intervention, with the distinct possibility that more intervention might be necessary to overcome crises.

In this view, government policies—including redistributive social policies—are not superstructures built on top of some economic base. Rather, they are constitutive of the capitalist economy—without them, there would be no functioning capitalist society. Hence, it no longer makes sense to speak of a contradiction between government policies and some essential logic of accumulation because the latter is a meaningless abstraction. Some government economic policies are more effective than others, but the explanation for the less effective ones has to be sought at a more concrete level of analysis than interference with the basic logic of the economy.

Analyzing the Diversity of Capitalist Institutional Arrangements

The diversity of the conditions under which capitalism has flourished provides considerable support for this line of argument. If the economy were autonomous and had a single logic, one would expect that there would be a very narrow range of difference in governmental policies and institutional arrangements among capitalist countries. But the reality is that capitalism flourishes in such diverse settings as Social Democratic Sweden and authoritarian South Korea. The extent of government regulation, the rates of taxation, and the nature of social policies varies across different capitalist countries far more than can be explained by different levels of development or different positions within the world economy.

The explanation for this diversity is not difficult to see. Individual capitalists tend to be opportunistic and pragmatic. While they might have a tendency to prefer the minimal state of laissez-faire ideology, they also tend to adapt to the political realities that they face. If their efforts to shape the political environment to their liking are unsuccessful, they will generally figure out ways to make profits in the new circumstances. It is precisely this adaptability of capital that makes it understandable how capitalism has flourished despite the enormous growth of the state in the twentieth century.

But while private ownership of capital is consistent with a broad range of different governmental policies, any particular set of policies must have some coherence if stable growth is to be achieved. If, for example, policies that encouraged production of consumer goods were combined with policies that restricted the growth of domestic and international markets, then one would anticipate serious problems and little growth. This idea of the need for some coherence in the institutional environment in which capitalists operate is captured in the concept of "social structures of accumulation."[14]

According to Gordon et al., each long period of capitalist expansion involves a particular set of social arrangements to sustain the dynamic of capitalist accumulation. The "social structure of accumulation" comprises particular configurations of urban growth, particular types of financial and governmental mechanisms for structuring demand, and specific ways of organizing the relations between workers and employers. It is the social structures of accumulation that assure that economic logics aggregate into a coherent and sustainable whole. As long as we remember that there is not one unique social structure of accumulation at a given moment, but multiple possibilities, then this conceptualization reinforces the Polanyian idea that one cannot simply separate out economic development from the political-economic context that makes it possible.

If, for example, we consider the experience of the Depression of the thirties in the United States, it becomes clear that a host of government policies laid the basis for a new period of capitalist expansion after World War II. The combination of social insurance programs and the extensive federal role in subsidizing suburbanization played a key role in supporting aggregate demand. Similarly, social insurance provisions and the recognition of industrial unions created the conditions for a relatively successful period of labor management relations in basic industry.

That the specific social structures of accumulation that were put in place in the thirties and forties ultimately came to grief in the sixties and seventies is not evidence that there was too much interference in the free market. Rather, social structures of accumulation are always time-limited in their effectiveness. As with the development of organisms, there is a process of growth and decay shaped by several factors. Particular patterns of social and economic development will face a law of diminishing returns—as, for example, when suburban development becomes increasingly problematic because available empty land is so far from the central city. And over an extended period of time, people will also become dissatisfied with some of the institutional arrangements that are part of particular social structures of accumulation. Industrial employees might grow restive with particular ways of organizing the workplace or a feminist movement might emerge that challenges the established place of women in the society. Finally, some of the positive synergies that occurred during the phase of expansion can turn negative under changing historical circumstances, as when a structure of accumulation that relied heavily on cheap energy faces systematic oil price rises.[15] Through these dynamics, particular social structures of accumulation become dysfunctional—they produce slower growth and more political-economic difficulties. The combination of vested interests and a general resistance to change makes it unlikely that decaying social structures of accumulation will be effectively reformed. Usually, dramatic political-economic deterioration is necessary before forces are mobilized to establish new social structures of accumulation.

In short, the political-economic difficulties that both leftists and rightists have identified as a product of the conflict between state intervention and the logic of the economy can better be understood as the result of decaying social structures of accumulation. This latter diagnosis leads to very different prescriptions. Whereas the conventional view sees the necessity of a reduction in the government's role in the economy, and particularly a sharp reduction in its efforts to redistribute income, a focus on decaying social structures of accumulation suggests that an expanded role of the state, and particularly an increased role of the state in redistributing income to the less well-off, could be part of the new social structures of accumulation. Whereas redistributive social policies were central to the last period of expansion because of the tendency of the society's capacity to produce to outstrip market-generated demand, it seems logical to suggest that they could be even more central to new social structures of accumulation in a period when computerization has the potential to expand output far faster than employment.[16]

The International Dimension

However, any argument that stresses the multiplicity of possibilities for organizing particular capitalist societies must deal with the issue of the world economy. As was noted earlier, the rediscovery of the ways in which the international economy constrains national choices played a key role in the revival of the economistic fallacy. These constraints have been seen as part of the fundamental economic structure of capitalism; according to this view, they cannot be altered without significant costs in reduced efficiency. I argue to the contrary that these constraints are actually political and ideological; they have little to do with efficiency and they can be altered without significant efficiency costs.

The pressures of the world economy fall into two categories—the impact of competition in international trade and the impact of international capital movements. While there are obvious interactions between these dimensions, they can be discussed separately.

The standard argument that is made about international trade is simply an extension of the argument that wage levels are critical to international competitiveness. It is argued that a country that has more generous social policies will be forced to have higher tax rates to finance these benefits. If these higher taxes fall on firms that produce products that are internationally traded, the firms will be at a competitive disadvantage in relation to firms from countries with lower taxes and less generous social policies.

One problem with this argument, as with many popular economic ideas, is that it traces out only one side of a causal sequence. The positive effects on economic efficiency of social policies are completely neglected, even though it is well known that higher levels of health, education, and general welfare are associated with higher levels of output per employee in manufacturing.[17] Sweden, for example, was able to "afford" more developed social welfare spending through most of the post–World War II period while maintaining a very strong position in international trade. The reason was that Swedish industry was able to use the high-quality "human capital" in the society to produce goods that were internationally competitive by virtue of their technological sophistication and quality.

Furthermore, the experience of the United States in terms of medical care suggests that the failure of the government to take an active role in delivering social services can be even more damaging to international competitiveness. It is well known that health-care costs for employees is one of the largest expense items for American automobile firms.[18] It seems highly likely that had the United States instead created a system of national health insurance, the burden on industries in international competition would be less great than it is now.

The conventional argument also forgets that productivity gains in internationally competitive production are closely linked to overall rates of economic growth.[19] If redistributive social policies contribute to rapid economic growth in a particular country, it is possible that that country's industries will improve their international competitiveness more rapidly than firms in another country that remains bogged down in slow growth.[20]

Above all, this conventional wisdom vastly exaggerates the importance of wage costs—both direct and indirect—in determining international competitiveness. Tyson and Zysman stress the possibility that

comparative advantage in modern mass-production sectors will hinge not on wage rates but on the operational control of complex systems that reduce per-unit labor costs substantially. In this regard, comparing Japanese labor requirements with U.S. labor requirements for production in a wide range of sectors is quite sobering. Also sobering is the fact that in technology-intensive products, the U.S. trade deficit with Japan increased from $2 billion in 1970 to $13.5 billion by the end of the 1970's.[21]

In short, in advanced economies, the international competitiveness of a country's products is influenced by many factors, including a broad range of government policies. And in the face of adversity, there are strategies to pursue for improved trade performance other than reductions in wages, benefits, and government welfare expenditures.

Arguments about capital movements tend to play a more central role in the conventional wisdom because the impact of capital movements can be much more immediate and dramatic than changes in a country's competitiveness in international trade. For example, a country that institutes generous social policies that require higher taxes on business or that imposes stricter regulations on business than its neighbors will likely experience significant capital flight. Not only will international capital be less likely to invest in such a country, but domestic capital is likely to seek safer and more lucrative opportunities abroad. In its mild form, such net capital outflows can lead to a domestic economic slowdown, a negative balance of payments, and a deterioration in the value of the country's currency. This devalued currency, in turn, means a relative reduction in the citizenry's standard of living. When capital outflows accelerate, the result can be even more serious economic turmoil that usually can force either a change of government or a change of governmental policy.

For adherents of the economistic fallacy, these consequences flow directly from the negative efficiency consequences of the original governmental actions. The increase in taxes or the increase in regulations will impose such burdens on firms that they will not be able to achieve adequate profit levels, so that they have no choice but to shift to foreign investments. It is here, also, that the trade arguments are invoked. Because it is assumed that the government moves will assure a deterioration in the international competitiveness of domestic industry, it would make little sense for a shrewd businessperson to invest there rather than abroad.

But with investments, as with trade, tha actual effects of any particular set of governmental initiatives are extremely difficult to predict. Again, redistributive policies might strengthen the domestic market and create all kinds of new investment opportunities. Forms of regulation might spawn new industries, as in pollution control, and even contribute to greater consumer and business confidence. One thinks, for example, of the negative investment climate created by proximity to toxic waste dumps.

The classic example of this unpredictability were Roosevelt's New Deal reforms. While the business community was almost unanimous in its condemnation of Roosevelt's initiatives on the grounds that he was destroying the conditions for an efficient capitalist order, the reality was that the reforms created the conditions for the great post–World War II economic expansion. There was, to say the least, a large gap between what was perceived to be efficient in the short term and what was efficient over the long term.

The point, however, is that the actual effects of more generous social policies on the country's international trade and investment position are basically irrelevant. Usually domestic and international business will not wait to see whether the policies strengthen or weaken the balance of payments; they will proceed immediately as though the impact of the policies will be negative. In most circumstances, they are then able to make the prediction into a self-fulfilling prophecy. If producers have predicted that higher taxes will be inflationary, they can then prove the accuracy of this forecast by accelerating the pace of price rises. If they have warned of negative effects on the trade balance, these too can be produced by "leads and lags" in payments that are justified through the imminence of a devaluation. If business has warned of an outflow of capital and a reduction in international investment, these too can be arranged by signaling that the business climate has turned bad under the new government.

The claim, however, is that each of these prophecies is soundly based in an economic theory that emphasizes the international trade and capital constraints on domestic economic actions. The reality is that both the self-fulfilling prophecies and the economic theory must be understood for what they are—stratagems in an ongoing political struggle. The business community tends to oppose redistributive social policies and higher taxes for very simple reasons. Redistributive policies can improve the bargaining power of certain sectors of the labor force with a possible negative effect on profit levels. Similarly, higher taxes appear to threaten profit levels and the income of the wealthy. For any particular firm, the impact on profits is not inevitable—it simply means that greater effort might be necessary to generate the same amount of profit. But an inconvenience for particular capitalists is not the same as impairing the logic of capitalism. The gap between system logic and short-term self-interest emerges when capitalists who are "inconvenienced" by various types of government intervention are forced to be more aggressive and imaginative in finding ways to turn a profit, thus contributing to the efficiency with which the society produces.[22]

But in opposing these types of measures, the business community uses its two complementary weapons—the self-fulfilling prophecy and the claims of economic theory. If business simply warned on the basis of theory that a particular policy would have disastrous consequences without being able to confirm its own predictions, it would not be taken seriously. Alternatively, if the business community fulfilled its own prophecies without the support of a persuasive theory that explained why those outcomes were inevitable, its maneuvers would likely be seen as obvious power plays. And there would be the opportunity to respond to such power plays in the realm of politics. In short, the special potency of economic theory is that it gives business arguments that appear to lie outside of politics and that preclude, in advance, political responses.

To be sure, even if the veil of economic ideology were stripped away, governments would be able to respond effectively to some, but not all, of the self-fulfilling prophecies. If business raises prices to fulfill a prediction of inflation, price controls could be imposed or a tax incentive scheme could be enacted that rewarded those firms that limited their price increases. Through such measures a government could gain time to demonstrate that the actual economic effects of its policies are positive. However, if capital flight and massive disinvestment are predicted, it is difficult—in most cases—for a single government, acting alone, to respond effectively. Even if capital controls are imposed to slow the flight of domestic capital, it is fairly certain that there will be a net and sizable loss of international capital, which can represent a crippling blow to a government's prospects.

However, much depends at this point on which government is involved. If we are discussing the United States government, it is difficult to foresee conditions under which it would be unable to pursue alternative policy directions because of the pressures of flight capital. Even in a period of significant domestic reforms, the United States would still appear a safer haven for international capital than most other places in the world. In addition, the United States has the capacity to mobilize its allies and international institutions such as the IMF to help it resist speculative pressures against the dollar. Moreover, the United States has on earlier occasions successfully controlled the outflow of capital by its own international banks and multinational corporations.[23]

The real problem comes with less powerful countries who find their domestic plans foiled by international capital movements. But it is in these cases that most analysts make the mistake of assuming that the free movement of international capital is a fundamental and necessary part of a capitalist world economy. Even without returning to the age of mercantilism, it must be recalled that capitalism flourished at the domestic level through the two World Wars despite substantial controls over international capital movements. Moreover, the early plans of J.M. Keynes and Harry Dexter White for the postwar international monetary order contemplated substantial controls over international capital mobility. White, in particular, feared that the free movement of capital could doom efforts within particular countries to pursue full-employment policies, so he proposed international arrangements through which other countries would agree to repatriate flight capital that left a country in violation of its domestic capital controls.[24] While these plans were not implemented, their demise reflected the political balance of forces at the time—particularly, the power of internationally oriented business in the United States—rather than the fundamental logic of the system. Moreover, despite the triumph of those forces favoring the free movement of capital, it was not until 1958 that most European countries restored the convertibility of their currencies. Hence, much of the postwar recovery of European capitalism occurred under a system of controls over the outflow of capital.

In fact, the experience of the past twenty years suggests that too much freedom for international capital movements is irrational even on capitalist terms. The huge quantities of "stateless" capital in the Eurodollar market that quickly shift from one currency to another have created turmoil in the currency markets and have repeatedly interfered with the effectiveness of national economic policies. And on numerous occasions, major countries have found it necessary to peg interest rates at excessively high rates—with the resulting slowdown in growth and increases in unemployment—simply because of the pressures of international capital markets. While it was once hoped that the shift in the seventies from fixed exchange rates to flexible rates would make possible international monetary stability even with these massive pools of speculative capital, the experience of the past ten years has demonstrated that floating rates have not solved the problem.

Moreover, the free movement of international capital has also created significant problems of instability in international banking. During the seventies, the international banks fell over each other making excessive loans to Third World countries creating the present debt crisis. And there is continuing fear of a spreading international financial crisis resulting from the failure of a subsidiary or offshore bank that is subject to little or no regulation by national banking authorities.

These problems have created strong pressures for increased regulation of international banking and even some establishment figures have made policy proposals designed to discourage speculative capital flows.[25] The point is that the degree to which the international economic order regulates and restricts international capital flows is itself a matter of political choice, and the efficiency arguments for complete freedom of capital movement are deeply flawed.[26] Hence, it is a political possibility that the international monetary order be reformed to limit speculative capital flows or to establish means to offset such flows.[27] Such reforms would result in a reduction in the political leverage that comes from the threat or reality of massive capital flight. Governments would then have expanded possibilities for pursuing alternative domestic policies.

In sum, the international argument has the same flaws as the domestic one—it mistakes the political preferences of an extremely powerful interest group for the fundamental logic of an economic system. In doing so, it simply reinforces the political strength of business by denying the real political choices that are available for organizing the international economic order and national political economies.

Conclusion

The issue of whether one sees the constraints on domestic freedom of action as economic or political has important practical consequences. If one accepts the position that reforms such as the expansion of social welfare actually interfere with the fundamental logic of a capitalist order, it becomes very difficult to defend those reforms from conservative attack. One can argue that over the long term the only way to protect those reforms is through a break with the capitalist system, but this does not provide much strategic guidance in the short term. On the contrary, since the left is agreeing that these reforms contribute to the problems of the economy—inflation, slow growth, unemployment—it follows that the citizenry is acting rationally when it supports the right-wing attacks on the reforms. In a context in which the immediate transition to socialism is not possible, it follows that the best way to enhance the collective welfare is by trading off the reforms for the promise of faster economic growth.

This is, I would argue, what has happened in the past decade in the United States. While one can easily exaggerate the influence of leftist ideas, the wide dissemination of the accumulation versus legitimation perspective within academia and activist circles has had the effect of persuading key groups of the futility of resisting the Reaganite attacks on the all-too-limited American welfare state. The very notion that Reagan's policies were necessary for American capitalism had the effect of disempowering those who were in a position to resist those policies.

If, on the contrary, the left had stressed that the constraints are political and that there are multiple ways to make a capitalist economy work, the possibilities for effective resistance would have been greater. Rather than perceiving Reaganite policies as reflecting some economic necessity, it would have been possible to formulate alternative policies for responding to the economic problems. With such alternative frameworks, it might then be possible to build broader political alliances while also empowering the victims of the cutbacks to fight both to protect earlier gains and to win new concessions.

Because the struggle to protect the remnants of the welfare state continues, it is not too late to break the chains of the economistic fallacy. The costs are slight and the benefits could be enormous.

Notes and Index

Notes

CHAPTER 1
Acknowledgments: I am grateful to Gene Burns, G. William Domhoff, Carole Joffe, Frances Fox Piven, and David Plotke for comments on earlier drafts of this chapter.

1. Lawrence Goodwyn, *The Populist Moment* (New York: Oxford, 1978). On one strand of distrust of business interests in academic thought, see Richard Hofstadter, *The Progressive Historians* (New York: Knopf, 1968).
2. Phyllis Schlafly, *A Choice Not an Echo* (Alton, Ill.: Pere Marquette Press, 1964); Gary Allen, *None Dare Call it Conspiracy* (Rossmoor, Calif.: Concord Press, 1971).
3. David Riesman, Nathan Glazer, and Reuel Denney, *The Lonely Crowd* (Garden City, N.Y.: Doubleday, 1953), 246–258; Robert Dahl, *Who Governs?* (New Haven: Yale University Press, 1961); Arnold Rose, *The Power Structure* (New York: Oxford, 1967).
4. Todd Gitlin, "Local Pluralism as Theory and Ideology," *Studies on the Left* 5, 3 (1965): 21–45; Shin'ya Ono, "The Limits of Bourgeois Pluralism," *Studies on the Left* 5, 3 (1965): 46–72. These were followed by G. William Domhoff's widely read *Who Rules America?* (Englewood Cliffs, N.J.: Prentice-Hall, 1967).
5. For a classic but only half-serious analysis of this group, see Richard A. Rovere, *The American Establishment and Other Reports* (New York: Harcourt, Brace, 1962), 3–21.
6. From the perspective of the 1980s, the Nixon administration appears quite liberal in maintaining low levels of unemployment, in advancing important initiatives in the area of environmental regulation, and in increasing Social Security payments. Nevertheless, it must be recalled that Nixon quickly moved to dismantle many of the War on Poverty programs, ending a period in which it seemed that the problems of black poverty would be addressed through reform efforts.
7. One solution was to define Nixon as representing Southern Rim capitalists who were Corporate Conservatives who then came into conflict with the traditional Eastern Corporate Liberal wing of the capitalist class. See, for example, Carl

Oglesby, *The Yankee and Cowboy War* (Kansas City, Mo.: Sheed Andrews and McNeel, 1976). Such formulations, however, created as many problems as they solved.

8. Nicos Poulantzas, "The Problem of the Capitalist State," *New Left Review* 58 (Nov.–Dec., 1969): 67–78.

9. Poulantzas' 1969 article as quoted by Martin Carnoy, *The State and Political Theory* (Princeton: Princeton University Press, 1984), 106.

10. G. William Domhoff, "Corporate-Liberal Theory and the Social Security Act: A Chapter in the Sociology of Knowledge," *Politics & Society*, forthcoming.

11. Examples of work influenced by Poulantzas include Isaac Balbus, "Ruling Elite Theory vs. Marxist Class Analysis," *Monthly Review* 23, 1 (1971): 36–46; David Gold, Clarence Lo, and Erik Olin Wright, "Recent Developments in Marxist Theories of the State," *Monthly Review* 27, 5, 6 (1975): 29–43, 36–51.

12. Adam Przeworski, "The Ethical Materialism of John Roemer," *Politics & Society* 11, 3 (1982): 289–313.

13. Ralph Miliband, "The Capitalist State: Reply to Nicos Poulantzas, " *New Left Review* 59 (1970).

14. Carnoy, *The State and Political Theory*, 106.

15. Key works of the business dominance perspective include the many works of G. William Domhoff, especially *The Higher Circles* (New York: Random House, 1970); *The Powers that Be* (New York: Random House, 1978); *Who Rules America Now?* (Englewood Cliffs, N.J.: Prentice-Hall, 1983). Significant recent contributions include Michael Useem, *The Inner Circle* (New York: Oxford, 1984); Beth Mintz and Michael Schwartz, *The Power Structure of American Business* (Chicago: University of Chicago Press, 1985); Thomas Ferguson and Joel Rogers, *Right Turn: The Decline of the Democrats and the Future of American Politics* (New York: Hill and Wang, 1986).

16. See, for example, G. William Domhoff, "Social Clubs, Policy-Planning Groups, and Corporations: A Network Study of Ruling-Class Cohesiveness," *Insurgent Sociologist* 5, 3 (spring 1975): 173–184, and *The Powers That Be*, 61–127; Mintz and Schwartz, *Power Structure*; Useem, *Inner Circle*.

17. Leonard Silk and David Vogel, *Ethics and Profits* (New York: Simon and Schuster, 1976); Francis X. Sutton et al., *The American Business Creed* (Cambridge, Mass.: Harvard University Press, 1956), especially chap. 9.

18. As I argue in Chapter 5, this question of linkage grows ever more important as the role of the state expands. The irony is that the broader the scope of state intervention, the more that business needs the "free market" ideology.

19. Karl Polanyi, *The Great Transformation* (Boston: Beacon, 1957 [1944]). For more on Polanyi's contribution, see Fred Block and Margaret Somers, "Beyond the Economistic Fallacy: The Holistic Social Science of Karl Polanyi," in *Vision and Method in Historical Sociology*, ed. Theda Skocpol (New York: Cambridge University Press, 1984), 47–84.

20. Karl Marx, *Capital*, vol. 1, (New York: Dutton, 1930), chaps. 8, 15.

21. See Fred Block, "Rethinking the Political Economy of the Welfare State," in *The Mean Season: The Attack on the Welfare State*, ed. Fred Block, Richard A. Cloward, Barbara Ehrenreich, and Frances Fox Piven (New York: Pantheon, 1987).

22. See Daniel Sipe, "A Moment of the State: the Enactment of the National Labor Relations Act, 1935," unpublished Ph.D. dissertation, Department of History, University of Pennsylvania, 1981.

23. Sometimes business dominance analysts use an even looser criterion to make their case—the involvement of key business representatives in the negotiation of a particular piece of legislation or of a particular executive branch policy. But such involvement proves very little about business dominance. It could be that the involvement is simply a form of damage control; businesspeople are trying to win small concessions on policy proposals that they oppose but are unable to block.

24. To his credit, Domhoff has devoted an article to one such negative case—the Wagner Act, which established the contemporary framework of collective bargaining, "The Wagner Act and Theories of the State: A New Analysis Based on Class-Segment Theory," *Political Power and Social Theory*, forthcoming.

25. For recent reviews of the literature on state theory, see Carnoy, *State and Political Theory*; Bob Jessop, *The Capitalist State* (New York: New York University Press, 1982); Robert R. Alford and Roger Friedland, *Powers of Theory* (Cambridge: Cambridge University Press, 1985).

26. The debate over the origins of the Social Security Act is a good illustration of these problems. The debate began with Jill Quadagno, "Welfare Capitalism and the Social Security Act of 1935," *American Sociological Review* 49 (Oct. 1984): 632–647. It continues with Theda Skocpol and Edwin Amenta, "Did Capitalists Shape Social Security?" *American Sociological Review* 50 (Aug. 1985): 572–575; Jill Quadagno, "Two Models of Welfare State Development: Reply to Skocpol and Amenta," *American Sociological Review* 50 (Aug. 1985): 575–578; G. William Domhoff, "On 'Welfare Capitalism and the Social Security Act of 1935,'" *American Sociological Review* 51 (June 1986): 445–446; G. William Domhoff, "'Corporate Liberal' Theory and the Social Security Acts."

27. The obvious exception are international bankers who have a substantial and immediate stake in international monetary issues. For the general argument about the exceptionality of international monetary issues, see Stepen D. Krasner, "United States Commercial and Monetary Policy: Unravelling the Paradox of External Strength and Internal Weakness," in *Between Power and Plenty*, ed. Peter J. Katzenstein (Madison: University of Wisconsin Press, 1978), 51–87.

28. It is entirely possible, therefore, that a business dominance framework is more successful at making sense of politics the further one moves away from the national level. Harvey Molotch has written persuasively of the role of real estate dominated growth coalitions in urban politics. See Harvey Molotch, "The City as a Growth Machine," *American Journal of Sociology* 82, 2 (1976): 309–330; "Growth Elite Constraints and Strategies," in *Business Elites and Urban Development*, ed. Scott Cummings (New York: Macmillan, forthcoming).

29. David Plotke, Ernesto Laclau, and Chantal Mouffe, "Recasting Marxism: Hegemony and New Political Movements," *Socialist Review* 66 (Nov.–Dec. 1982): 92–113; David Plotke, "The Democratic Political Order, 1932–1972," unpublished Ph.D. dissertation, Department of Sociology, University of California, Berkeley, 1985; Ernesto Laclau and Chantal Mouffe, *Hegemony and Socialist Strategy* (London: New Left Books, 1985).

30. Adam Przeworski, "Proletariat into a Class: The Process of Class Formation from Karl Kautsky's *The Class Struggle* to Recent Controversies," *Politics & Society* 7, 4 (1977): 343–401.

31. A similar emphasis on the indeterminacy of social outcomes has been developed by scholars in the Critical Legal Studies movement. I have been influenced particularly by Duncan Kennedy, "The Role of Law in Economic

Thought: Essays on the Fetishism of Commodities," *American University Law Review* 34, 4 (summer 1985): 939–1001.

32. Among her major pieces of work are *States and Social Revolution* (Cambridge: Cambridge University Press, 1979); "Political Response to Capitalist Crisis: Neo-Marxist Theories of the State and the Case of the New Deal," *Politics & Society* 10, 1 (1980): 155–201; Theda Skocpol and Kenneth Finegold, "State Capacity and Economic Intervention in the Early New Deal," *Political Science Quarterly* 97 (1982): 255–278; Peter B. Evans, Deitrich Rueschemeyer, and Theda Skocpol, *Bringing the State Back In* (Cambridge: Cambridge University Press, 1985); Margaret Weir, Ann Shola Orloff, and Theda Skocpol, *The Politics of Social Policy in the United States* (Princeton: Princeton University Press, forthcoming).

33. Margaret Weir and Theda Skocpol, "State Structures and the Possibilities for 'Keynesian' Responses to the Great Depression in Sweden, Britain and the United States," in *Bringing the State Back In*, ed. Evans et al., 107–163.

34. Skocpol has indicated a recognition of this problem by shifting from the term state-centered to the term polity-centered.

35. A classic instance is John Zysman's study of how the French state's interventions in the French electronic industry were counterproductive, *Political Strategies for Industrial Order* (Berkeley: University of California Press, 1977).

36. Charles Lindblom, *Politics and Markets* (New York: Basic Books, 1977).

37. Stephen Krasner, *Defending the National Interest* (Princeton: Princeton University Press, 1978).

38. The invisibility of these arrangements is by no means universal. There are individuals who are able to see and analyze these hidden relations of power, but the problem is that such analyses are unlikely to be widely influential at the time that they are produced.

39. Barbara Ehrenreich, "Life without Father: Reconsidering Socialist-Feminist Theory," *Socialist Review* 73 (Jan.–Feb. 1984): 48–57.

40. C. Wright Mills, *The Power Elite* (New York: Oxford, 1956).

41. For a sampling of responses, see G. William Domhoff and Hoyte B. Ballard, *C. Wright Mills and the Power Elite* (Boston: Beacon, 1968).

42. See, for example, James O'Connor, *The Fiscal Crisis of the State* (New York: St. Martin's, 1973).

43. The records of both the Reagan and Thatcher administrations in economic policy are mixed, and the evaluation of their relative successes is itself an issue of considerable political debate and conflict. See Joel Krieger, *Reagan, Thatcher and the Politics of Decline* (New York: Oxford, 1986), especially chap. 8. However, in comparison with the 1950s and 1960s, it seems clear that the 1980s have been a more troubled period for macroeconomic policies.

44. Peter J. Katzenstein, *Small States in World Markets* (Ithaca: Cornell University Press, 1985); John H. Goldthorpe, ed., *Order and Conflict in Contemporary Capitalism* (Oxford: Clarendon Press, 1984).

45. Chalmers Johnson, *MITI and the Japanese Miracle* (Stanford: Stanford University Press, 1982).

46. Mark Kesselman, "Capitalist Austerity versus Socialist 'Rigueur': Does It Make a Difference? The Case of France," *New Political Science* 12 (summer 1983): 37–55.

47. Postbureaucratic forms of work organization refers to efforts to overcome the hierarchical chain of command and narrow specialization of classic bureaucracies. These trends are analyzed in Chapters 6 and 8.

48. The account of postindustrial transition in Chapter 6 revolves around the

emergence of new productive forces, and it uses the classical Marxist schema of the conflict between productive forces and social relations. This is a more deterministic and evolutionary version of the argument than I would make today. Although we argued in that essay that it will take conscious political efforts to forge a postindustrial society, the emphasis on the importance of politics is undercut by the seemingly inevitable dynamic of emergent productive forces.

The determinism of the argument can be stripped away by shifting the analytic focus to the concepts that are used to order our experiences. The concept of "industrial society" is a way of thinking about how different social institutions and social practices fit together; it represents the society's understanding of itself. The problem is that a number of empirically observable social trends that accelerated beginning in the 1960s were radically inconsistent with the concept of "industrial society." This began a period of postindustrial transition in which the society struggled to develop a new concept of itself, a new way to create some order out of the complexity of social institutions and social practices.

49. Computed from 1984 Personal Consumer Expenditures, see Block, "Rethinking the Political Economy of Welfare."

50. This point is made clearly in Goran Therborn, *Why Some Peoples Are More Unemployed Than Others* (London: Verso, 1986).

51. The emphasis on debureaucratizing the state is a political alternative to the emphasis in Chapter 5 on taking advantage of the tensions between state managers and capitalists. Moreover, from my current perspective, the argument of Chapter 5 overstates the imminent danger to capitalists of a further expansion of the state's regulatory power.

52. Warren G. Bennis and Philip E. Slater, *The Temporary Society* (New York: Harper and Row, 1968); F. E. Emery and E. L. Trist, *Towards a Social Ecology* (New York: Plenum, 1975); Larry Hirschhorn, *Beyond Mechanization* (Cambridge, Mass.: MIT Press, 1984).

53. For a powerful critique of the welfare system along these lines that proposes a debureaucratizing alternative, see William H. Simon, "Legality, Bureaucracy and Class in the Welfare System," *Yale Law Journal* 92, 7 (June 1983): 1198–1269. For a case study of how debureaucratized workers are indispensable to the production of another kind of social service, see Carole Joffe, *The Regulation of Sexuality* (Philadelphia: Temple University Press, 1986).

54. Steven Kelman, *Regulating America, Regulating Sweden* (Cambridge, Mass.: MIT Press, 1981).

55. This example makes clear that the National Labor Relations Act represented an early experiment with this new model. The federal government by granting union recognition provided resources and formal legal protection to a nonstate entity that was then able to pursue a general social interest—more balanced relations between workers and management. However, the courts and the National Labor Relations Board pursued a procedural rather than a substantive conception of the role of government regulation, with the result that much of the radical potential of the legislation was lost. See Karl Klare, "Judicial Deradicalization of the Wagner Act and the Origins of Modern Legal Consciousness, 1937–1941," *Minnesota Law Review*, 62 (1978): 265–339.

56. Frances Fox Piven and Richard A. Cloward, *Regulating the Poor* (New York: Random House, 1971).

57. The Swedish Active Labor Market Policy that emphasizes retraining efforts and improved linkage of individuals to job vacancies would fit within the framework of debureaucratization. See Rudolf Meidner, "Sweden: Approaching

the Limits of Active Labour Market Policy," in *Public Policies to Combat Unemployment in a Period of Economic Stagnation*, ed. K. Gerlach, W. Peters, and W. Sengenberger (Frankfurt: Campus Verlag, 1984), 247–265.

58. Albert Hirschman, *Shifting Involvements* (Princeton: Princeton University Press, 1982).

59. For the tensions within the tradition, see Alvin Gouldner, *The Two Marxisms* (New York: Seabury, 1980); Melvin Rader, *Marx's Interpretation of History* (New York: Oxford, 1979).

60. The term is from Dick Howard and Karl E. Klare, *The Unknown Dimension: European Marxism since Lenin* (New York: Basic Books, 1972).

61. "Transcend" is the inadequate English translation of the German *Aufhebung* which conveys the ideas of preservation, of destruction, and of moving to a higher level.

CHAPTER 2

Acknowledgment: I would like to acknowledge the assistance of Carole Joffe and Sheldon Messinger in the preparation of this article. An earlier version of this paper was given as part of the Political Economy of the World System program at the American Sociological Association meetings, August 1975.

1. Arthur M. Schlesinger, Jr., *The Age of Jackson* (Boston: Little Brown, 1946), 505.

2. Some examples of work strongly influenced by corporate liberal theory by subject: Welfare and antipoverty programs—Frances Fox Piven and Richard A. Cloward, *Regulating the Poor* (New York: Pantheon, 1971); Robert Allen, *Black Awakening in Capitalist America* (Garden City, N.Y.: Doubleday, 1970). Education—Samuel Bowles and Herbert Gintis, "Capitalist Education in the United States," *Socialist Revolution* (July–Sept. 1975): 101–138; David Cohen and Marvin Lazerson, "Education and the Corporate Order," *Socialist Revolution* (Mar.–Apr. 1972): 47–72; Michael Katz, *Class, Bureaucracy, and Schools* (New York: Praeger, 1971). Social services—Jeffrey H. Galper, *The Politics of Social Services* (Englewood Cliffs, N.J.: Prentice-Hall, 1975). Deviance—Anthony M. Platt, *The Child Savers* (Chicago: University of Chicago Press, 1969). In this paper, I am abstracting a common set of themes from a variety of studies. Most of the authors avoid the pitfalls that I am describing when they analyze specific policies. However, they have contributed to a way of thinking that, I would argue, leads to problematic conclusions.

3. An inverted functionalism because it self-consciously rejects the conservatism implicit in much traditional functionalist analysis.

4. Gabriel Kolko, *Triumph of Conservatism* (1963; reprint, Chicago: Quadrangle, 1967). Kolko had first developed his argument in a study of the railroad industry, published as *Railroads and Regulations, 1877–1916* (Princeton: Princeton University Press, 1965).

5. James Weinstein, *The Corporate Ideal in the Liberal State: 1900–1918* (Boston: Beacon, 1968). Weinstein was clearly influenced by William Appleman Williams, *The Tragedy of American Diplomacy* (1959; reprint, New York: Delta, 1962) and *The Contours of American History* (1961; reprint, Chicago: Quadrangle, 1966), who had already laid the basis for the new theory in his own work on American foreign policy. Much of the early development and elaboration of the theory of corporate liberalism went on in the pages of *Studies on the Left* throughout the early sixties.

For a selection of some of the major articles, see James Weinstein and David Eakins, *For a New America* (New York: Vintage, 1970).

6. Kirkpatrick Sale, *SDS* (New York: Vintage, 1974).

7. Carl Oglesby and Richard Shaull, *Containment and Change* (New York: Macmillan, 1967).

8. See, for example, Gabriel Kolko, *The Politics of War* (New York: Random House, 1968), and Gabriel Kolko and Joyce Kolko, *The Limits of Power* (New York: Harper and Row, 1972).

9. The relationship between the theory of corporate liberalism and Marxism is complex, especially because there are so many varieties of Marxism. The theory of corporate liberalism originated as a critique of both liberalism and the orthodox Marxism of the Communist International. Gradually, the theory of corporate liberalism has been incorporated into much contemporary Neo-Marxist discourse. I am arguing that this incorporation is harmful to the attempt to construct a Neo-Marxist theory of capitalism. Finally, I would argue that the theory of corporate liberalism directly conflicts with Marx's analysis of politics in *The Eighteenth Brumaire of Louis Bonaparte* (1852; reprint, New York: International, 1963).

10. Alan Wolfe, *The Seamy Side of Democracy* (New York: David McKay, 1973).

11. Steve Weissman, "Cowboys and Crooks," in *Big Brother and the Holding Company*, ed. Steve Weissman (Palo Alto: Ramparts, 1974); Kirkpatrick Sale, "The World Behind Watergate," in *Big Brother*, ed. Weissman, 277–296.

12. Stephen Johnson, "How the West Was Won: Last Shootout for the Yankee-Cowboy Theory," *Insurgent Sociologist* (Winter 1975): 61–93; Weissman, "Cowboys and Crooks."

13. James O'Connor, *The Fiscal Crisis of the State* (New York: St. Martin's, 1973).

14. See, for example, Fred Block, "Watergate," *Socialist Revolution* (May–June 1973): 3–17.

15. O'Connor, *Fiscal Crisis*; Stanley Aronowitz, "Modernizing Capitalism," *Social Policy* (May–June 1975): 19–24; James Crotty and Raford Boddy, "Who Will Plan the Planned Economy?" *The Progressive* (Feb. 1975): 15–19.

16. Robert Heilbroner, "The American Plan," *New York Times Magazine* (Jan. 25, 1976): 35–40; *Business Week*, "A New Push Behind Economic Planning" (March 10, 1975): 21–22.

17. I have monitored the *Wall Street Journal* and *Business Week* for the past three years for such evidence.

18. Heilbroner, "The American Plan."

19. "Murphy of G.M. Lambastes National Economic Plan," *New York Times* (June 24, 1975).

20. "Bridling at the FTC's Product Line Reports," *Business Week* (Aug. 11, 1975): 17–18.

21. William Nordhaus, "The Falling Share of Profits," *Brookings Papers on Economic Activity* 1 (1974): 169–208.

22. Ingrid Lehmann, "Corporate Capitalism and the Liberal State: The Kolko-Weinstein thesis," *Kapitalistate* (spring 1975): 159–166.

23. Murray Edelman, *The Symbolic Uses of Politics* (Urbana: University of Illinois Press, 1964), 24.

24. See, for example, Robert Engler, *The Politics of Oil* (Chicago: University of Chicago Press, 1967), 319–323.

25. Aaron B. Wildavsky, *The Politics of the Budgetary Process* (Boston: Little Brown, 1964).

26. The centrality of this autonomy to the modern corporation is stressed by John Kenneth Galbraith, *The New Industrial State* (Boston: Houghton Mifflin, 1967).

27. Richard Barnet and Ronald Muller, *Global Reach* (New York: Simon and Schuster, 1974), 258–259.

28. There is some evidence that the French planning process, which has often been seen as a model of capitalist planning, has been undermined recently by the global ambitions of French corporations. Some of these corporations grew to their present size and strength through the active cooperation of the planning authorities. But once these firms are large enough to become multinationals, they lose interest in a planning process that is national in its focus, Charles-Albert Michalet, "France," in *Big Business and the State*, ed. Raymond Vernon (Cambridge, Mass.: Harvard University Press, 1974), 105–125.

29. By conservative reform, I mean reforms that strengthen a system of production for private profit.

CHAPTER 3
Acknowledgement: In addition to the *SR* collectives, I would like to thank the McNeil Marxist Group, Clarence Lo, and Theda Skocpol for their help on this article.

1. For two surveys of recent Marxist work on the state—one polemical and the other dispassionate—see Alan Wolfe, "New Directions in the Marxist Theory of Politics," *Politics and Society* 4, 2 (1974), and David Gold, Clarence Y. H. Lo, and Erik Olin Wright, "Recent Developments in Marxist Theories of the Capitalist State," parts 1 and 2, *Monthly Review* (Oct. and Nov. 1975).

2. For critiques of such interpretations of Watergate, see Steve Weissman, "Cowboys and Crooks," in *Big Brother and the Holding Company: The World Behind Watergate*, ed. Steve Weissman (Palo Alto: Ramparts, 1974), 297–310; and Stephen Johnson, "How the West Was Won: Last Shootout for the Yankee-Cowboy Theory," *Insurgent Socialist* (Winter 1975): 61–93.

3. My analysis has been influenced by the arguments of Nicos Poulantzas, particularly in his "Problems of the Capitalist State," *New Left Review* 58 (Nov.–Dec. 1969). However, my analysis differs from Poulantzas' in two important respects. He tends to attribute consciousness to particular fractions of the ruling class and he fails to explain adequately the mechanisms by which the state is structurally a capitalist state. In this regard, my position is closer to that of Claus Offe in a number of articles, including "Structural Problems of the Capitalist State," in *German Political Studies*, ed. Klaus von Beyme (Beverly Hills, Calif.: Sage Publications, 1976); and Claus Offe and Volker Ronge, "Theses on the Theory of the State," *New German Critique* 6 (fall 1975).

4. By "rationalization" and "capitalist reform," I am referring primarily to the use of the state in new ways to overcome economic contradictions and to facilitate the integration of the working class. Rationalization must be distinguished from strategies of forcing the working class to bear the costs of economic contradictions through dramatic reductions in living standards combined with severe political repression.

5. Each of these categories requires some definition: "Capitalist class" or "ruling class" is used to refer to the individuals and families that own or control a certain quantity of capital. The cut-off point would vary by country or period, and it would necessarily be somewhat arbitrary, but the point is to distinguish be-

tween small businesses and large capitalist firms. The "managers of the state apparatus" include the leading figures of both the legislative and executive branches. This includes the highest-ranking civil servants, as well as appointed and elected politicians. "Working class" is being used in the broad sense. It includes most of those who sell their labor for wages, unwaged workers, and the unemployed.

6. In *The German Ideology*, Marx and Engels talk about a division of labor and of interests between capitalists and the producers of bourgeois ideology: "so that inside this class one part appears as the thinkers of the class (its active, conceptive ideologists, who make the perfection of the illusion of the class about itself their chief source of livelihood), while the others' attitude to these ideas and illusions is more passive and receptive, because they are in reality the active members of this class and have less time to make up illusions and ideas about themselves." In Robert C. Tucker, ed., *The Marx–Engels Reader* (New York: Norton, 1972), 136–137. This suggests an analogous division of labor between capitalists and state managers. In both cases, however, treating ideologists or state managers as part of the ruling class violates the idea that class is determined by one's relation to the means of production. In short, Marx and Engels in this passage are using the notion of the ruling class in a polemical sense.

7. "The Eighteenth Brumaire," in ibid., 502.

8. Ibid., 462.

9. It is beyond the scope of this essay to explore the dynamics of authoritarian rule in capitalist societies. However, it is important to give some content to the familiar Marxist thesis that authoritarian rule is a second-best solution for capitalism, as compared with parliamentarism, and is only resorted to when the threat of revolution is serious. Part of the answer is that authoritarian regimes are less reliable in serving the general interests of capital because the structural mechanisms described here do not operate in the same way in the absence of parliamentarism.

10. For a critique of corporate liberal theory, see Chapter 2.

11. An obvious example here is the commitment to maintaining "full employment." This was a concession granted to the working class in the aftermath of the Great Depression, but it has proved increasingly costly for the developed capitalist nations.

12. They also have the option of responding to pressures through severe repression. The choice between concessions and repression is made by the state managers on the basis of their perceptions of the general environment and their political orientations.

13. These arguments all assume that some significant degree of national mobilization has occurred. In this sense, the business confidence veto was far stronger during Vietnam than during Korea. (In fact, it can be argued that the Johnson administration's desire to continue escalating in Vietnam ran afoul of declining business confidence.) In some cases, the business community's lack of enthusiasm for a war can prevent mobilization efforts from getting off the ground in time. This was clearly an element in the French collapse during World War II. But how does business confidence evaluate wars? I would suggest that the answer lies in terms of short-term considerations rather than an evaluation of the nation's long-term international position. In conditions of weak demand, the outbreak of major wars generally leads to a decline in business confidence.

14. This was the case with the New Deal. The Roosevelt administration

simply stumbled on some of the elements necessary for a rationalization of the economy. The open-ended nature of the process is indicated by the fact that full recovery was not achieved until the mobilization for World War II.

15. This kind of selection process was carried out by the Conservative government that came to power in Britain in 1951 after Labour had presided over postwar reconstruction. The dangers involved in the selection process are indicated by the fact that Britain's long-term prospects as a capitalist nation might have been improved by the retention of more of the Labour reforms.

16. See, for example, Stanley Aronowitz, "Modernizing Capitalism," *Social Policy* (May–June 1975), and James Crotty and Raford Boddy, "Who Will Plan the Planned Economy?" *The Progressive* (Feb. 1975). Such analyses tend to assume that the contradictions of advanced capitalism can be solved or effectively eased through state action. The possibility exists that this is not the case. While it is virtually impossible to reach a conclusion on that issue, one can debate whether such expanded state intervention will even be attempted.

CHAPTER 4
Acknowledgement: I am grateful to David Plotke, Michael Reich, and Robert Keohane for their comments on earlier drafts of this paper.

1. Karl Kautsky, " Ultra-Imperialism," *New Left Review*, no. 59 (1970, originally published in 1914): 41–46; V. I. Lenin, *Imperialism* (New York, 1939, originally published in 1917). The issue was joined most directly in a debate between Martin Nicolaus and Ernest Mandel in *New Left Review* at the end of the 1960s. See Ernest Mandel, "Where Is America Going?" *New Left Review* no. 54 (1969): 3–15; Martin Nicolaus, "The Universal Contradiction," *New Left Review* no. 59 (1970): 3–18; Ernest Mandel, "The Laws of Unequal Development," ibid., 19–40. Mandel's views are also developed in *Europe vs. America?* (London, 1970), and *Late Capitalism* (London, 1975), chap. 10. For other contributions to the debate, see Bob Rowthorn, "Imperialism in the Seventies—Unity or Rivalry," *New Left Review* no. 69 (1971): 31–54; Marty Landsberg, "Multinational Corporations and the Crisis of Capitalism," *Insurgent Sociologist* 7 (1976): 19–33; Nicos Poulantzas, "Internationalization of Capitalist Relations and the Nation-States," *Economy and Society* 3 (1974): 145–179.

2. This argument is suggested by Landsberg, *Insurgent Sociologist* 7 (1976): 19–33; and by Stephen Hymer, "The Internationalization of Capital," *Journal of Economic Issues* 6 (1972): 91–112. It is developed explicitly in Jeff Frieden, "The Trilateral Commission: Economics and Politics in the 1970s," *Monthly Review* 29 (1977): 1–18.

3. Ibid. For the Trilateral Commission's commitment to international cooperation and its opposition to neomercantilism, see its periodic reports, issued as *Trilateral Commission Task Force Reports: 1–7* (New York, 1977).

4. While the commission originally sponsored the study, it dissociated itself from the study's conclusions. For a discussion of this aspect of Trilateralism, see Alan Wolfe, *The Limits of Legitimacy* (New York, 1977).

5. Elizabeth Drew, "Brzezinski," *New Yorker* (May 1, 1978): 109.

6. See The Editors, "Comment on Frieden," *Monthly Review* 29 (1977): 19–22.

7. The Editors, "Emerging Currency and Trade Wars," *Monthly Review* 29 (1978): 1–7. Note that Sweezy and Magdoff do not explicitly address the relationship between capital and the state in the development of this policy, but a corporate interest in a depreciating dollar is implied.

8. Germany and Japan refused to stimulate their economies for fear that Keynesian measures would generate more inflation than real growth. Both countries preferred to wait for export demand to pull their economies toward a faster rate of growth. Their suspicion of Keynesian fiscal measures seems well founded because both economies seem to require structural changes to open the way to a resumption of rapid growth. For a discussion of the German case, see Fred Block, "The Stalemate of European Capitalism: Eurocommunism and the Postwar Order," in *The Politics of Eurocommunism*, ed. Carl Boggs and David Plotke (Boston: South End Press, 1980).

9. This was clearly a factor in the Japanese case. Estimates at the beginning of April 1978 were that the Japanese government had absorbed $11 billion in dollars since September 1977. "This enormous amount of liquidity has the potential of creating a severe burst of inflation in Japan." *New York Times* (Apr. 2, 1978).

10. West Germany has found another way to respond to the dilemmas created by a declining dollar. West Germany and France have attempted during 1978 to revive the project of monetary unification within the EEC. Their current plan, the European Monetary System, envisions greater stability among European currencies supported by a $20 billion fund. The immediate goal is to keep West German goods from being priced out of European markets as a result of the mark's rise against the dollar. Still, this cannot be understood simply as a retaliatory action since it is linked to the historical project of European economic integration, and U.S. policymakers are divided in their assessment of whether the Franco-German plan is against U.S. interests.

11. The principal source for the critique of instrumental views of the state is David Gold, Clarence Lo, and Erik Wright, "Recent Developments in the Marxist Theory of the State," *Monthly Review* 27 (Oct. 1975): 29–43, and (Nov. 1975): 36–51.

12. See Chapter 3. By state managers, I am referring to the more powerful figures at the top of the state apparatus, whether they be in the legislative, executive, or judicial branches. To be sure, this is a heterogenous group whose interests are by no means uniform, but they share enough in common so that it is reasonable to speak of the interests of state managers. Finally, the interests of state managers involve a complex combination of personal interests, as with politicians who want to remain in office, and institutional interests—defense of the state apparatus or of particular bureaucratic entities within it. Although conflicts do emerge between personal and institutional interests, these two types of interests are generally mutually reinforcing.

13. I do not mean to suggest a simple relationship between unemployment and political crisis, but it does seem true, particularly in conditions of advanced capitalism, that rising and continuing unemployment undermine the legitimacy of government.

14. See James O'Connor, *The Fiscal Crisis of the State* (New York, 1973), and Wolfe, *Limits of Legitimacy*.

15. Emphasis on the national security component of the administration's choice of reference-pricing builds on an argument of Robert Keohane, "United States Foreign Economic Policy toward other Advanced Capitalist States: The Struggle to Make Others Adjust," 91–122, in *Eagle Entangled*, ed. Kenneth Oye, Donald Rothchild, and Robert Lieber (New York: Longman, 1979).

16. This point—the difference between particular interests and general interests—is essential. Another way of stating it is that these multinational firms depend upon the power of their home state to support them in their international

activities. At the same time, they also wish to maximize their own freedom from interference by that and other states. In this sense, their advocacy of international-ism is not simply ideological. This tension is captured well by Richard Barnet and Ronald Müller, *Global Reach* (New York, 1974), especially chap. 4. But it is precisely the dependence of firms on their home states that the neo-Kautskians fail to take into account. For a discussion of this weakness of neo-Kautskian scenarios, see Fred Block, *The Origins of International Economic Disorder* (Berkeley, 1977), 212–215.

17. The term *peace interest* is Karl Polanyi's, drawn from his discussion of the role of international banks in maintaining peace in Europe in the second half of the nineteenth century. See Karl Polanyi, *The Great Transformation* (Boston, 1957), 9–14. Bruce M. Russett and Elizabeth C. Hanson, *Interest and Ideology* (San Francis-co, 1975) provide some limited but suggestive evidence, based on surveys of internationally oriented businessmen, that supports this argument.

18. An editorial in *Business Week* argued for a moderation in the administra-tion's policies in the issues of Sept. 11 and Sept. 25, 1971. Hints of domestic business opposition to Connally's policies are provided in Robert Solomon, *The International Monetary System, 1945–1976* (New York, 1977), 200–201.

19. See, for example, *Wall Street Journal* (Mar. 8, 30, 1978) and *Business Week* (Mar. 6, 1978).

20. *Wall Street Journal* (Apr. 20, 1978).

21. Mihaly Vajda develops this argument in reference to the nazi regime in Germany after 1936. He argues that its pursuit of a more aggressive foreign policy was not in the interests of the business community, but that community had lost its capacity to resist. See Mihaly Vajda, *Fascism as a Mass Movement* (London, 1976), chap. 14.

CHAPTER 5
Acknowledgement: This paper has grown out of discussions with Karl Klare, Theda Skocpol, Larry Hirschhorn, Margaret Somers, and David Plotke.

1. The remarks are from an interview with Poulantzas by Stuart Hall and Alan Hunt that was published in *Marxism Today* (July 1979), and reprinted in *Socialist Review* 48 (Nov.–Dec. 1979). The quoted passage is on p. 67.

2. The seriousness of the challenge derives from Poulantzas' own enormous contribution to the revival of Marxist theorizing on the state.

3. Bob Jessop, "Recent Theories of the Capitalist State," *Cambridge Journal of Economics* (1977): 356.

4. Nicos Poulantzas, "The Problem of the Capitalist State," *New Left Review* 58 (Nov.–Dec. 1969): 73.

5. Mouzelis criticizes Poulantzas' interpretation of the 1967 military coup in Greece along precisely these lines. See Nicos Mouzelis, "Capitalism and Dic-tatorship in Post-war Greece," *New Left Review* 96 (Mar.–Apr. 1976).

6. The condensation notion is elaborated in Nicos Poulantzas, *State, Power, Socialism* (New York: New Left Books/Shocken, 1978).

7. For purposes of this paper, I am using the term *class* to mean social groups that have a common relation, direct or mediated, to the means of production. Since class does not exhaust the forms of structured inequality in human society, referring only to class involves some simplification.

8. In the Asiatic Mode of Production and in contemporary state Socialist societies, the degree to which state power is unconstrained is particularly high.

Yet even in these instances, there are social groups that can place limits on the exercise of state power. For a recent discussion that argues that Marx and Engels recognized the autonomy of the state in the Asiatic Mode of Production but had trouble reconciling it with the rest of their theory, see Alvin Gouldner, *The Two Marxisms*, (New York: Seabury, 1980).

It should also be noted that the thrust of my argument is consistent with the famous passage in the *Grundrisse:* "In all forms of society there is one specific kind of production which predominates over the rest, whose relations thus assign rank and influence to the others. It is a general illumination which bathes all the other colours and modifies their particularity. It is a particular ether which determines the specific gravity of every being which has materialised within it." Karl Marx, *Grundrisse* (New York: Vintage, 1973), 106–107. Yet it must be acknowledged that much of Marx's work is not consistent with this particular passage.

9. State managers are those at the peak of the executive and legislative branches of the state apparatus. Sometimes occupants of these positions are on loan from capitalist firms, but they operate in a situation that tends to be dominated by people for whom politics is a vocation, whether advancement comes through pursuit of elective or appointive offices. It is my hypothesis that such temporary state managers tend to adapt to the ways of thinking appropriate to their new occupational situation, just as a corporate executive would alter his or her views in accordance with a shift from one type of firm to another.

10. This *modus vivendi* explains the historical power of the Marxist formulations that see the state as an executive committee of the bourgeoisie. The problem, however, comes in those periods in which the *modus vivendi* breaks down or is strained.

11. This qualification is necessary because one option for state managers in less developed nations has been to serve as the clients of more powerful nations. In this case, their nation's standing in the world system is irrelevant; what is more important is the standing of the regime of which they are clients.

12. This dynamic has played an important role in the extension of citizenship rights through the nineteenth and early twentieth centuries.

13. This argument is made at greater length in Chapter 3 and in Charles Lindblom, *Politics and Markets* (New York: Basic, 1977).

14. On this point, see Ralph Miliband, *The State in Capitalist Society* (New York: Basic, 1969).

15. Karl Polanyi, *The Great Transformation* (Boston: Beacon, 1957). While Polanyi lacks an explicit theory of the state, his book is an important source for my argument.

16. I do not mean to exaggerate the insight and understanding that state managers bring to these tasks. Their understanding of the overall situation tends to be limited, and their actions tend to be crisis-oriented. This is not surprising since they are necessarily preoccupied with short-term problems of maintaining their political position.

17. For a useful case study, see Karl Klare, "Judicial Deradicalization of the Wagner Act and the Origins of Modern Legal Consciousness," *Minnesota Law Review* 62 (1978): 265–339.

18. I am following here the argument of Mihaly Vajda, *Fascism as a Mass Movement* (London: Allison and Busby, 1976).

19. One is reminded here of Marx's description of the French state in the Brumaire where he is stressing the state's freedom of action: "It is immediately

obvious that in a country like France, where the executive power commands an army of officials numbering more than half a million individuals and therefore constantly maintains an immense mass of interests and livelihoods in the most absolute dependence; where the state enmeshes, controls, regulates, superintends and tutors civil society from its most comprehensive manifestations of life down to its most insignificant stirrings, from its most general modes of being to the private existence of individuals, where through the most extraordinary centralization this parasitic body acquires a ubiquity, an omniscience, a capacity for accelerated mobility and an elasticity which finds a counterpart only in the helpless dependence, in the loose shapelessness of the actual body politic—it is obvious that in such a country the National Assembly forfeits all real influence when it loses command of the ministerial posts . . ." Karl Marx, *The Eighteenth Brumaire of Louis Bonaparte* (New York: International Publishers, 1963), 61–62.

20. For a longer discussion of the limits of Eurocommunist strategies, see Fred Block, "The Stalemate of European Capitalism: Eurocommunism and the Postwar Order," *Socialist Review* 43 (Jan.–Feb. 1979).

21. Block, "The Stalemate of European Capitalism." See Chapter 6. I am also drawing on discussions of the contradictions of centralized planning in Lindblom, *Politics and Markets*, and Radovan Richta et al., *Civilization at the Crossroads* (White Plains, N.Y.: International Arts and Sciences Press, 1969).

22. Such views are expressed in Poulantzas, *State, Power, Socialism*; Ernest Mandel, *Late Capitalism* (London: New Left Books, 1975), Bob Jessop, "Capitalism and Democracy: The Best Possible Political Shell," in *Power and the State,* ed. Gary Littlejohn et al. (New York: St. Martin's, 1978), and in a number of American writings that center on the role of the Trilateral Commission that are collected in Holly Sklar, ed., *Trilaterialism* (Boston: South End Press, 1981).

23. Alan Wolfe noted in an unpublished paper that just as Marxists have developed an extremely sophisticated theory of the state, capitalists have reverted to crude instrumentalism. Yet this is only part of the story.

24. A recent illustration of this was intense corporate resistance in the United States to efforts by the Federal Trade Commission to obtain profit information by product line.

25. This is also Polanyi's theme in *The Great Transformation* that I have sought to extend into the post-war period in *The Origins of International Economic Disorder* (Berkeley: University of California Press, 1977).

26. James O'Connor, *The Fiscal Crisis of the State* (New York: St. Martin's, 1973).

27. Theda Skocpol, *States and Social Revolutions* (Cambridge: Cambridge University Press, 1979). This brief summary of her argument applies most completely to the French Revolution.

CHAPTER 6

Acknowledgement: In developing these ideas, we owe a substantial intellectual debt to Martin Sklar, although our thinking has diverged in important ways from his formulations. A large number of people read earlier versions of this manuscript and have helped us clarify our ideas. We particularly want to thank Jeffrey Escoffier, David Gold, Jim Hawley, Karl Klare, Jim Mulherin, Bill Tabb, Marc Weiss, Alan Wolfe, and Eli Zaretsky. This essay elaborates on themes developed by L. Hirschhorn in a number of articles, see particularly "Toward a Political

Economy of the Service Society," Working Paper no. 229, Institute for Urban and Regional Development, University of California, Berkeley (IURD): "The Social Crisis," Parts I and II, Working Papers no. 251, 252, IURD; "Social Services and Disaccumulationist Capitalism," *International Journal of Health Services* (May 1979); "The Political Economy of Social Service Rationalization," *Contemporary Crisis* (winter 1978).

    1. Karl Marx, "Preface to the Contribution to the Critique of Political Economy," in Robert Tucker, ed., *The Marx-Engels Reader* (New York: Norton, 1972), 3–6.

    2. While this essay analyzes capitalist society, particularly the United States, a parallel analysis could be developed of the state Socialist societies as they face the problem of postindustrial transition. For an important attempt at such an analysis, see Radovan Richta et al., *Civilization at the Crossroads* (White Plains, N.Y.: International Arts and Sciences Press, 1969). Daniel Bell, the theorist most closely identified with postindustrialism, has written extensively and provocatively on the emergence of postindustrial technologies. See his *The Coming of Post-Industrial Society* (New York: Basic Books, 1973. Yet he examines these technologies of production and decision-making in a narrow frame—without asking how they reorganize people's experiences of and commitments to work. His analysis is consequently a reified one and not surprisingly he sees the new technologies as simply intense or extreme extensions of the classical industrial principles of specialization and efficiency. However, when one examines the new technologies within the framework of their impact on the organization and experience of work, it becomes clear that the new technologies break down specialization and redefine efficiency (curiously, Marshall McLuhan has always been more sensitive here). Because Bell pursues a narrow approach he winds up bifurcating the moments of development in social life and work life. If currents of work life do *not* represent a *rupture* with past developments, the obvious crisis of social life has other roots. Social conflict then becomes the conflict between two principles—the "Dionysian principle" of social life and the efficiency principle of work life, (echoing the old Gesellschaft-Gemeinschaft dichotomy within a postindustrial frame). In contrast we argue that social crisis is rooted in a total social system in conflict with itself, that it produces crisis through the contradiction between its present and its potential future. Ours is a *developmental* argument while Bell's is ultimately a *functionalist* one. That is why opponents of the concept of an historical rupture have found much solace in the limits of Bell's argument.

    3. For some of the key works of the Neo-Marxist tradition to which we refer, see Serge Mallet, *Essays on the New Working Class* (St. Louis: Telos Press, 1975); Andre Gorz, *Strategy for Labor* (Boston: Beacon, 1967); Martin Nicolaus, "The Unknown Marx," in *The New Left Reader*, ed. Carl Oglesby (New York: Grove Press, 1969); Martin J. Sklar, "On the Proletarian Revolution and the End of Political-Economic Society," *Radical America* (May–June 1969). Other important statements of this position in the United States are the editorials in the first two issues of *Socialist Revolution* (Jan.–Feb. and Mar.–Apr. 1970); the neglected study by Greg Calvert and Carol Nieman, *A Disrupted History: The New Left and the New Capitalism* (New York: Random House, 1971); a more recent book by Trent Schroyer, *The Critique of Domination* (Boston: Beacon, 1973); and an essay that links these Neo-Marxist themes to the underground tradition of European Marxism by Karl Klare, "The Critique of Everyday Life, the New Left, and the Unrecognizable

Marxism," in *The Unknown Dimension*, Dick Howard and Karl Klare eds., (New York: Basic Books, 1972). The most important writer to continue this line of argument into the 1970s is Alain Touraine, see *The Postindustrial Society* (New York: Random House, 1971) and *The May Movement* (New York: Random House, 1971).

4. Our use of the term "economism" is broader than the standard Leninist usage; we are referring to the assumption that economic grievances are the principle concerns around which people can be mobilized. In this sense, most current Marxist political activity reflects the first pitfall. The other tendency frequently appears in the pages of *Telos*, see particularly, "Symposium on Class," *Telos* (summer 1976), and "Internal Polemics," *Telos* (spring 1977).

5. *The Great Transformation* (Boston: Beacon, 1957), 77–110.

6. David McLellan, ed., *The Grundrisse* (New York: Harper and Row, 1971), 142.

7. McLellan, ibid.

8. McLellan, ibid.

9. McLellan, ibid.

10. McLellan, ibid., 148.

11. Sklar, "On the Proletarian Revolution."

12. John Kendrick, *Productivity Trends in the United States* (Princeton: Princeton University Press, 1961), 314.

13. Richta, *Civilization*, 303. Note that since labor and capital saving technologies have been introduced into capital goods production, one would suspect that the process of capital cheapening has been even more dramatic in value terms, that is, in the amount of labor time embodied in the amount of capital required to produce a unit of output.

14. The calculations of Edward P. Denison on the sources of economic growth provide a rough approximation of the impact of new productive forces. His data show, for example, that education and the advance of knowledge account for 43 percent of total economic growth in the period from 1929 to 1957, and more than 50 percent in the period from 1948 to 1969. See Edward F. Denison, *The Sources of Economic Growth in the United States* (New York: Committee for Economic Development, 1962), 266, and *Accounting for United States Economic Growth, 1929–1969* (Washington: Brookings, 1974), 79–83, 111.

15. In sum, the introduction of new technologies does not follow some logic of its own, but is a function of the specific social relations of capitalism.

16. A similar argument is made by Gabriel Kolko, *Main Currents of Modern American History* (New York: Harper and Row, 1976), 100–105, 144.

17. Sklar, "On the Proletarian Revolution,"23–36.

18. This argument is developed at greater length in Hirschhorn, "Toward A Political Economy of the Service Society," 32–39. Two valuable recent studies analyze the cultural ambivalences of the twenties, although their emphasis is on the successful containment of cultural change: Stuart Ewen, *Captains of Consciousness* (New York: McGraw-Hill, 1976), and Paula Fass, *The Damned and the Beautiful: American Youth in the 1920s* (New York: Oxford, 1977). For an analysis that stresses the tensions between these cultural changes and the logic of capitalism, see Daniel Bell, *The Cultural Contradictions of Capitalism* (New York: Basic Books, 1976), especially 54–84.

19. Some evidence for the progressive consolidation of a linear life course is provided in John Modell, Frank Furstenberg, and Theodore Hirschberg, "Social

Change and Life-Course Development in Historical Perspective," *Journal of Family History* (Sept. 1976); John Modell, Frank Furstenberg, and Douglas Strong, "The Timing of Marriage in the Transition to Adulthood: Continuity and Change, 1860–1975," *American Journal of Sociology, Special Issue: Turning Points: Historical and Sociological Essays on The Family* (University of Chicago Press).

20. The breakdown of the linear life course and the emergence of the fluid life cycle is discussed in Larry Hirschhorn, "Social Policy and the Life Cycle: A Developmental Perspective," *Social Service Review* (Sept. 1977); also Larry Hirschhorn, "Toward an Analytic History of the Life-Course," unpublished manuscript; Fred Block, "The New Left Grows Up," *Working Papers for a New Society* (Sept.–Oct. 1978).

21. From 1966 to 1977, the New England, Middle Atlantic and Great Lakes Regions lost 1.4 million manufacturing jobs. While there has been some compensating growth in manufacturing employment in other regions of the country, many displaced workers are unwilling or unable to move long distances in search of new jobs. *Business Week* (Nov. 14, 1977), 142–152.

22. For the impact of unemployment on family life, see Frank Furstenberg, "Work Experience and Family Life," in *Work and the Quality of Life*, James O'Toole, ed., (Cambridge, Mass.: MIT Press, 1974).

23. Trends in "participation rates" in the labor force for older and younger men since World War II can be found in U.S. Department of Labor, *Report to the President,1975* (Washington, 1975), 204–205. Trends for the last fifty years can be found in U.S. Bureau of Census, *Historical Statistics of the United States from Colonial Times to the Present* (Washington, 1975), 132.

24. Sar A. Levitan and Richard S. Belous, *Shorter Hours, Shorter Weeks* (Baltimore: John Hopkins University Press, 1977), 7–16.

25. To be sure, the actual amount of time devoted to housework has probably not declined over the past fifty years, but the nature of the tasks has shifted. Chauffering children, for example, has a different meaning than baking. In this sense, the declining capacity of housework to organize the lives of women is not a quantitative issue so much as a qualitative one. For data and arguments relevant to this question, see Richard Edwards, Michael Reich, Thomas Weisskopf, eds., *The Capitalist System* (Englewood Cliffs, N.J.: Prentice-Hall, 1978), chap. 9.

26. For an elaboration of these arguments, see Barbara Epstein, "Feminism and the Contemporary Family," *Socialist Review* (May–June, 1978).

27. See Braverman, *Labor and Monopoly Capital* (New York: Monthly Review Press, 1974), especially chap. 4 and 5.

28. A recent Bureau of the Census report cited in the *New York Times* (Feb. 10, 1977) found that 32 percent of all workers has switched careers between 1965 and 1970. The number is very high and suggests the need for statistical classifications that can differentiate between real and spurious changes. Yet the high number does indicate that career switching is becoming more normal. The recent rapid growth in adult education on college campuses is another sign of the growth in career switching. One study in 1972 found that close to thirty million adult Americans were engaged in some form of study. See Commission of Non-Traditional Study, *Diversity by Design* (San Francisco: Jossey Bass, 1973), 82. Seymour Sarason, *Work, Aging and Social Change* (New York: Free Press, 1977), chap. 11, also presents some sketchy evidence for increases in career switching. For a discussion of rising absenteeism rates, see Judson Gooding, *The Job Revolution* (New York: Walker Press, 1972).

29. James O'Toole, "The Reserve Army of the Unemployed," *Change* (May–June 1975); Ivar Berg and Marcia Freedman, "The American Workplace: Illusions and Realities," *Change* (Nov. 1977).

30. Ivar Berg, *Education and Jobs: The Great Training Robbery* (New York: Praeger, 1970).

31. Marx anticipated this shift: "The worker no longer inserts transformed natural objects as intermediaries between the material and himself; he now inserts the natural process that he has transformed into an industrial one between himself and inorganic nature, over which he has achieved mastery. He is no longer the pincipal agent of the production process: he exists alongside it." McLellan, *The Grundrisse*, 142.

32. This idea of compensating satisfactions in tedious work is developed by W. Baldamus, *Efficiency and Effort* (London: Tavistock Press, 1961), 57–65.

33. The phenomena of work discontent in automated settings based on an uneven balance between engagement and displacement is discussed in Larry Hirschhorn, "The Social Crisis, Part II," 33–43.

34. For an introduction to the vast literature on these experiments, see Louis E. Davis and James C. Taylor, *Design of Jobs* (Middlesex, Eng.: Penguin, 1972); Louis E. Davis and Albert B. Cherns, *The Quality of Working Life*, vol. II (New York: Free Press, 1975). At this point and others, our analysis of the labor process diverges from Braverman's. His emphasis on the single process of deskilling misses much of the complexity of contemporary work settings. Not only do many workers experience skill upgrading as a result of new technologies and new forms of work organization, but Braverman also tends to exaggerate the compatibility between advanced technologies and a deskilled workforce. The empirical evidence he relies on comes from a study by James Bright of the impact of automation on skill levels that was done in the mid-fifties, before most of the major advances in automated and semiautomated technologies. While we do not know of more recent studies that pose the same question in relation to a variety of different technologies, there is evidence to suggest the limits of Braverman's argument. For example, much of the contemporary personnel management literature deals with problems of training and teaching people how to learn. See the journal, *Training and Development Review*, for an indication of the importance of these issues at both blue-collar and white-collar levels.

35. Management training and development has become an increasingly complex affair. Today the emphasis is on "continuous learning" to cope with organizational change. Robert Pearse dates to the mid-sixties the explicit formulation and diffusion of what he calls an "adult educational view" of management development: see also Rensis Likert, "New Patterns of Management," in *Management and Motivation*, ed. Victor Vroom and Edward L. Pielci (Middlesex, Eng.: Penguin, 1970). For a general discussion of the problems of labor and management in advanced technological settings, see Charles Walker, ed., *Technology, Industry and Man: The Age of Acceleration* (New York: McGraw-Hill, 1968), chap. 7–8.

36. This argument is developed by Warren Bennis and Philip Slater, *The Temporary Society* (New York: Harper and Row, 1968).

37. Christina Maslach, "Burn-Out," *Human Behavior* (Sept. 1976).

38. See the *New York Times* (Apr. 10, 1977).

39. See, for example, Bell, *Cultural Contradictions*, Russell Jacoby, *Social Amnesia* (Boston: Beacon, 1975); Christopher Lasch, *Haven in a Heartless World* (New York: Basic Books, 1977), especially chap. 8.

40. The major statement of this position is James O'Connor, *The Fiscal Crisis of the State* (New York: St. Martin's, 1973), which builds on the analysis of Paul Baran and Paul Sweezy, *Monopoly Capital* (New York: Monthly Review Press, 1966).

41. See, for example, Harry Magdoff and Paul Sweezy, "The Long Run Decline in Liquidity," *Monthly Review* (Sept. 1970), and "The Debt Economy," *Business Week* (Oct. 12, 1974).

42. For accounts of the implementation of Keynesian policies in the United States, see Fred Block, *The Origins of International Economic Disorder* (Berkeley: University of California Press, 1977), chap. 3–4, and David A. Gold, "The Rise and Decline of the Keynesian Coalition," *Kapitalistate* (fall 1977).

43. On the destructive impact of military Keynesianism on the domestic economy, see Seymour Melman, *The Permanent War Economy* (New York: Simon and Schuster, 1974).

44. On the contradictory nature of austerity policies, see Hirschhorn, "The Political Economy of Social Service Rationalization," 74–79.

45. On the Kondratieff perspective, see Ernest Mandel, *Late Capitalism* (London: New Left Books, 1975), chap. 4; Richard B. Day, "The Theory of Long Waves," *New Left Review* (Sept.–Oct. 1976); David A. Gold, "Accumulation and Economic Crisis in the United States," unpublished.

46. Serge Mallet makes this point in terms of migrant laborers in Western Europe. Mallet, Essays, 52–53.

47. Institute for Labor Education and Research, "Labor Unions in Transition," in *U.S. Capitalism in Crisis*, ed. Union for Radical Political Economics, (New York: URPE, 1978).

48. Between 1972 and 1977, the number of individuals receiving disability benefits under Social Security jumped by 45 percent from 1.8 million to 2.8 million." *Wall Street Journal* (Jan. 30, 1978).

49. The idea of reproduction costs is borrowed from David A. Gold and James O'Connor.

50. It is beyond the scope of the present essay to address the nature of the state in the current period. Our tendency, however, is to be skeptical of the state's capacity to intervene successfully to resolve economic and social contradictions in the absence of powerful social movements advocating one kind of reorganization or another. In short, the state itself is mired in the paralysis that results from the blocking of new productive forces. Some sense of this paralysis is provided in Chapter 3, and Alan Wolfe, *The Limits of Legitimacy* (New York: Free Press, 1977), part II.

51. This argument is developed at length in Hirschhorn, "The Political Economy of Social Service Rationalization," 72–73.

52. Again, we are not able to address this issue of regional economic differences. Suffice it to say that we are skeptical of claims that Southern and Southwestern economic vitality is great enough to overcome the relative stagnation in other regions.

53. Our discussion of economic crisis has generally neglected the international dimension. We have addressed these issues in other places; see Fred Block and Larry Hirschhorn, "The International Monetary Crisis," *Socialist Revolution* (Sept.–Oct., 1972) and Block, *Origins*. A full discussion of the international impact of the emergence of new productive forces would begin with the argument that the contradictions created by the emergence of new productive forces are experienced throughout the world capitalist system. In particular, the world depression of the thirties was a direct result of the economic transformation in the United

States. Similarly, the problems of accumulation in the current period in Western Europe and Japan and in Eastern Europe and the Soviet Union can be understood in terms of the conflict between new productive forces and capitalist or bureaucratic socialist social relations. Finally, the problems of accumulation in the underdeveloped world today are closely linked to the labor saving nature of the technologies being used in those societies, indicating that the problem of labor surplus is a global one.

CHAPTER 7

1. Dan Luria and Jack Russell, *Rational Reindustrialization* (Detroit: Widgetripper, 1981), and "Rebuilding Detroit: A Rational Reindustrialization Strategy," *Socialist Review* 63–64 (May–Aug. 1982). Barry Bluestone and Bennett Harrison also use the concept in their book *The Deindustrialization of America* (New York: Basic Books, 1982).

2. *Liberation*, April 1964.

3. Leonard Silk, "Military Surge as Spur to Jobs," *New York Times* (Sept. 17, 1982).

4. International Labour Office, *Yearbook of Labour Statistics*.

5. One source makes the probably exaggerated estimate that four million Japanese workers are kept on payrolls with nothing to do. See Colin Hines and Graham Searles, *Automatic Unemployment* (London: Earth Resources Research, 1979), 30.

6. United Nations, *Yearbook of Industrial Statistics*.

7. United States Department of Commerce, *U.S. Direct Investment Abroad, 1977*.

8. Mick McLean, *The Electronic Industry* (Paris: OECD, 1980).

9. A given quantity of yarn could be produced in 1950 by 1/500th of the labor time that was needed in 1850. Roy Rothwell and Walter Zegveld, *Technical Change and Employment* (New York: St. Martin's Press, 1979).

10. Calculated from data in Edward F. Denison, *Why Growth Rates Differ* (Washington: Brookings, 1967), and Statistical Office of the European Community, *Labor Costs in Industry* and *Population and Employment*.

11. Dieter Ernst, *Restructuring World Industry in a Period of Crisis—The Role of Innovation*, UNIDO Working Paper, Dec. 1981.

12. McLean, *Electronics Industry*.

13. Gunter Friedrichs, "Microelectronics and Macroeconomics," in *Microelectronics and Society: For Better or for Worse*, ed. Gunter Friedrichs and Adam Schaff (Oxford: Pergamon Press, 1982), 191.

14. United States Department of Labor, *Employment and Earnings*.

15. "Detroit's Jobs That Will Never Come Back," *Business Week* (May 23, 1983).

16. My argument rests on the premise that Taylorist forms of work organization that attempt to radically simplify labor are decreasingly effective in the current industrial context. For slightly different arguments to this effect, see Larry Hirschhorn, "The Soul of a New Worker," *Working Papers*, Jan.–Feb. 1982, and *Beyond Mechanization* (Cambridge, Mass: MIT Press, 1984); Charles Sabel, *Work and Politics* (Cambridge: Cambridge University Press, 1982); Charles Heckscher, "Democracy at Work," doctoral dissertation, Department of Sociology, Harvard University, 1981; Robert Reich, *The Next American Frontier* (New York: Times Books, 1983).

17. Sabel, *Work and Politics*, chap. 5.

18. The theory underlying this alternative model is developed in Chapter 6.

19. While new technologies are likely to displace labor in parts of the "service" sector such as banking, insurance, and certain types of retailing, it seems probable that private service employment in the United States economy will continue to expand. The problem, however, is that it is unlikely that private service employment can expand fast enough to make much dent in the unemployment rate in a context where even mainstream analysts argue that there are as many as 17 million people who would enter the labor force if there were a chance to get a job. On the latter point, see Eli Ginzberg, "The Job Problem," *Scientific American* (Nov. 1977).

20. Such measures have been adopted in very limited form through plans in which employers are encouraged to cut working hours rather than resorting to layoffs, and employees are compensated for shorter hours through the unemployment insurance system. See Fred Best and James Mattesich, "Short-time Compensation Systems in California and Europe," *Monthly Labor Review* (July 1980).

21. Seymour Sarason, *Work, Aging, and Social Change* (New York: Free Press, 1977), 269–272.

22. For an extended discussion of the centrality of some of these reforms to democratic theory, see Philip Green, "Considerations on the Democratic Division of Labor," *Politics & Society* 12,4 (1983).

CHAPTER 8

Acknowledgement: This paper was prepared with support from the Program for the Assessment and Revitalization of the Social Sciences at the University of Pennsylvania. I am particularly grateful for the research assistance of Gene Burns that was made possible by that support. Albert Ando, Almarin Phillips, and Edward Herman made valuable comments on earlier versions of the paper but are in no way responsible for the final product. I am also grateful for comments and suggestions from Larry Hirschhorn, Candace Howes, Jerry Jacobs, Karl Klare, and Magali Sarfatti-Larson. William Dickens and Michael McKee were helpful in providing data.

1. One of the few dissenters from this line of argument has been Robert Heilbroner in his essay, "The Deficit," *The New Yorker* (July 30, 1984).

2. Simon Kuznets, "National Income and Industrial Structure," *Economic Change* (New York: Norton, 1953), 145–91.

3. This is a major theme in Daniel Bell, *The Coming of Post-Industrial Society* (New York: Basic Books, 1973).

4. This argument is elaborated by Alvin Toffler, in *The Third Wave* (New York: Bantam, 1980), and by Charles Sabel, in *Work and Politics* (Cambridge: Cambridge University Press, 1982), chap. 5.

5. Larry Hirschhorn, *Beyond Mechanization* (Cambridge, Mass.: MIT Press, 1984).

6. See Chapter 6.

7. See Richard Ruggles, "The United States National Income Accounts 1947–77: Their Conceptual Basis and Evolution," in *The U.S. National Income and Product Accounts*, ed. Murray F. Foss (Chicago: University of Chicago Press, 1983), 15–104.

8. J.R. Norsworthy, Michael J. Harper, and Kent Kunze, "The Slowdown in Productivity Growth: Analysis of Some Contibuting Factors," *Brookings Papers on Economic Activity* 2 (1979): 387–421.

9. To be sure, most professional economists stressed the inadequacy of new

investment or the consequences of government regulation, but politicians and some economists, including Arthur Burns (cited in Edward F. Denison, *Accounting for Slower Growth* [Washington: Brookings, 1979], 134) blamed the productivity crisis on the decline of the work ethic.

10. Charles S. Morris, "Productivity Slowdown: A Sectoral Analysis," *Economic Review* (Apr. 1984): 4. See also Michael Darby, "The U.S. Productivity Slowdown: A Case of Statistical Myopia," *American Economic Review* (June 1984): 301–22.

11. Randall K. Filer, "The Downturn in Productivity Growth: A New Look at its Nature and Causes," in *Lagging Productivity Growth: Causes and Remedies*, ed. Shlomo Maital and Noah M. Meltz (Cambridge, Mass.: Ballinger, 1980), 111.

12. William T. Dickens, "The Productivity Crisis: Secular or Cyclical?" *Economic Letters* 9 (1982): 37–42.

13. Denison, *Accounting for Slower Growth*.

14. Cited in Maital and Meltz, *Lagging Productivity Growth*, 274.

15. This periodization is commonly used since the years involved represent business cycle peaks. The analysis is confined to private GNP because measurements of government contributions to GNP are problematic. Employment is measured as hours actually worked, omitting paid leaves and paid vacation time.

16. Harry Magdoff and Paul Sweezy argue that the entire productivity shortfall can be explained by slower growth. "Productivity Slowdown: A False Alarm," *Monthly Review* 31, 2 (June 1979): 1–12. A similar argument with empirical support is made by Albert Szymanski, "Productivity Growth and Capitalist Stagnation," *Science and Society* 48, 3 (fall 1984): 295–322. See also Victor Perlo, "The False Claim of Declining Productivity and Its Political Use," *Science and Society* 46, 3 (fall 1982): 284–327.

17. The decision to restrict business investment to tangibles precluded any concept of investment in "human capital." Hence, educational expenditures were treated simply as consumption. This decision was hardly surprising in that the flowering of a "human capital" theory occurred well after the system of national income accounting was in place.

More recently, George Jaszi, for many years the head of the BEA, was unable to offer a theoretical justification for limiting BEA investment to tangible capital. He argued, rather, on the basis of the practical difficulty of delineating a boundary between intangible capital and other forms of expenditure. This is certainly an issue, but conventions could easily be developed to make such distinctions as they have with other problematic boundaries. For Jaszi's argument, see "Comment," in *The Measurement of Economic and Social Performance*, ed. Milton Moss (New York: NBER, 1973), 84–99.

18. John Kendrick, *The Formation and Stocks of Total Capital* (New York: NBER, 1976), 29.

19. Robert Eisner, "The Total Income System of Accounts," *Survey of Current Business* (Jan. 1985): 27–28. Eisner's system of accounts makes many other changes in the traditional accounting scheme including estimates of the value of unpaid household labor. But the largest component in the increase of investment is the inclusion of intangible investment in education and training.

20. The term *services* will be used, unless specified otherwise, to conform to the Commerce Department's Standard Industrial Classification codes 70–80, a category that includes medical services, legal services, repair services, miscel-

laneous business services, entertainment, personal services. There are other service industries—communications, trade finance, insurance, real estate, and transportation—that are categorized separately in the SIC system.

21. "A Productivity Drop That Nobody Believes," *Business Week* (Feb. 25, 1980): 77, 80.

22. T.P. Hill, *The Measurement of the Real Product* (Paris: OECD, 1971), 47.

23. For further discussions of this series, see Jack Gottsegen and Richard C. Ziemer, "Comparisons of Federal Reserve and OBE Measures of Real Manufacturing Output, 1947–1964," in *The Industrial Composition of Income and Product*, ed. John Kenrick (New York: NBER, 1968), 225–347; and U.S., Department of Commerce, Office of Business Economics, "GNP by Major Industries: Concepts and Methods," mimeo.

24. There is also a problem with those quality changes that are associated with increased costs of production. If those who compile the price index are not aware of the quality change, they will treat the price change as purely inflationary, and the change will not be reflected in higher levels of measured output. One recent defense of BLS techniques (John F. Early and James H. Sinclair, "Quality Adjustments in the Producer Price Indexes," in *The U.S. National Income and Product Accounts*, ed. Foss, 107–42) noted that in 1976 out of 108,756 price observations in the construction of the producers price index, only 455 instances of quality change were located. As Zvi Griliches commented in the same volume (pp. 143–144), this finding "implies that out of about 10,000 different commodities and varieties priced one encountered only 455 comparability problems during one year. Either many true comparability problems are not reported or the PPI [Producers Price Index] by design excludes most of the rapidly changing commodity areas from its purview. I assume that both are true." In short, there is good reason to assume that most quality changes are inadequately measured. However, for purposes of this discussion, the emphasis will be on "costless" quality changes.

25. John Kendrick, *Productivity Trends in the United States* (Princeton: Princeton University Press, 1961), 30.

26. Zvi Griliches, "Comment," in *The U.S. National Income and Product Accounts*, ed. Foss, 142–45.

27. Zvi Griliches, ed., *Price Indexes and Quality Change* (Cambridge, Mass.: Harvard University Press, 1971).

28. Albert Rees, "Improving the Concepts and Techniques of Productivity Measurement," *Monthly Labor Review* (Sept. 1979): 24.

29. James Martin, *Application Development without Programmers* (Englewood Cliffs, N.J.: Prentice-Hall, 1982), 3. See also Sol Triebwasser, "Impact of Semiconductor Microelectronics," *Computer Technology: Status, Limits, Alternatives* (New York: Institute of Electrical and Electronic Engineers, 1978), cited in William J. Baumol, "Productivity Policy and the Service Sector," Discussion Paper no. 1, Fishman-Davidson Center for the Study of the Service Sector, University of Pennsylvania, Apr. 1984.

30. Michael J. McKee, "Computer Prices in the National Accounts: Are Our Economic Problems a Computer Error?" unpublished paper.

31. Martin Neil Baily, "The Productivity Growth Slowdown by Industry," *Brookings Papers on Economic Activity* 2 (1982): 442.

32. Daniel Creamer, *Gross National Product Data Improvement Project Report* (Washington: Department of Commerce, 1977), 144.

33. These figures, and others on manufacturing value added, are from U.S. Department of Commerce, *Census of Manufacturing* and *Annual Survey of Manufacturing*.

34. A. Harvey Belitsky, "Metalworking Machinery," in U.S., Bureau of Labor Statistics, *A BLS Reader on Productivity* (Washington: USGPO, 1983), 177.

35. John Duke and Horst Brand, "Cyclical Behavior of Productivity in the Machine Tool Industry," in BLS, *A BLS Reader on Productivity*, 89.

36. Tom Boucher, "Technical Change, Capital Investment, and Productivity in U.S. Metalworking Industries," in *Aggregate and Industry-Level Productivity Analyses*, ed. Ali Dogramaci and Nabil R. Adams (Boston: Martinus Nijhoff, 1981), 115.

37. Gordon's findings are reported in Stanley Engerman and Sherwin Rosen, "New Books on the Measurement of Capital," in *The Measurement of Capital*, ed. Dan Usher (Chicago: University of Chicago Press, 1980), 153–70.

38. Hirschhorn, *Beyond Mechanization*; Sabel, *Work and Politics* argues that destandardization is a consumer-driven process. Nevertheless, technological advances facilitate the satisfaction of consumer demands for more diverse products.

39. Kendrick, *Formation and Stocks of Total Capital*, and Eisner, "The Total Income System of Accounts." See also F. Thomas Juster, "A Framework for the Measurement of Economic and Social Performance," in *The Measurement of Economic and Social Performance*, ed. Milton Moss (New York: NBER, 1973), 23–84.

40. Engerman and Rosen, "New Books on the Measurement of Capital," 158.

41. John Kendrick, "Survey of the Factors Contributing to the Decline in U.S. Productivity Growth," in Federal Reserve Bank of Boston, *The Decline in Productivity Growth* (Boston: Federal Reserve Bank, 1980), 1–21.

42. Eisner, "Total Income Systems of Accounts," 45.

43. Baumol, "Productivity Policy and the Service Sector," 6. Data are from the 1970 and 1980 Census. While the $2.7 billion figure covers a longer period than 1973–1979 and includes public-sector expenditures, it is also the case that the census category of computer programmers is narrow for these purposes. Many of those who are counted separately in the category of computer analysts are also involved directly in the production of software.

44. These data come from the Department of Commerce, *Input Output Studies of the U.S. Economy*. The deflator for services is taken from U.S., Department of Commerce, *National Income and Product Accounts*. Note that these calculations omit an important component of service capital, namely, engineering and architectural services, which are counted separately among miscellaneous services. Recent, disaggregated data on the size of this category are not available.

45. The methodology is described in Martin Marimont, "Measuring Real Output for Industries Providing Services: OBE Concepts and Methods," in *Production and Productivity in the Service Industries*, ed. Victor Fuchs (New York: Columbia University Press, 1969). In the GNP originating series, business services in 1977 are $38.1 billion in current dollars and $26 billion in constant dollars. These data—Gross Product by Sector or Industry of Origin—at this level of disaggregation are unpublished but are available from the U.S. Department of Commerce, Bureau of Economic Analysis, on request.

46. John A. Gorman, "Alternative Measures of the Real Output and Productivity of Commercial Banks," in *Production and Productivity*, ed. Victor Fuchs, 155–89.

47. Horst Brand and John Duke, "Productivity in Commercial Banking: Computers Spur the Advance," in U.S., BLS, *Reader on Productivity*, 58–66.

48. The assumption that productivity accelerated at the same time that employment also expanded is plausible in light of the rapid growth in recent years in the quantity and diversity of financial services provided to individuals. The employment data and the data for recalculations are from U.S., Department of Commerce, *National Income and Product Accounts*.

49. The data are from Edward F. Denison, "The Shift to Services and the Rate of Productivity Change," *Survey of Current Business* (May 1973): 37–63, and from unpublished data from the U.S. Bureau of Economic Analysis. While Denison's article is designed to debunk the argument that the shift to services is an explanation of slower productivity growth, his argument is marred by a failure to look at the problems of measuring output in the service industries.

50. Hill, *Measurement of Real Product*, 56–57.

51. Data are from *National Income and Product Accounts*.

52. Kuznets, "National Income and Industrial Structure," 162.

53. There are other adjustments that are made between the two series, but the subtraction of services purchased from outside of manufacturing appears to be the most consequential. See Gottsegen and Ziemer, "Comparisons of Federal Reserve and OBE Measures."

54. The GNP originating series shows a decline in manufacturing productivity growth from 4.4 percent in 1960–1966 to 1.6 percent in 1973–1979. The value-added figures produce a change from 4.7 percent to 2.6 percent. These calculations use figures on employment measured in hours engaged in production from *National Income and Product Accounts*. Other data are from *Census of Manufacturers* and the *Annual Survey of Manufacturers*.

Yet it seems obvious that the manufacturing value-added measure is closer to the original intention of productivity analysis than the GNP originating figures. If one were measuring output in physical terms—tons of steel—whether or not an industry was buying more business services would be irrelevant to measures of tons of steel per employee hour.

55. "If the present contribution of past research and development and education expenditures equalled present outlays, there would of course be no significant distortion in the measurement of total economic activity. However, if these expenditures are increasing substantially there will be a systematic understatement of total economic activity, and also an understatement of profits resulting from current productive activity." Nancy Ruggles and Richard Ruggles, *The Design of Economic Accounts* (New York: NBER, 1970), 44.

56. Robert P. Parker, "Improved Adjustments for Misreporting of Tax Return Information Used to Estimate the National Income and Product Accounts, 1977," *Survey of Current Business* (June 1984): 17–25.

57. Exceptions include: Eisner, "Total Income System of Accounts"; and Irving Kravis, "Discussion," in *Production and Productivity in Service Industries*, ed. Fuchs, 86: "I believe that on both these issues—the scope of economic activity and the treatment of quality change—the practice of national income accountants and of price index makers has become rigidified around compromises that were necessary and reasonable thirty years ago but can no longer be justified."

58. Hirschhorn, *Beyond Mechanization*. For the economy as a whole, see the data on training in Eisner, "Total Income System of Accounts."

59. Seymour Melman, "Alternatives for the Organization of Work in Comput-

er-Assisted Manufacturing," *Annals of the New York Academy of Science* 426 (Nov. 1984): 83–90. See also the case studies in Barry Wilkinson, *The Shopfloor Politics of New Technology* (London: Heinemann, 1983).

60. John D. Baxter, "*Kanban* Works Wonders, but Will It Work in U.S. Industry?" *Iron Age* 225, 16 (June 1982): 44–48. See also Michael J. Piore and Charles F. Sabel, *The Second Industrial Divide* (New York: Basic Books, 1984). Their notion of flexible specialization draws on the Japanese experience.

61. For an exploration of the importance of a number of job design variables, see Peter S. Albin, "Job Design within Changing Patterns of Technical Development," in *American Jobs and the Changing Industrial Structure*, ed. E. Collins and L. Tanner (Cambridge, Mass.: Ballinger, 1984). For quality control in chip production, see William G. Oldham, "The Fabrication of Microelectronic Circuits," in *The Microelectronics Revolution*, ed. Tom Forrester (Cambridge, Mass.: MIT Press, 1981), 42–61.

62. Studies of productivity now often evaluate the changing quality of the labor input into the economy. Rather than simply measuring the labor input in hours, adjustments are made for differences in wage levels on the assumption that earnings "are proportional to the marginal products of labor, per hour of work. . . ." Denison, *Accounting for Slower Growth*, 33. This method ignores the controversy over whether differences in wages result from discrimination or differences in actual effectiveness. But the underlying assumption is that the quality of labor is a function of individual characteristics brought to the workplace rather than of the organizational environment in which the labor is employed.

63. Tom Boucher, "Technical Change, Capital Investment, and Productivity in U.S. Metalworking Industries," in *Aggregate and Industry-Level Productivity Analyses*, ed. Ali Dogramaci and Nabil R. Adams (Boston: Martinus Nijhoff, 1981), 99.

64. For more discussion of alternative policy directions, see Chapter 7 and Fred Block, "Technological Change and Employment: New Perspectives on an Old Controversy," *Economia & Lavoro* 18, 3 (July–Sept. 1984): 3–21.

65. Actually, the discovery that the economy was more productive in the 1973–1979 period—the "bad old days" of extensive government regulation and high social spending—would be little comfort to conservatives. However, the arguments of this paper can also be used to show that growth of GNP during the Reagan years has been even better than previously believed.

66. The development of the new price index for computers is discussed in articles in the *Survey of Current Business* in December 1985, January 1986, and March 1986.

CHAPTER 9

Acknowledgment: Some of the arguments in this essay were first developed in "Social Policy and Accumulation: A Critique of the New Consensus," pp. 13–31 in *Stagnation and Renewal in Social Policy*, ed. Martin Rein, Gosta Esping-Anderson, and Lee Rainwater (Armonk, N.Y., 1987). I am also indebted to Erik Olin Wright, Karl Klare, David Plotke, and the Editors of *Theory and Society* for suggestions that were incorporated at various stages of this article's evolution.

1. For an important exception, see Teresa Amott and Joel Krieger, "Thatcher and Reagan: State Theory and the 'Hyper-Capitalist' Regime," *New Political Science* 8 (spring 1982): 9–37.

2. Key works include Jürgen Habermas, *Legitimation Crisis* (Boston: Beacon, 1975); James O'Connor, *The Fiscal Crisis of the State* (New York: St. Martin's, 1973); Alan Wolfe, *The Limits of Legitimacy* (New York: Free Press, 1978); Samuel Bowles and Herbert Gintis, "The Crisis of Liberal Democratic Capitalism," *Politics & Society* 11, 1 (1982): 51–93; and some of the essays included in Claus Offe, *Contradictions of the Welfare State* (Cambridge, Mass.: MIT Press, 1984.)

3. This convergence has also been noted by Michael Piore and Charles Sabel, *The Second Industrial Divide* (New York: Basic Books, 1984), and by Robert Kuttner, *The Economic Illusion: False Choices Between Prosperity and Social Justice* (Boston: Houghton Mifflin, 1984).

4. See R. Bacon and W. Eltis, *Britain's Economic Problems: Too Few Producers* (London: Macmillan, 1978); Organization for Economic Cooperation and Development, *Towards Full Employment and Price Stability* (Paris: OECD, 1977); George Gilder, *Wealth and Poverty* (New York: Basic Books, 1981).

5. See, particularly, Wolfe, *Limits of Legitimacy*, chap. 10.

6. For an influential statement of these arguments, see Barry Bluestone and Bennett Harrison, *The Deindustrialization of America* (New York: Basic Books, 1982), especially chap. 6.

7. The original publication was in 1944, but references are to the Beacon Press edition, Boston, 1957. For an extended discussion of Polanyi's thought, see Fred Block and Margaret Somers, "Beyond the Economistic Fallacy: The Holistic Social Science of Karl Polanyi," in *Vision and Method in Historical Sociology*, ed. Theda Skocpol (New York: Cambridge University Press, 1984).

8. Polanyi, *Transformation*, 63–67.

9. Polanyi, *Transformation*, 77–85.

10. Polanyi, *Transformation*, 73.

11. Polanyi, *Transformation*, 165–166.

12. Volume 1, chap. 8, 15.

13. See Adam Przeworski, "The Ethical Materialism of John Roemer," *Politics & Society* 11, 3 (1982): 289–313, for a critique of the Marxist tendency to see the economy as a self-operating automaton.

14. See David Gordon, Richard Edwards, and Michael Reich, *Segmented Work, Divided Workers* (New York: Cambridge University Press, 1982). While I make use of their concept, there is much in their argument with which I disagree.

15. This list of factors is far from complete; it is meant only to be illustrative.

16. The argument is that if computerization reduces the demand for labor while output rises, there could be a significant shortfall in demand. While such an outcome is not inevitable, a weakening of the labor market from technological displacement can reduce employee bargaining power so that wage gains fail to keep pace with the growth of output. On problems of employment generation in advanced capitalism, see Chapter 7 and Fred Block, "Technological Change and Employment: New Perspectives on an Old Controversy," *Economia & Lavoro* (Aug.–Sept. 1984).

17. See Denison's classic work in growth accounting, Edward F. Denison, *Accounting for United States Economic Growth, 1929–1969* (Washington: Brookings, 1974).

18. In 1984, Chrysler Corporation budgeted $460 million for health-insurance premiums. This amounts to $5,000 per employee or $275 per vehicle. "Chrysler Program Saves Millions in Health Costs," *New York Times* (April 29, 1985).

19. "In general, there is a logical correlation between increases in production

and in productivity, with productivity speeding up as production accelerates and slowing down as production is retarded." Harry Magdoff and Paul Sweezy, "Productivity Slowdown: A False Alarm," *Monthly Review* 31, 2 (June 1979): 11.

20. The actual outcome depends, of course, on other variables such as the rate of inflation, exchange rates, and the propensity to import. But my point is that the impact of social policies on international competitiveness is indeterminate and depends on other variables some of which can be effectively manipulated by governments.

21. Laura Tyson and John Zysman, "American Industry in International Competition," in *American Industry in International Competition: Government Policies and Corporate Strategies*, ed. Zysman and Tyson (Ithaca: Cornell University Press, 1983), 33.

22. This now neglected line of argument has a distinguished lineage in the economics literature. For example, in his classic study of manufacturing employment, Fabricant argues that reductions in the length of the working day imposed by government or unions can have the effect of inducing greater entrepreneurial effort by the employer. Solomon Fabricant, *Employment in Manufacturing, 1899–1939* (New York: NBER, 1942) 13.

23. The system of capital controls imposed during the Vietnam War is described briefly in Fred Block, *The Origins of International Economic Disorder* (Berkeley: University of California Press, 1977) 182–184.

24. Block, *Origins*, 42–46.

25. While the Reagan administration's obstinate commitment to free markets and deregulation has discouraged initiatives in this direction, steps were being taken in the late seventies toward greater international cooperation to regulate banking. See Hugo Colje, "Bank Supervision on a Consolidated Basis," *The Banker* (June 1980): 29–34. Robert Dunn writes that, "Prohibitions or limitations on capital flows have been widely discussed as a possible route to a less volatile exchange market . . . ," and he reports a proposal by James Tobin to discourage speculative capital flows by taxing exchange market transactions. Robert M. Dunn Jr., *The Many Disappointments of Flexible Exchange Rates*, Princeton Essays in International Finance, no. 154, Dec. 1983, 24–26.

26. The argument that the new technologies of capital transfer make controls impossible is clearly specious. The reality is that such electronic transfers leave more traces than traditional currency transactions.

27. The natural coalition for such reforms would bring together progressive social forces in Western Europe and the United States with Third World nations that are currently suffering from their indebtedness to international banks.

Index